Comparative Romanticisms

Studies in German Literature, Linguistics, and Culture

Edited by James Hardin
(*South Carolina*)

COMPARATIVE ROMANTICISMS

POWER, GENDER, SUBJECTIVITY

Edited by
Larry H. Peer
and
Diane Long Hoeveler

CAMDEN HOUSE

Copyright © 1998 Larry H. Peer and Diane Long Hoeveler

All Rights Reserved. Except as permitted under current legislation, no part of this work may be photocopied, stored in a retrieval system, published, performed in public, adapted, broadcast, transmitted, recorded, or reproduced in any form or by any means, without the prior permission of the copyright owner.

First published 1998
Camden House
Drawer 2025
Columbia, SC 29202–2025 USA

Camden House is an imprint of Boydell & Brewer Inc.
PO Box 41026, Rochester, NY 14604–4126 USA
and of Boydell & Brewer Limited
PO Box 9, Woodbridge, Suffolk IP12 3DF, UK

ISBN: 1–57113–170–1

Library of Congress Cataloging-in-Publication Data

Comparative romanticisms : power, gender, subjectivity / edited by
  Larry H. Peer and Diane Long Hoeveler.
    p.   cm. – (Studies in German literature, linguistics, and culture)
  Includes bibliographical references and index.
  ISBN 1-57113-170-1 (alk. paper)
    1. Romanticism. 2. Comparative literature. I. Peer, Larry H.
II. Hoeveler, Diane Long. III. Series: Studies in German literature, linguistics, and culture (Unnumbered)
PN603.C66 1998
809'.9145—dc21   97-46703
                                                                  CIP

This publication is printed on acid-free paper.
Printed in the United States of America

Table of Contents

Acknowledgments ix

Introduction

Larry H. Peer and Diane Long Hoeveler
A Lens for Comparative Romanticisms 1

Power

Stephen C. Behrendt
Remapping the Landscape: The Romantic Literary
Community Revisited 11

Clark Davis
Mutual Trust and the Friendly Loan:
Melville, Money, and Romantic Faith 33

Richard Kaplan
Romantic and Realist Rubble: The Foundation for a New
National Literature in Dostoevsky's *Poor Folk* and Melville's *Pierre* 47

Margaret Reid
From Revolutionary Legends to *The Scarlet Letter*:
Casting Characters for Early American Romanticism 59

Karen Karbiener
The Unexpress'd: Walt Whitman's Late
Thoughts on Richard Wagner 81

Gender

Diane Long Hoeveler
The Female Gothic, Beating Fantasies, and
the Civilizing Process 103

Donelle R. Ruwe
The Canon-Maker: Felicia Hemans
and Torquato Tasso's Sister 133

Debbie Lopez
"Ungraspable Phantoms": Keats's Lamia
and Melville's Yillah 159

Julie Costello
Aesthetic Discourses and Maternal Subjects:
Enlightenment Roots, Schlegelian Revisions 171

Subjectivity

Larry H. Peer
Pushkin and *Romantizm* 191

Fred V. Randel
Romantic Poetry and Civic Space
in the Wordsworthian Cave 199

Michael J. Call
Atala's Body: Girodet and the Representation
of Chateaubriand's Romantic Christianity 211

Heather I. Sullivan
The Postponed Narratives of Desire in Ludwig Tieck's
Novel *Franz Sternbalds Wanderungen* 223

Notes on Contributors 235

Index 239

Acknowledgments

The authors are indebted to a number of anonymous colleagues who read the manuscript and to Camden House personnel for their untiring devotion to getting things right. They also wish to express gratitude to those whose personal commitment to this project was steady and informed, including Katalin Kalmár-Abbott, keyboarder *extraordinaire*, and to family *prodigieux*.

The reproduction of Girodet's burial scene from Chateaubriand's *Atala* is used courtesy of the Louvre, Paris (March, 1998).

Introduction: A Lens for Comparative Romanticisms

Larry H. Peer and
Diane Long Hoeveler

Critical approaches to anything, especially Romanticism, may well run aground on the fallacies of absolutism and relativism. An approach that disdains interrelations between literary movements, generations, periods, and both cross-linguistic and interdisciplinary sources and influences will tend to submit any concept or conceptual framework to a dogmatic and authoritarian set of preconceptions, where even the use of terms may be garbled. Opposite to this absolutism is the referral of Romanticism exclusively to a particular critical lens with its explicit and implicit selection of biases that ignore the dynamic continuance of the movement and that negate any way of understanding the multi-faceted dimensions of its significance.

Many Romantics sensed this twin problem. An interesting way to look at this phenomenon is to remember Goethe in his student years at Leipzig, where he first became acquainted with the writings of Spinoza. Goethe admired Spinoza as an advocate of liberalism and toleration, as one who had insisted on perspective rather than dogmatism in both conclusions about the world and the method by which those conclusions were made. The essence of Spinoza's metaphysical and ethical views is that reality, in order to be known, must be conceived of as a whole, where our understanding of each part of the whole depends upon the relationship of that part to all other parts in a single, self-explaining system. One of the philosopher's great propositions is that there cannot exist two things either having the same nature or having no relationship to any other thing. Thus, all things depend for their coming into our perception upon both that which is in and of itself the uniqueness of the thing as well as upon that which relates the thing to other things. For the human intellect to perceive the essence of anything, the whole to which it is related must be perceived. That this does not usually happen is the cause of both intellectual fallacy and moral failure. Goethe's pantheist organology derives directly from Spinoza's account of human perception and lies at the base of Romantic theory.

It happens that Spinoza developed *his* system by frequent contact with a group of devoted disciples and leading European philosophers, particularly Leibniz. Spinoza was a lens-maker by profession; Leibniz seized upon the premises of optical theory and the use of optical instruments in his arguments about human perception. For both, the lens was the object symbol of theory, of the promises and pitfalls of human perception. Having already postulated differential and integral calculus by the time he visited Spinoza at The Hague, Leibniz spent the next several years of his life developing theories of knowledge and truth that resulted in hundreds of essays and dozens of key encounters with other thinkers that in turn spurred them on to great discoveries and formulations. In his time a belief arose that he was the last universal genius, a judgement about Goethe that the great minds of Europe were to make three generations later.

The central point of Leibniz's thought is that there are only two types of statements, those that state necessary truth and those that express contingent truth. The first establishes truth in reference by being self-evidently non-contradictory, and the second establishes truth by means other than that which is mere non-contradictory. In "right" thinking, therefore, we must always either perceive that which is self-evidently non-contradictory (usually not possible to any "perceptor" but God) or perceive that which is based upon a hypothesis showing the greatest number of effects deducible from the smallest number of causes. That is, in checking the validity of our perceptions, and the things we say based upon those perceptions, we must have "sufficient reason" for seeing things as we do.

The individual mind, according to Leibniz, is like a mathematical point on which all possible perceptions converge as do lines of reference. But there is always a relationship between one mind's "mathematical point" and all other minds; thus, avoiding the relativism of reference to merely one's own point and the absolutism of reference to all possible points (for Leibniz only God can "refer" in this way) involves recognizing that we are seeing everything from a particular point of view, or through a particular lens. This does not mean that each perception is wrong, only that each one is contingent. Truth would be a harmonious and ordered intermeshing of perceptions revealed, as it were, by a series of lenses mathematically positioned in three dimensions.

Of course, it would be wrong to say that the group of essays in this book (or any group, no matter how large or varied) provides a harmonious and ordered intermeshing of perceptions about Romanticism. We may view this collection of views as a lens, but a Goethean or Romantic lens more like the organic lens of the human eye, flexing, adjusting, and squinting, than like the ground and fixed lenses of Spinoza and Leibniz. These papers attempt to refocus on Romanticism without trying to invent a new synthesis for the movement. The editors have selected thirteen essays from a variety of older and newer scholarly voices that represent a rethinking of key Romantic texts and interrelations through the lens of three fundamental theoretical issues: power, gender, and subjectivity. They call for a newly comparative sense of Romanticism that avoids the kind of critical explication of these issues limited to single national, linguistic, or cultural traditions, or seen through too narrowly applied contemporary theoretical "-isms."

An important line of recent Romanticism scholarship proceeds from the view that discourse and its texts create and manipulate socio-economic power, and control ideology. The first five essays in this collection deal with how Romantic discourse determines what comes to be seen as ideologically normal in the nineteenth century. Romantic texts speak by observing an unspoken set of regulations, and the discursive power of the movement is reflected in intertextual relations that cross, for example, between such diverse voices as Melville, Dostoevsky, Whitman, and Richard Wagner, and form a Romantic literary community extending in subtle ways across many language traditions. The first essay, for example, Stephen C. Behrendt's "Remapping the Landscape: The Romantic Literary Community Revisited," suggests that our scholarly responsibility might be to seek a considerably greater common ground upon which to see a reformulated and comparative Romanticism. He shows conclusively that what we designate as Romanticism today (particularly through an Anglo-American lens) cannot function as our designation for Romanticism in the future. This new Romanticism will need to include not only fiction, but theater, books on science, a study of morals and ecomonics, the pan-European periodical canon, and so on. This new and varied discourse will give us a completely different picture from the one we in the Anglo-American tradition have grown accustomed to see. Of course, our recovery of Romantic women writers is an exciting development in the last decade, but numerous male writers need to be recovered as well: and they will be recovered when we come to a deeper understanding of the artistic, social, and cultural ethos of Europe as a whole. It is clear that we need to encourage an expanding and cross-linguistic view of Romanticism, understanding (for example) the British version in broader terms than that of Regency culture. Behrendt's essay desires an interconnectedness called for a generation ago and practiced by René Wellek and other comparatists, as well as by the English Romantics themselves.

Melville's attempt to understand the power of language comes from his reading of British writers, especially Wordsworth. Clark Davis shows how Melville's view of language is linked to concerns of social and economic power. Thus, even widely read American writers of the 1850s participate in a Romantic transformation of language begun by the English Romantics two generations earlier.

Richard Kaplan shows how the sentimentalism associated with Romanticism is routinely and systematically attacked by such authors as Dostoyevsky and Melville. In fact, the confusing of sentimentalism with Romanticism represents the homogenizing of that which such writers simply did not understand in the first place. It is a commonplace that many nineteenth-century works parody sentimentalism but this essay details a number of ways in which the attack on sentimentalism proceeded, including poking fun at the rhetoric of Romanticism, intensifying the superficial sentimentality of pseudo-Romantic feeling, and turning the melodrama as a genre inside out for realist purposes. No two works serve as critiques of late Romantic sentiment better than Melville's *Pierre* and Dostoyevsky's *Poor Folk*.

Recent scholarship has probed the problem of finding the beginnings of Romanticism in America, and Margaret Reid's essay "From Revolutionary Legends to *The Scarlet Letter*: Casting Characters for Early American Romanticism" adds to the debate. Her thesis is that the developing cultural story of America becomes an agent of mediation between the violent and disordered experience of lived history and the highest ideals of the Romantic imagination. The freedom at the core of Romanticism was valorized by constant use of the early American tradition of storytelling.

Karen Karbiener's essay suggests that Walt Whitman's relationship to Richard Wagner was more than merely that of the influence of a composer on a music lover. Pointing out that Whitman respected and admired Wagner, Karbiener suggests that Whitman was actually intimidated and threatened by the German's power and universality.

The next four essays explore international aspects of Romantic gender reformulation, moving between writers such as Felicia Hemans, Keats, the Schlegel brothers, and the European gothic novelists, and show how Romantic discourse and ideology begin to break down eighteenth-century notions of womanhood, particularly taboos about expressing female passion and transcending social positioning. This group of essays also reveals the paradox of some Romantic writers unwittingly reformulating pre-Romantic male-dominated cultural customs, in spite of the often brilliant strategies they invent to deflate and replace these earlier norms.

In "The Female Gothic, Beating Fantasies, and the Civilizing Process," Diane Long Hoeveler deftly dissects the "female gothic pattern" so central to Romantic fantasy but so little understood in contemporary criticism. The pattern is formed by a "persecuted heroine trapped in a house diffused with manic oedipal anxieties" who is attacked by random social, economic, or cultural compulsions. Hoeveler finds that this pattern actually goes beyond female writers and the female readership, offering the discovery that nineteenth-century female gothic writing is not radically different from other Romantic works because its highly ideological signifying system does not decode or encode any especially distinguishable experience. The notion that Romantic women writers were careful manipulators of their world view is an important neo-Freudian re-reading of central cultural constructs such as family, socio-economic power, and personal survival.

Hemans's Romanticism and her relationship to European developments of the period are the subjects of Donelle R. Ruwe's "The Canon-Maker: Felicia Hemans and Torquato Tasso's Sister." By reflecting primarily on Hemans's translation and commentary on Goethe's *Torquato Tasso*, Ruwe shows how the entire Hemans canon has been framed by a reinscribing of old masters within a kind of domesticity. Seeing Hemans in a European context shows how a traditional model of canonicity develops into a new version in which canonicity is formed by educational institutions.

An interesting view of Romantic personality is suggested through the lens of Debbie Lopez's essay on Keats and Melville. Referring to an imaginary encounter with various English Romantic poets, including a hideously fat Byron (now reconciled with his wife), a politically converted Shelley, and a dead Wordsworth, Lopez shows how as recreated images these figures are thrown into ironic perspective with the struggle Keats had in writing *Lamia*. Then, by drawing upon a typological relationship with Melville and Hawthorne, Lopez shows that Keats' *Lamia* is not only a female demon but also a fabulous monster, perhaps the "monster" of Romanticism itself.

Julie Costello in "Aesthetic Discourses and Maternal Subjects: Enlightenment, Roots, Schlegelian Revisions" provides an interesting view of the aesthetic discourse of the female. She shows how most recent studies of the gendered social and literary dynamics of British Romantic literature have dealt almost exclusively with Romanticism's idealization of the female. Most apparent in Friedrich Schlegel's novel *Lucinde*, although not exclusively there, is the valorization of female experience per se, and the recognition that gender relations are de facto characterized by a misunderstanding. That becomes the prime source of creative energy.

The problem of Romantic subjectivity has been viewed in a number of ways by contemporary critics, but the final four essays in this book posit comparative ideas about how Romantic texts are both open (requiring readers' collaboration in producing meaning and significance) and closed (in control of limited possible readings). Without invoking the language of reader-response, phenomenological, or semiotic theory, these essays suggest that key Romantic conventions about subjectivity move between a diverse group of artists, including Pushkin, Chateaubriand, Girodet, and Tieck.

Larry H. Peer's essay on Pushkin shows that most European Romantic poets were deeply immersed in continental philosophy and the periodical literature of the day, so that for them the term Romanticism (in its numerous national variants) maintained a cluster of meanings somewhat at odds with the way the term is often used today. Romanticism for the Romantics meant anti-sentimentality, anti-picturesqueness, and anti-exclusion. Pushkin is a key example of this view of the movement and use of the word, and the Russian is aligned with Friedrich Schlegel, Hegel, and Manzoni in his concern with the tenets of Romanticism as well as the use of the term itself.

Fred V. Randel's essay increases our understanding of the Romantic response to fierce ideological battles that were determined, in some ways, by the political, social, and economic climate of the day. By focusing on the image of the cave, Randel shows clearly that the typical Romantic way of surviving these battles was to find or create a separation from the factions in order to find a personal and ideological utopia in the projections of their thinking. For this reason many of the Romantics and Romantic heroes were loners who had a more profound historical and prophetic vision of societal possibilities than other souls. All Romantic poets lean toward the contemplative solitaries of the monastic tradition, and the ethos of Romanticism itself cannot help but seek a numinous encounter outside established traditions. We thus may understand more completely the Romantic fascination with hermits, and how such a fascination serves both personal and poetic purposes.

The thematic ontology of Chateaubriand's novel *Atala* is the subject of Michael J. Call's "Atala's Body: Girodet and the Representation of Chateaubriand's Romantic Christianity." The French author claimed to be demonstrating through his Christian epic the harmony of Christian and the Enlightenment's humanistic ideals. But Call shows that *Atala* fails to be this reconciliation, just as Girodet's painting of the burial scene from the epic fails. When Romantic writers or painters drew upon traditional Christian symbolism and sentiment they produced a deconstruction of Christianity. Thus for Chateaubriand Romanticism cannot be a harmony of Christian and Enlightenment ideals, but rather the deconstruction of the attempt to make a reconciliation at all.

Heather I. Sullivan's essay on Tieck's *Franz Sternbalds Wanderungen* demonstrates how the novel both follows and departs from the pulp fiction traditions of its time. Especially in terms of narratology, the novel is about fragmentation and the inability to use both the supernatural and the popular in a harmonious way. Tieck's desire to yet impossibility share self-representation with the world of popular readers is, he believes, the ultimate Romantic difficulty.

Each of these essays offers, in its own way, analyses of the convergences encoded in the typological system we now call Romanticism. Each essay in turn represents a line of reference that can be read as a convergence with several or all of the others. Such convergences tug at the muscles focusing the critical lens, and provide an elucidation through which future views may be directed.

POWER

Remapping the Landscape: The Romantic Literary Community Revisited

Stephen C. Behrendt

Critical discourse and scholarly inquiry across the entire spectrum of Romanticism has made it startlingly clear that we stand at a remarkable moment in the history of Romanticism studies, a moment that is as exciting as it is challenging and unsettling. This historical moment invites us to think about our field in new ways, ways that may be significantly different from the ways many of us have become accustomed to thinking about Romanticism, ways that may even contradict one another in wholly irreconcilable ways. Even those of us who have enthusiastically embraced the recovery of marginalized or even erased writers, of both sexes and of all races, classes, and national or ethnic affiliations, have an enormous amount of work still to do. For instance, we need to start thinking more deeply and systematically not about Romanticism (singular), but rather about Romanticism*s* (plural). In the process we need to question anew why what we call "Romanticism" happened (and continues to happen) at different times in different places. It happened early in Germany and England, for instance, and later in France and America. Moreover, what is usually called Romanticism seems to have happened at slightly different moments in the various arts, so that Romanticism in literature may precede Romanticism in visual art or music in one culture but not in another. Further still, for all the convenience that comes with characterizing periods as Romantic (or Neoclassical, or naturalistic, or whatever), we need to pay far more serious attention to the fact that at any historical moment within Romanticism there is always active in the culture generally a powerful counter-impulse that engages in its own discourse with that burgeoning Romanticism. Indeed, I have come in recent years to talk and write not so much about "British Romantic poetry," for instance, as about "British poetry of the Romantic period." Shifting the nomenclature in that fashion, as many of us have begun to do, at the very least permits us to foreground the *diversity* that is everywhere the hallmark of Romantic writing communities, and to begin to move away from monolithic conceptions and categories that have dominated critical and literary-historical discussions of Romanticism for the last century and a half.

To talk about "Comparative Romanticisms," as we find ourselves doing increasingly in the modern global community, is to talk about Comparative Literature, as well as about comparative arts and comparative cultures. It is to become not just interdisciplinary but cosmopolitan in a way that is still unfamiliar for many of us who were trained in individual national literatures, and often with little but a nodding acquaintance with the other arts—both the "fine arts" and the popular arts. One of the great gains that will inevitably come as more of us begin to acclimate ourselves to this wider, cross-cultural and interdisciplinary environment of inquiry will be a more sophisticated appreciation for the ways in which Romanticism in all its varieties *resists* the easy categorization that has always been implicit in a quantitative term like "the Romantic period."

And then there is the matter of periodization. Simply looking at the range of different chronological parameters that have appeared in the titles of anthologies of British Romantic literature alone in recent years is instructive: not only are we beginning to see a "long" Romantic period, so in fact are we seeing a period that is ever less a real *period*. Indeed, the very label, Romantic, has become sufficiently problematical that it is not even used in the title of Anne Mellor and Richard Matlack's new anthology, which simply offers us British Literature and a set of inclusive dates.[1]

Further still, it used to be easy to demarcate the British Romantic era by citing the productive years of the six canonical male poets, which fairly neatly gave us approximately 1789 to 1832 (convenient—until students ask why a *literary* period should come to be delineated by dates most often associated with *political* events, and those in two different nations, to boot). But when we factor in the women, the chronological parameters change dramatically. Poets like Helen Maria Williams and Charlotte Smith are publishing important Romantic poems already in the early 1780s, and Letitia Elizabeth Landon and Felicia Hemans continue to publish well after 1830. It may be time to go back to thinking not about a Romantic period but about a Romantic movement—or even several of them. Indeed, it will be healthiest and most productive for all of us if we address instead a Romantic "ethos," and leave behind the red herring of periodicity. For it is, ultimately, an ethos, an inner spirit (however diverse) and constellation of related manifestations, that enables us to see why elder writers like Chaucer, Calderón, and Shakespeare, and like Theodore Roethke, Alice Fulton, Gary Snyder, and Emily Grosholz in our own times, may appropriately be regarded as "Romantic" writers.

In what follows I shall focus almost exclusively upon British literature, in part because even that body of writing offers more than enough challenges and complications to consider. But the issues I explore here bear implications for other national Romanticisms, and for comparative Romantics studies that range across various cultures and arts, just as they do across national and cultural borders. I have no illusions, though, about arriving at definitive answers to the questions I want to raise, for we need for some time to concern ourselves more with asking better questions than with defending answers to less troublesome questions. Therefore, like Charles Ives's musical composition, what follows is also something of an Unanswered Question, one whose many component questions stand as invitations to further dialogue, further questioning.

I would like to suggest that in comparing some of the various models of Romanticism available to us at the present historical moment, we begin by looking for some of the common ground upon which we might begin constructing a modified, reformulated Romanticism. What we designate as Romanticism in the future will almost certainly be very different from what we have understood by that term for the better part of a century and a half. This new Romanticism will need to include fiction, which we will need to re-examine on the basis of very different criteria than have traditionally been used to assess—and then to dismiss—most of Romantic fiction. It will need to consider as well the most overlooked of all Romantic literature, that written for the theatre, and which exerted enormous formative influence not just on literary creation but also on the public awareness of how and why characters are exhibited and actions transpire in time and place. And it will need, too, to re-evaluate the vigorous non-fictional prose that accompanied the rapid expansion of the print medium. In this category I include not just formal discursive prose works on science, history, philosophy, literary criticism, religion, morals and economics, but also the vast body of writing in the periodical press—the dailies, weeklies, quarterlies, and the like—where "voices" and subjects, policies and parties, engaged in a remarkable multivocal discourse that itself fed and shaped the expanding public consciousness that accompanied the expansion of literacy. All this varied discourse is going to present us with a very different picture from the one we have grown accustomed to seeing. Marilyn Butler was absolutely correct when she observed that "poets we have installed as canonical look more interesting individually, and far more understandable as groups, when we restore some of their lost peers."[2] In reassessing Romanticism we must immerse ourselves in examining, mediating, and reformulating the often very different premises that underlie important studies like Clifford Siskin's *Historicity of Romantic Discourse*, J. R. Jackson's *Historical Criticism and the Meaning of Texts*, and the influential work that has been published since the mid-eighties especially by scholars like Butler, Marjorie Levinson, Stuart Curran, and Jerome McGann,[3] to name only the most conspicuous. At the same time, though, we must heed Levinson's caution against reformulating the Romantic past so as to make it "continuous with the present rather than *related* to it,"[4] for re-inventing the past in terms of new theoretical and historical methodologies so that it seems to prefigure ourselves and our times risks subjecting that past to ideological distortions comparable to those we have come to decry.

The most exciting development in recent Romantics studies is without question the recovery of the women writers of the period. Many reasonable political and ideological impulses have led scholars like Anne Mellor and Marlon Ross (and anthologizers like Jennifer Breen and Andrew Ashfield) to *separate* male and female writers to varying degrees, and to assign gender-specific labels to the alternative Romanticisms they would seem to represent.[5] But I believe a compelling case exists for remapping the landscape in such a way as to accommodate and enfranchise within a single, diverse fabric many of the threads that have been separated—most often along gender lines—in recent critical discourse. Anne Mellor in fact moves in this direction in *Romanticism and Gender*, as do Stuart Curran and Jerome McGann—if his *New Oxford Book of Romantic Period Verse* is any indication.[6] At the same time, new anthologies, those traditionally troubled sites of canon petrification, hold the potential to advance this important cause in significant ways if only by including male and female, canonical and non-canonical, authors between the covers of a single textbook.[7]

In the meantime, let me suggest that once we begin to rethink British Romanticism by re-historicizing both the literary and extra-literary materials and their cultural contexts, the old distinction between "first" and "second generation" Romantics may prove to be more important, more profound, than we have usually understood. The more one views the literary scene up to the beginning of the Regency, especially when the non-canonical materials are added to the mix, the more we see in the arts and in social culture alike the culmination of the literary, artistic, socio-politico-economic, and cultural ethos of "the eighteenth century." What follows ushers in the "modern" period by breaking dramatically with what had gone before. The younger Romantics' rejection of Wordsworth—especially in the aftermath of *The Excursion* in 1814—is symptomatic of a much more profound disruption and then reorientation of culture that takes place in the decade of the Regency. This reorientation shifts British culture—and its aesthetic artifacts—away from an earlier paradigm organized around Sentiment, engagement, and the paradigm of a self-sustaining social unit, and toward a new one characterized by anxiety, irony, dislocation, and social dysfunction, which is in many ways an *inversion* of that culture of Sentiment. Siskin has written that the end of the eighteenth century saw the replacement of a "fiction of community as the basis for communication" with a "fiction of communication as the basis for a new human community."[8] The formulation is as culturally insightful as it is rhetorically neat, especially in light of what Benedict Anderson has written about how "imagined communities" had come to be constructed with greater ease and effect by the time of the Romantic period as a result of the rise of what he calls "print-capitalism." "Print-capitalism gave a new fixity to language," Anderson writes,[9] and we can trace in Romantic writing how this fixity of language encouraged among an expanding and diversifying reading public a new sort of identification—even solidarity—with a writing community that seemed in many respects nearer their own interests and concerns than previous ones had historically been. Regency culture encouraged the formation of new, non-biological families, real and symbolic, that replaced the dysfunctional biological ones that had been rendered failures by a bewildering array of new cultural and societal pressures.

We need to study more carefully the disruption of the community that had characterized the later eighteenth century as well as the non-overlapping subcommunities produced during the Regency. As one means of beginning to define both the earlier community and those that began to supplant it, we might consider to what extent Romanticism might fruitfully be delineated by the ways in which writers and citizens alike position themselves, at various points in the period, in relation to an axis whose poles are the Sentimental and the Sublime. Doing so enables us to recognize one common ground explored by most of the writers of the Romantic period, male and female, major and minor, radical and reactionary. In both these terms, the Sentimental and the Sublime, and in what they connote, we are provided with touchstones for a very substantial portion of Romantic writing. Paradoxically, it is on this very point that so much of the current debate about separate female and male Romanticisms (or literary traditions) generally begins to fragment, shearing off on tracks that seem to move ever further apart. And yet it is quite possible to see, particularly—but not exclusively—in the poetry a common interest in exploring a range of human emotion and human response that appears to be tied directly to eighteenth-century notions of sentiment and the sublime.

Consider, for instance, two passages; the first is from Burke's *Enquiry on the Sublime and the Beautiful*:

> Whatever ... is in any sort terrible, or is conversant about terrible objects, ... or operates in a manner analogous to terror, is a source of the *sublime*; that is, it is productive of the strongest emotion which the mind is capable of feeling. (I, vii.)[10]

The second is from Wollstonecraft's *Mary, A Fiction*:

> Sensibility is the most exquisite feeling of which the human soul is susceptible.[11]

Even granting that Wollstonecraft's word is sensibility rather than sentiment, the similarity of the terminology and the mutual emphasis on feeling is strikingly instructive. In *The Culture of Sensibility* G. J. Barker-Benfield makes sensibility virtually synonymous with the term "generous feelings" in a way that is especially helpful here.[12] For Barker-Benfield's discussion helps us to appreciate what a short step it is from formulations like Burke's and Wollstonecraft's to William Wordsworth's well-known phrase about poetry as "the spontaneous overflow of powerful feelings."[13]

Of course, the sentimental was regarded from the first both as a desirable affective response to external (and internal) stimuli *and* as a vehicle for stimulating such responses. In both cases, sentiment and the Sentimental were closely associated with education, as is abundantly clear in a work like Sterne's *Sentimental Journey* (1768). There Yorick describes the purpose of his continental journey in terms of education:

> 'tis a quiet journey of the heart in pursuit of NATURE, and those affections which rise out of her, which make us love each other—and the world, better than we do.[14]

The insistently human (and humane) focus of this variety of education feeds directly into the impulses behind much of what we typically think of as the Romantic ethos. The key term is probably "affections," a ubiquitous term in Romantic writing generally that recurs as part of a constellation of telltale semantic indicators of sentiment including "sensations," "fibres," "vibrations," and "thrill."[15]

Underlying these conceptions is the notion of sympathy frequently articulated in the eighteenth century, as it is for instance by David Hume, who asserted already in 1739 that "moral good and moral evil are certainly distinguish'd by our *sentiments*, not by *reason*." Moreover, Hume set out what would become a central tenet of Romantic thought when he observed that it is "the principle of *sympathy*" that "produces our sentiment of morals" and that enables us to "enter into the sentiments of the rich and poor, and partake of their pleasures and uneasiness," producing in the process an "agreeable idea or impression" that "is connected with love, which is an agreeable passion."[16] The echoes of this confluence of sentiment, sympathy, and morals are unmistakable some eighty years later in Percy Shelley's *Defence of Poetry*:

> The great secret of morals is Love; or a going out of our own nature, and an identification of ourselves with the beautiful which exists in thought, action, or person, not our own. A man, to be greatly good, must imagine intensely and comprehensively; he must put himself in the place of another and of many others; the pains and pleasures of his species must become his own.[17]

Notice that Shelley appeals to the whole emotional range of human response: not just joy is shared, but also suffering. Of signal importance here, even in the words of this "second generation Romantic," is the explicit appeal to that *community* of human experience that is accessed by means of the workings of sympathy upon and within the consciousness. That appeal inscribes a line that includes Hume, Burke, Wordsworth, and a host of others, including important women poets like Charlotte Turner Smith, Mary Darby Robinson, and Joanna Baillie, as well as minor poets like Samuel Jackson Pratt, who appealed in an 1801 poem called "Bread" to the "blest muse of SYMPATHY":

> No idle plumage pluck'd from fancy's wing,
> No playful bubbles from the fabled spring,

> Thy bard now seeks. Ah no! far other themes
> Than verdant meads, or fiction's fairy dreams,
> Now prompt the numbers: TRUTHS, that may impart
> A touch of mercy to the hardest heart;
> Teach Avarice to feel the social sigh,
> And bathe his cheek in dews of charity.[18]

Indeed, already in 1781 Pratt had published a poem with the telling title of *Sympathy; or, a Sketch of the Social Passion*.[19] In that poem he had asserted that in all of nature

> . . . Instinct, Sympathy, or what you will,
> A first great principle, is active still.
> Shines out of ev'ry element the soul,
> And deep pervading, animates the whole. (p. 15)

This powerful communitarian impulse, which according to Pratt works everywhere for the purposes of good, he calls "the Sympathetic Principle, or Social Principle" (p. iii):

> This then is clear, while human kind exist,
> The social principle must still subsist,
> In strict dependency of one on all,
> As run the binding links from great to small. (p. 51)

The notion of interconnectedness articulated in Pratt's verses prefigures by some two centuries Siskin's observation that representing experience in first-person terms made communication seem to the Romantics to be a condition for dwelling with others, and that the first-person gesture did not just *invite* the reader to be also a writer: it *made* the reader into a writer, casting her or him explicitly in that role and thus manufacturing one of those "implied communities" that *seemed* to be an actual one rather than an artificially-induced one.[20] The vehicle for achieving this experiential fusion is sympathy, its agent is imagination, and its "trigger mechanism" is sentiment.

Thinking about sentiment as an intellectual and aesthetic "throughline" or *leitmotif* in writing of the Romantic period can help us uncover areas of consensus where many have usually found not logical continuity but what they have instead perceived simply as failure, whether intellectual or artistic. I think, for instance, of Coleridge's much-lambasted 1794 poem to a young ass.[21] This poem turns *precisely* on this particular sort of sentimental response, both to the suffering creature and to the situation in general as Coleridge formulates it, that originates in the "sympathy" both Burke and Hume talk about, and which in turn lies at the heart of the notion of love Shelley subsequently articulates in the *Defence*. It is no coincidence either that Sterne had turned in *A Sentimental Journey* to "a dead ass" for the signal disruption to the journey of his post-chaise.[22] Indeed, Sterne's interpolated tale of the dead ass turns upon a sympathetic response that Coleridge's poem subsequently replicates, with the poor beast's owner saying of a bit of bread that "this, should have been thy portion, . . . hadst thou been alive to have shared it with me." Indeed, Sterne's poor rustic even takes a bit of the bread and when he had "laid it upon the bit of his ass's bridle—looked wistfully at the little arrangement he had made—and then gave a sigh."[23] Coleridge's poem likewise draws for its full effect upon that same element of sentimental response which Hume defined as "sympathy." Interestingly, it was this very rhetorical posture that contemporary critics seized upon for particular emphasis when they ridiculed the poem. When Coleridge's speaker declares "I hail thee *Brother*" ("spite of the fool's scorn," Coleridge writes, getting the jump on his critics; line 26), he makes a point about human community that is quite in keeping with Hume's theories and Sterne's practices.

At the same time, many of the works written in the 1780s and 90s by Williams, Wordsworth, Robinson, Coleridge, Southey, and Barbauld present what seem at first to be intensely personal rejoinders to extra-aesthetic political and social events that proceed in each case from the author's own essentially "sentimental" response to these events. Each author then invites her or his audience to internalize, to share, and to act upon these in the public arena of society as a whole. That these documents, which seem so sincere and so spontaneous, are in fact deliberately composed and revised *poems* by means of which their authors manipulate their readers' subsequent responses in carefully calculated fashion merely underscores their authors' typically undervalued rhetorical sophistication. The many poems from the 1790s in particular that center upon social issues—poems on wanderers, on displaced or ostracized individuals, on the poor, on the handicapped, on widows (war widows and otherwise), on orphans, and so forth—all appeal to the reader's ability *and willingness* to enter into community with these unfortunate individuals: to "make the pains and pleasures of [their] species . . . become [their] own." Even the most "sublime" of the traditionally canonized Romantic poems (like the "Intimations" ode, or—in the next generation—like *Prometheus Unbound*) substantially reprocess this essentially eighteenth-century complex of sentiment and sympathy, however they may metamorphose and elevate it.

A particularly strong appeal to this strain of sentiment is mounted in the war poetry of the 1790s, during which time the fashionableness of the French Revolution and the associated republican aspirations crested and began to give way to the disillusionment born of war, suffering, cynicism, and the European descent into new totalitarianism. Amid all the predictable jingoistic verse—whatever its particular affiliation—appear a great many poems that explicitly take up the plight of the victims of war and revolution. Poems assume the voices of wives, daughters, and sisters, effectively mining the rich vein of sympathy precisely because the trauma addressed in the poems was so palpable an issue to the readership. Both the physical effects and the psychological and societal effects of the wars against the Revolution and subsequently against Napoleon were so profound and so widely shared that sympathy was virtually guaranteed.[24] Elizabeth Moody's ballad is typical in the universality of the experience it recounts:

> Ah, William, wherefore didst thou go
> To foreign lands to meet the foe?
> Why, won by war's deceitful charms,
> Didst thou forsake thy Anna's arms?[25]

Note how Moody enhances this universality of experience by rendering it in conventionally domesticized, gendered fashion through the traditional Christian names, the trope on seduction, and the apparently innocent pun on "arms" in the final line of this stanza. Poems of this sort—and there are many of them—help to define the tenor of the period, and its growing emphasis on community. Images of the home, of the family, of the hearth and the domestic circle—all of which regularly stand in for implied figurations of the nation—constitute a large and powerful presence within the Romantic ethos in the 1790s.

Nor is this all. The attribute of "domesticity" typically assigned to poetry by women (where it is customarily praised) and to—less frequently—poetry by men (where it is generally dismissed or ridiculed) likewise owes much to this complicated matrix of sentiment and sympathy. Anne Mellor suggests in *Romanticism and Gender* that a major difference between masculine Romanticism and feminine Romanticism, especially in prose fiction, derives from the woman writer's preference for themes of community and sharing—for "domestic affections"—and for an ultimately logical and integrative approach to self, other, and others (a.k.a "society"), as opposed to the more isolationistic, hierarchical, and exploitative themes and subjects to be found in the male writer's works. But the themes that Mellor and others associate with the woman writer are in fact present also in a great deal of writing by men, though both their immediate forms and their rhetorical (and intellectual) emphases may be different. Moreover, they are present in poetry and in prose fiction, and they emerge perhaps even more strikingly in dramatic literature, where the sentimental import is underscored by the shift away from the relative reserve of Neoclassical drama (and theatre practice) and toward the broader and more emotional style of Romantic theatre in which melodrama played an increasing part. The blurring of gendered expectations to which these facts point, together with the resistance of all writing of the Romantic period to consistent division along gender lines in subject, form, or function, further argues for considering women and men writers together within a single more flexible and more generously conceived literary community.

One final point about the function of sentiment in Romantic writing. The resolutions of Romantic tales (whether in verse, prose, or drama) are often uncommonly grim, especially—but again *not exclusively*—in works by women authors. That is, in poems both long and short by writers like Helen Maria Williams, Charlotte Smith, Letitia Landon, and Felicia Hemans; in fiction by authors like Mary Robinson, Charlotte Smith (again), Susan Ferrier, Amelia Opie, and Mary Shelley; and in plays by dramatists like Joanna Baillie and Mary Pix; *and* in poems, novels, and plays by their male contemporaries—the final scene often is one of death, either literal or figurative. Often in women's writings encounters with death faced by the protagonist, the narrator, or the authorial persona are particularly stark, both in their physical and emotional detailing and in the abruptness with which death arrives on the scene in virtually the final words of the work.[26] Less often, but often enough to remark, something of the sort occurs in the men's writing (P. B. Shelley's early romance, *Zastrozzi*, for instance, or his later drama, *The Cenci*). What does this suggest about the community-building that is so central to so many Romantic literary works? Is the human condition *really* so bleak as these conclusions seem to imply? Is that storybook Romanticism we once heard so much about—that soaring optimism, that idealistic aspiration—all an illusion, a charade? Or do we need again to rethink our characterizations, our assumptions, and our conditioned responses?

Part of the answer undoubtedly lies in the converging terminology of sentiment and the Sublime. The common ground lies in the superabundance of affective response, of emotion, of feeling. Of course, the subject of death—both in the abstract and in the local and particularized—has historically been regarded as at once the most terrible and the most chastening of subjects. Furthermore, the history of art—right up through today's media productions—provides ample evidence of the perennial appeal of death as a theme. Not for nothing was the term "tearjerker" coined for works in all media which exploit their audience's emotional responses for all they're worth. But this is merely a pop-culture version of the more traditionally legitimized version of tear-jerking we associate with the tradition of *memento mori* and the *ars moriendi*. I observed earlier that the function of sentiment in a project of *education* always involves the author and the reader; the same is true in the case of writing about death.

When Robinson's or Smith's or Landon's poems end with proleptic visions of their speaker's oblivion—often a consciously *desired* oblivion (Landon's *Improvisatrice*, for instance, or any number of Smith's *Elegiac Sonnets*), which makes the sentiment the more terrible in the Burkean sense—they deliberately link the sentimental and the sublime. Death is of course at once the most common and the most extraordinary event in human experience. But for the earlier Romantics death bore special relevance. For they were writing in the wake of increasingly destructive wars first against France, then against the American colonies, and then against Revolutionary France. Given the already considerable mortality rates that were a fact of late eighteenth-century life, the inevitable slaughter that goes with war ensured that death—often sudden death—touched virtually every social unit. If the central impulse of Romantic thought involves the primacy of human community, then the principal threat to that integrative Eden that humanity is ever at work to reconstruct must inevitably be death.

This plain fact informs one aspect of what has often been called "the Romantic dilemma," the fact that however much we may formulate our private, imaginative Edens, we all live nevertheless in temporal, public Wildernesses. This central lesson of Coleridge's "Kubla Khan" is repeated everywhere in Romantic writing. Its very inescapability makes it all the more compelling. Writer after writer confronts this terrible enigma of human existence. And here women's writing is especially illuminating in its particular foregrounding of the notion of *community*. Anne Grant's poignant "Familiar Epistle" invokes the intimate community of experience shared by the recipient of her verse letter (and by extension subsequent public readers), while Joanna Baillie's poems on the seasons literally reproduce for us the internal and external (or public) dynamics of the rural family unit,[27] which stands in stark contrast to the increasingly common dysfunctional family shattered on the rocks of post-Industrial Revolution dislocation, depersonalization, and urbanization. Mary Robinson's and Anne Hunter's poems to and about their daughters address the same dynamic of community, whose fragility is paradoxically underscored by the immediate or proleptic references to new, altered communities betokened by marriages and births.[28] But then, Coleridge's "Frost at Midnight" is in its own way no less about making and unmaking. Indeed, at the center of Wordsworth's famous claim that the poet "is a man speaking to men"[29] lies the implied truth that all persons are potentially poets and that they therefore constitute at least *potentially* a self-sustaining integrated community, if they will only realize that this is so, a community whose common social bonds are activated by acts of imagination that set in motion societal acts that inform interpersonal relations in the public world.

Moreover, it is clear from Wordsworth's remarks in the Preface to the *Lyrical Ballads* that he expects his poems to serve an educational purpose. It is equally clear that Wordsworth expects his reader's educational experience to be grounded in significant measure in that area most associated with sentiment: the feelings and "affections." He writes: "I have therefore to request, that the Reader would abide independently by his own *feelings*, and that if he finds himself *affected* he would not suffer such conjectures [as arise from what the reader thinks *others* might think] to interfere with his pleasure" (my emphases).[30] The masculinist terminology notwithstanding, Wordsworth's point is clear: the immediate, unvitiated individual response is the most valid one, and the surest route to an appropriately responsive reading leads through the feelings rather than the "meddling intellect."

I suggested earlier that the most important dividing-line in British Romanticism may lie along the historical and cultural fault line inscribed by the beginning of the Regency. As early as 1810 the sort of communitarian writing we associate with the so-called "early Romantics" and their eighteenth-century forebears begins to give way to a more deeply skeptical sort of writing that increasingly questions the viability of community in any sense. This is the lesson Byron teaches in his profoundly ambivalent poetry, where impulses toward community are subverted or parodied when they are not flatly rejected—even at the same time the fundamental attraction of those impulses is everywhere reinforced. It is the lesson we find, too, in Letitia Landon's remarkable *Improvisatrice* of 1825 and in Felicia Hemans's *Records of Woman* (1828). While Anne Mellor rejects the stance Landon typically adopts in her poems because it denies the sustaining authenticity of the woman's inner life,[31] that stance nevertheless reveals—like the one often taken by Byron's protagonists—the hazard to one's inner self inevitably posed by *any* attempt to live a life of interpersonal community, *whatever* the terms of that life, and whether one is female or male, as Mary Shelley's *Frankenstein* demonstrates with particular poignancy.[32] It is this growing anxiety about the potentially *destructive* nature of the effort to extend oneself and establish community—whether of sentiment, of affections, or of plain practical social necessity—that introduces a new and ominous note to Romantic writing during the Regency and afterwards. As William Hone and George Cruikshank demonstrated in devastating fashion in *The Political House that Jack Built* (1819),[33] the whole notion of an integrated, dynamic, and salutary community (and here the nation may be seen also to figure the domestic family) is revealed as a sham, an illusion. Where the nation should be "maternal and nurturing" in its devotion to protecting the family (whether figured as nuclear family or as the Nation), Hone and Cruikshank reveal that it is instead "aggressive and self-indulgent."[34] "The Family," whether we regard it as domestic social unit, national body, or ideological ideal, seemed by the later Regency to be a dying institution, as appeared painfully obvious to the shocked public when Princess Charlotte Augusta, the Prince Regent's only child, died after bearing a stillborn son on 6 November 1817. Hence it is little surprise that the fatalism—indeed the utter nihilism—that is everywhere a hallmark of Byron's *Don Juan* lurks in the wings of the theatre of later Regency consciousness, spilling out ever more uncontrollably into the dominant mind-set of the age.

How great was the rupture with a past built on a benevolent moral, social, and economic meritocracy is indicated by a long anonymous poem from 1819 called *The Political Dessert*, where public cynicism about war profiteering in post-war England is plainly evident:

X.

> Time was, when there was work and bread enough,
>   Ere war had pour'd its fellest evils forth;
> When land was tax'd, as well as other stuff,
>   Yet all things were not mortgag'd to their worth;

> Where, less dependent, man met no rebuff
>   Unmerited, nor slighted his free birth,
> No one's displeasure dreaded, no one's spite,
> While speaking, writing, norwhile acting right.
>
> XI.
>
> E'en in the midst of the late, bloody war,
>   Which cost each week a million pound,
> The portion spent at home, whatever for,
>   Fail'd not to give employ to all around.
> A peace, 'twas fear'd, as it's turned out, would mar
>   Their pickings, and all business greatly bound:
> 'Twas therefore wish'd the war might be eternal,
> Whether the cause were human, or infernal.[35]

What has broken down are the sympathetic bonds of community that once bound one citizen to another and made the welfare of one the concern of all. The new world of industrial capitalism that builds empires upon the blood of the citizens has already begun its inexorable process of transforming brothers and sisters into competitors.

The self-consuming and in many respects self-contradictory ethos of flamboyant doubt and *malaise* that characterizes the later Regency could only serve to propel to the surface the contrary, reactionary impulses that were to govern so much of the Victorian ethos that would succeed and supplant it. As the Victorian novelists would eventually labor to show their readers, "community" would have to be defined and sustained in a wholly different fashion in the modern urban, industrial world of anxiety and alienation in which the "later Romantics" already found themselves. In this light it is enormously instructive to remember that Dickens has David Copperfield declare repeatedly in the 1850 novel that his project is to "discipline" his heart, a thoroughly pragmatic objective that would have been as inconceivable to Sterne as it would have been to the early Romantics who built on the foundation that he and others had laid.

No doubt the Romantics themselves would have been puzzled—and not a little amused—by attempts to characterize them and their various projects with a single, one-size-fits-all label. By the first half of our own century, however, when the academic critical industry had gotten well into its project of marginalizing or erasing the vast majority of writers of the Romantic period and then trying to convince us that those few who remained on the page were THE Romantics, the utility of easy labels was clear. Indeed, it was much clearer then than it is now, when we have begun in earnest to interrogate such labels and the ideological forces that generate them. Was there ever a Romantic community, a common field of cultural turf? Probably there was, though not in the narrow, univocal sense the terminology implies. Certainly that is the implication of Percy Shelley's observation in the Preface to *Prometheus Unbound* that writers exist in a historical and cultural community—both of general publics and of writers in particular—that furnishes the forms of their art, to which "endowment of the age in which they live" individual writers contribute that genius which is "the uncommunicated lightning of their own mind."[36] What almost certainly did characterize this Romantic ethos was a sense of common cause—even when it was a deliberately adversarial one among participants whose ideological and intellectual agendas varied widely. What we now think of as the early Romantic period may have been the last time in Western history in which it was still possible to sustain a belief in an egalitarian, communitarian vision of a society grounded in the sort of *sympathy* Hume had described. In a very real sense that now, at the distance of two centuries, is often touching in its earnestness, the early Romantic writers devoted themselves and their works to educating their audiences in how to make it all happen, providing them with both models of response and texts conceived to awaken and exercise those affections, those moving soft sentiments, that would humanize readers and engender in them that humanizing sympathy. Their successors in the Regency and afterwards were less fortunate. It fell to them to begin educating *their* audiences in how to *cope* with the fact that it had not happened—and probably would not happen. The predicament they faced is summed up with particular poignancy by the remark that Lily Tomlin has made in our own time and in quite a different context: "Just remember, we're all in this alone."[37]

Notes

1. *English Literature, 1770-1835*. Ed. Richard Matlack and Anne K. Mellor (Fort Worth: Harcourt Brace Jovanovich, 1995).

2. Marilyn Butler, "Repossessing the Past: the Case for an Open Literary History," *Rethinking Historicism: Critical Readings in Romantic History*, ed. Marjorie Levinson (Oxford: Basil Blackwell, 1989), 72.

3. Clifford Siskin, *The Historicity of Romantic Discourse* (New York: Oxford UP, 1988); J. R. deJ. Jackson, *Historical Criticism and the Meaning of Texts* (London: Routledge, 1989); Marjorie Levinson, "The New Historicism: Back to the Future," *Rethinking Historicism: Critical Readings in Romantic History*, ed. Levinson (Oxford: Basil Blackwell, 1989), 18-63; Marilyn Butler, *Romantics, Rebels, and Reactionaries: English Literature and its Background, 1760-1830* (New York: Oxford UP, 1982), and "Repossessing the Past," *Rethinking Romanticism*, 64-84; Stuart Curran, *Poetic Form and British Romanticism* (New York: Oxford UP, 1986); Jerome J. McGann, *The Beauty of Inflections: Literary Investigations in Historical Method and Theory* (Oxford: Clarendon Press, 1985), and *Social Values and Poetic Acts: The Historical Judgment of Literary Work* (Cambridge: Harvard UP, 1988).

4. Levinson, "The New Historicism," 50.

5. Anne Mellor, *Romanticism and Gender* (New York: Routledge, 1993); Marlon Ross, *The Contours of Masculine Desire: Romanticism and the Rise of Women's Poetry* (New York: Oxford UP, 1989); *Women Romantic Poets, 1785-1832: An Anthology*, ed. Jennifer Breen (London: J. M. Dent, 1992), *Women Romantic Poets, 1770-1838: An Anthology*, ed. Andrew Ashfield (New York: St. Martin's, 1995).

6. Curran, *Poetic Form and British Romanticism*; *The New Oxford Book of Romantic Period Verse*, ed. Jerome J. McGann (Oxford: Oxford UP, 1993). See also *Romanticism: An Anthology*, ed. Duncan Wu (Oxford: Basil Blackwell, 1994).

7. A particularly good example is Matlack and Mellor's *English Literature, 1770-1835*.

8. Siskin, 68.

9. Benedict Anderson, *Imagined Communities: Reflections on the Origin and Spread of Nationalism* (London: Verso, 1983), 47; see especially chapter 3.

10. Edmund Burke, *A Philosophical Enquiry into the Origin of our Ideas of the Sublime and Beautiful* (1757), I, vii.

11. Mary Wollstonecraft, *"Mary" and "The Wrongs of Woman,"* ed. Gary Kelly (New York: Oxford UP, 1980), 53.

12. G. J. Barker-Benfield, *The Culture of Sensibility: Sex and Society in Eighteenth-Century Britain* (Chicago: U of Chicago P, 1992), xxx.

13. *William Wordsworth: The Poems*, ed. John O. Hayden, 2 vols. (New Haven: Yale UP, 1981), I: 886.

14. Laurence Sterne, *A Sentimental Journey through France and Italy, by Mr. Yorick*, ed. Gardner D. Stout, Jr. (Berkeley: U of California P, 1967), 219.

15. Barker-Benfield, 16-23. See, for instance, Wordsworth's Intimations Ode ("those first affections," line 149) or "Tintern Abbey" ("sensations sweet, / Felt in the blood, and felt along the heart," lines 27-28).

16. David Hume, *A Treatise of Human Nature*, ed. L. A. Selby-Bigge (Oxford: Clarendon Press, 1888), 577, 589, 362.

17. *Shelley's Poetry and Prose*, eds. Donald H. Reiman and Sharon B. Powers (New York: W. W. Norton, 1977), 487-88.

18. Mr. [Samuel Jackson] Pratt, *Bread; or, The Poor. A Poem* (London: Longman and Rees, T. Becket, 1801), 2.

19. [Samuel Jackson Pratt], *Sympathy; or, a Sketch of the Social Passion* (London: T. Cadell, 1781). I quote, below, from the fourth edition, re-titled *Sympathy. A Poem* (London: T. Cadell, 1781).

20. See Siskin, p. 82; I have taken Siskin's argument to what seems to me its logical next step.

21. "To a Young Ass, Its Mother being Tethered Near It"; first printed in *The Morning Chronicle*, 30 December 1794. *The Poems of Samuel Taylor Coleridge*, ed. Ernest Hartley Coleridge (London: Oxford UP, 1917), 74-76.

22. I would note here that what Siskin says about later eighteenth-century novels of Sensibility (like Sterne's *Sentimental Journey*), that "they have been marginalized by the literary institution because they suggest that feeling is *unavoidably* didactic" (90), is true also of the *poetry* of sensibility and of sentiment. Paradoxically, while a poem like Coleridge's continues to be the butt of humorous readings that deliberately avoid "getting" its point, other works of "high Romanticism" that engage in some of the same sentimental techniques and for much the same purposes (Wordsworth's Intimations Ode is merely one example), routinely escape castigation—at least on those grounds.

23. *Sentimental Journey*, 138. In "Repossessing the Past," 77, Butler cites this same poem in connection with her discussion of how Southey's *Thalaba the Destroyer* demonstrates how members of writing communities *and the cultural community they shared with their readers*, detected and manipulated references to one another's works in their own. I would add that the inclusion of inter-textual references which would be apparent to knowledgeable readers directly signals to those readers their membership in a community in which they are in fact employed as collaborative writers, as co-creators, and in which that membership is at once engineered and acknowledged by the originary author.

24. Indeed, some authors were able to write effectively on both sides of the issues, adjusting their positions as circumstances changed in the dark days of the Terror and afterward. "Recantation" could be turned to real political—and literary—profit, as we may see in the publication record during the 1790s of authors like Coleridge or Smith.

25. Mrs. [Elizabeth] Moody, "Anna's Complaint; Or the Miseries of War; Written in the Isle of Thanet, 1794"; first published in *The Universal Magazine* 96 (March 1795); reproduced in Betty T. Bennett, *British War Poetry in the Age of Romanticism: 1793-1815* (New York: Garland, 1976). Bennett's collection is a particularly rich treasury of primary material.

26. The poems of Smith (especially) and Robinson, and later of Hemans in *Records of Woman*, provide good examples.

27. Anne Grant, "A Familiar Epistle to a Friend" (1795); Joanna Baillie, "A Winter's Day," "A Summer's Day" (both 1790). All are reproduced in Jennifer Breen, *Women Romantic Poets, 1785-1832: An Anthology* (London: J. M. Dent, 1992), 86-93, 43-59.

28. For example, Robinson, "Ode to My Beloved Daughter," "Sonnet to my Beloved Daughter"; Hunter, "To My Daughter on Being Separated from Her on Her Marriage" (1802). Hunter's poem is in Breen, 118. Robinson's poems are in *The Poetical Works of the Late Mrs. Mary Robinson* (London: Jones and Co., 1824), 54, 188.

29. "Preface to *Lyrical Ballads*," *Poems*, I: 877.

30. *Poems*, I: 890.

31. Mellor, Chapter 6; esp. 112-13.

32. I have discussed this in a different context in "Mary Shelley, *Frankenstein*, and the Woman Writer's Fate," *Romantic Women Writers: Voices and Counter-voices*, eds. Paula R. Feldman and Theresa M. Kelley (Hanover: UP of New England, 1995), 69-87.

33. *The Political House that Jack Built* (London: William Hone, 1819); illustrations by George Cruikshank.

34. Michael Henry Scrivener, *Radical Shelley: The Philosophical Anarchism and Utopian Thought of Percy Bysshe Shelley* (Princeton: Princeton UP, 1982), 201-3.

35. [Anon.], *The Political Dessert* (London: W. Neely, 1819), 10.

36. *Shelley's Poetry and Prose*, 134.

37. *Quotable Women* (Philadelphia: Running Press, 1989).

Mutual Trust and the Friendly Loan: Melville, Money, and Romantic Faith

Clark Davis

> All the world over, the picturesque yields to the pocketesque.
> —Melville, "I and My Chimney"

The reader who sets out to understand what Herman Melville thought about the English Romantics will have a relatively short journey. In all of Melville's works, the space devoted directly or indirectly to nineteenth century English writers is small, especially when compared to the frequent comments, usually outright attacks, on American transcendentalism, Emerson, and the generally harmful effects of optimistic philosophies. Despite this paucity of reference, however, readers have managed to locate notable allusions to the major English Romantic poets, especially Wordsworth. In two works of the middle 1850s, for instance, Melville includes the author of *The Prelude* in his general broadside against Emerson and company, in each case by means of a brief parody of a Wordsworth poem.[1]

The first occurs in 1854 in a short story entitled "Cock-A-Doodle-Doo!" Written after the failure of Melville's seventh novel, *Pierre* (1852), the story, like the novel before it, takes aim at idealism, exposing the dangers involved when the physical world is denied in favor of a more pleasant idealization. Melville's figure for such thinking is the "magic cock" that crows like "the great bell of St. Paul's rung at a coronation," leading the story's narrator out of his "hypoes" and into a search for optimism.²

The parody—here of "Resolution and Independence"—appears early in the story, just after the gloomy narrator has been revitalized by the sound of the "triumphant thanksgiving of a cock-crow!" (271). Worried that the bird might limit his exaltations to the morning hours, the narrator adapts the poem's famous lines to the situation:

> . . . Of fine mornings,
> We fine lusty cocks begin our crows in gladness;
> But when eve does come we don't crow quite so much,
> For then cometh despondency and madness. (272)

According to Marvin Fisher, this relatively slight attack forms part of a more general revision of Wordsworth's poem. Aside from changing Wordsworth's "stock-dove, jay, magpie, and skylark" into the American rooster (the "lusty cock," pun intended), Melville ultimately equates Wordsworth's poetic optimism with a kind of madness.³ As the story concludes, the cock/poet crows magnificently, uplifting the spirits of his owner's family but doing little for their rapidly failing bodies. The narrator watches as Merrymusk—the poor sawyer who owns the rooster—dies happily, unaware that the cock's optimistic crowing has distracted him from the more mundane, physical concerns of his own and his family's sickness. In other words, Merrymusk's optimism, gained from the cock, has not only proved misleading; it is indirectly responsible for his own death and the death of his family.⁴

Three years later, in 1857, Melville took aim at Wordsworth again to make a similar point. The second parody appears in the even darker pages of *The Confidence-Man*, where "a somewhat elderly person, in the quaker dress" passes out handbills containing an ode with the following title: "Ode: On the Intimations of Distrust in Man, Unwillingly Inferred from Repeated Repulses, in Disinterested Endeavors to Procure His Confidence."⁵ Again, the poet is the voice of optimism—or in this case "confidence," that is, faith in the basic goodness of others—though the title of his ode seems more a lament than an attempt to inspire. Like many of the other passengers on board the *Fidèle*, the Quaker appears to be a kind of minor confidence-man, not one of the shape-shifting rhetoricians who exist only to destroy human faith, but an unconscious purveyor of hopeful philosophy who is sincere in his own faith but potentially harmful just the same. In this sense, the quaker helps demonstrate one of the novel's primary ironies: that even those with good intentions, the "disinterested" interest of the charitable soul, can still cause irreparable damage, if only by encouraging unchecked idealism.

The common ground between these two parodies may seem clear enough at first glance. The argument appears to go something like this: Melville, stung by his own failures, is taking out his frustrations on those who suggest that despair can be overcome simply by the application of faith and hope. He focuses on Wordsworth because his poems are well-known and because the sometimes inflated figure of the Romantic poet, like that of the Romantic philosopher, is an easy target.[6]

But while such an explanation may be accurate, it neglects a serious, if somewhat hidden element in Melville's attack. If we look closer at the parodies and their narrative contexts, we can see that Melville bases his criticisms of Wordsworth and optimism (or "confidence") not simply on a different perception of human nature but on a different interpretation of human relationships and language. For the Melville of the later 1850s, the question of faith or confidence in other human beings is often inseparable from his interpretation and criticism of financial relationships in America. Human interest is frequently corrupted by financial interest. Faith or trust, and the words that are their signs, are revealed to exist in a false economy continually undercut by the reality of material necessity. In these ironic Melvillian worlds, Wordsworthian hope seems impossible if not absurd because the language of optimism (and its counterpart faith or "credit") represents in part the failure of language itself, specifically the separation of sign and signification evident in the false money of loans.

It may not be immediately apparent in either of the parodies that money is a significant issue, but in both instances the problems of finance, particularly the ethics of loan-making and loan-taking, form a major element of the narrative background. In "Cock-A-Doodle-Doo!," for instance, the narrator, when he is not searching for the "majestic" cock, is being chased by a "lean rascal" of a dun who is symbolically related to the instruments of progress—particularly the locomotive—that have contributed to the narrator's pessimistic vision. Speaking of the railroad, the narrator wishes that

> ... fifty conspiring mountains would fall atop of him!
> And, while they were about it, would they would also fall atop of that smaller dunning fiend, my creditor, who frightens the life out of me more than any locomotive—a lantern-jawed rascal, who seems to run on a railroad track, too, and duns me even on Sunday, all the way to church and back, and comes and sits in the same pew with me, and pretending to be polite and hand me the prayer-book opened at the proper place, pokes his pesky bill under my nose in the very midst of my devotions, and so shoves himself between me and salvation; for how can one keep his temper on such occasions? (270)

It is precisely this conflict between the worldly, definite demands of money and the other-worldly, indefinite demands of spirit that supports the story's general attack on faith. To read the prayer book is, after all, to consent to the notion that language can and does transcend human limits. The "pesky bill" not only brings the narrator down to earth, ruining his devotions; it demands attention for an alternate system of symbolic relationships, one that refuses both transcendence and the spiritual plenum of knowledge and meaning. After all, the dun wishes to be *paid*, to see the symbolic money of credit translated into the material money of specie, and this demand directly contradicts the very notion of human credit or, more pointedly, "belief."

Even the ironic economics of "Resolution and Independence" fail to offer a practicable solution to the increasingly idealistic narrator. Though Merrymusk, like the leech gatherer, represents the symbolic "wealth" of the optimistic or persevering individual, his non-material riches prove harmful precisely because they are not tangible and because they lead their possessor away from the physical world. In a linguistic sense, they create what is clearly a false value, a symbolic wealth analogous to the loans that the narrator labors to repay. In this respect, the narrator learns the lesson of Wordsworth's poem all too well, and yet he fails to realize that in Melville's universe there is a price to pay for turning from the real to the ideal—a tangible, financial price, represented in part by the continued action of the bill collector. For while the narrator continues to search for Merrymusks's rooster, the dun initiates a lawsuit, finally forcing the narrator to "clap another mortgage on [his] estate" to pay his bills (278). And though this action offers him some temporary relief from the pressures of debt, the increased "interest" (both financial and legal) of the extended loan casts yet another shadow over the story's already ironic conclusion.

The Confidence-Man offers similar, if somewhat more sinister, examples of the conflation or confusion of symbolic and material values. In fact, the sudden shift from abstract to concrete—from an idea to its monetary expression—plays a crucial role in the confidence-man's seductive technique. A good example of this maneuver occurs early in the book when a "man in gray"—the confidence-man in one of his many disguises—sidles up to "a plump and pleasant [widow], whose aspect seems to hint that, if she have any weak point, it must be anything rather than her excellent heart" (43). She is reading "a small gilt testament" open to the thirteenth chapter of First Corinthians (the exhortation to charity) when the man in gray begins his seduction. Over the course of the subsequent conversation he gradually gains her confidence by exhibiting an immediate trust in her. This unexpected gift of belief eventually embarrasses the widow into a halting reciprocation:

> "No one can befriend me, who has not confidence."
> "But I—I have—at least to a degree—I mean that—"
> "Nay, nay, you have none—none at all. Pardon, I see it. No confidence. Fool, fond fool that I am to seek it!"
> "You are unjust sir," rejoins the good lady with heightened interest; "but it may be that something untoward in your experiences has unduly biased you. Not that I would cast reflections. Believe me, I—yes, yes—I may say—that—that—" (44)

At this point the man in gray has accomplished his goal. The widow is on the verge of admitting her trust in a stranger, but the trust she has conceived remains an abstraction, an idea with little material substance to give it specific value. In other words, at this point she is being asked for "credit" rather than cash. So the confidence-man, as is his practice, changes registers:

> "That you have confidence? Prove it. Let me have twenty dollars."
> "Twenty dollars!"
> "There I told you, madame, you had no confidence." (44-45)

As with most of the confidence-man's arguments, this claim seems justifiable, a simple request for proof. But the introduction of a specific monetary value in such an exchange changes the field dramatically. The widow is forced to choose between symbolic and material definitions of value, and that choice proves to be difficult and even perilous aboard the *Fidèle*. For in Melville's 1857 America, neither credit nor cash is a reliable indication of value. Credit or confidence depends upon mutual trust and is undermined by the confidence-man's lies. Cash, which should be reliable, is likewise subject to the symbolic fictions of counterfeiters. Again and again the individual faces an impossible choice, and neither "Cock-A-Doodle-Doo!" nor *The Confidence-Man*, as fictional worlds, contains the possibility of a compromise.

The most memorable and damning example of this condition occurs late in *The Confidence-Man* in a story told by one of the riverboat's passengers. Like most of the novel's many internal narratives, the story of China Aster is compromised by several layers of fictionality. The tale is told by a passenger named Egbert, disciple to the Emersonian Mark Winsome and long considered a fictional portrait of Henry Thoreau. Egbert has been challenged by the cosmopolitan (another possible confidence-man) to a sort of fictional dialogue; the two will pretend to be bosom-friends, one of whom will seek a loan from the other. "For brevity," as the cosmopolitan says, Egbert will be called "Frank" and the cosmopolitan, "Charlie." In the course of their discussion, as part of his attempt to argue against the giving of loans, Charlie/Egbert tells the story of China Aster—but not in his own words. It seems that "the original story-teller," as he puts it, "has so tyrannized over [him], that it is quite impossible . . . to repeat his incidents without sliding into his style" (207). Since the story he is about to tell concerns trust (both linguistic and financial), it seems clear that this elaborate distancing of narrator from narrative serves to remind us of the basic unreliability of words. By extension, it may very well also imply an inability to trust any system in which the value of the sign is dependent upon a mutually agreed upon meaning or set of meanings. If we cannot trust the storyteller, be he "Frank" or Charlie, how can we trust the banker whose hopeful narrative of a brighter future turns upon the mutual assumption of risk? If we cannot trust language itself, how can we trust the symbolic money of loans or the symbolic value of bank notes?[7]

Having thus thoroughly undermined his narrative, Melville then tells the story of a young candle maker, China Aster, who is persuaded by his lottery-winning friend, Orchis, to accept a friendly loan in order to invest in the production of expensive spermaceti candles. Though initially reluctant, China Aster dreams of success and takes the loan, only to endure a series of business failures that force him to take out additional loans to pay off the mounting interest. Eventually, China Aster sickens and dies, losing all his property to his creditors and leaving his wife and children in the care of the state.

The story has often been explained as an allegory of Melville's own financial failure as a writer, with possible echoes of his father's disastrous bankruptcy and related premature death. If such a context is accurate, the story of China Aster may well be Melville's most heartfelt complaint against the corruption of human relationships by the consuming powers of monetary credit and interest. After all, Orchis makes the initial loan out of pure benevolence and generosity of spirit, but as his own financial situation worsens, he transforms into the rapacious, heartless dun.[8] The symbolic wealth of his "confidence" yields to the pressing demand for "actual" as opposed to symbolic wealth. In this respect, China Aster, an unsuccessful business man, fails not only to read the market correctly but also to understand that in Melville's world Romantic promises cannot be kept because the symbolic values of money and language lose meaning in the face of material needs and physical realities.

The question Melville asks of Romanticism thus reduces to the relative powers of mind over matter. Is thought or language hardy enough to transform the harsher facts of existence, signs of poverty and loss, into signs of hope? Are the leech gatherer's "lofty utterance" and cheerful demeanor really adequate to provide the despondent poet with a source of hope "real" enough to sustain him through his "fears and fancies thick" of "Solitude, pain of heart, distress, and poverty"? Given his own experiences with money and credit, Melville apparently says "NO! in thunder," in part because he considers the language of the "well-housed, well-warmed, and well-fed" tainted by its preference for just such symbolism as the guise for its own ruthlessly materialistic economy.

"Poor Man's Pudding," Melville's companion piece to "Rich Man's Crumbs," makes the case most directly. In this sketch the poet Blandmour—a possible Wordsworthian caricature—offers the "philosophy" that "Nature, is in all things beneficient; and not only so, but considerate in her charities, as any discreet human philanthropist might be" (289). This natural charity consists in the readily available "substitute" for such things as manure for fertilizing fields, medicine for weak eyes and "other bodily harms," eggs, and, of course, pudding: "Come now, and if after this eating, you do not say that a 'Poor Man's Pudding' is as relishable as a rich man's, I will give up the point altogether; which briefly is: that, through kind Nature, the poor, out of their very poverty, extract comfort" (291). The audience for this remark is the tale's narrator, who takes a generally skeptical view of both nature and Blandmour's "point." Conducting his own investigation of the reality behind his friend's poetic sentiments, he discovers a way of life and a level of poverty that refuses all reference to Blandmour's vision. Indeed, Blandmour's words lose all meaning in the context of Farmer Coulter's damp, squalid cabin. This alteration becomes starkly clear when the narrator is offered the titular pudding of "rice, milk, and salt boiled together," and makes the mistake of venturing his friend's optimistic phrasing:

> "Ah, what they call 'Poor Man's Pudding,' I suppose you mean."
> A quick flush, half resentful, passed over her face.
> "*We* do not call it so, sir," she said, and was silent. (292-93)

The poor "do not call it so" out of pride, of course, but also out of a deeper understanding of the material basis of wealth. They do not call it so because for them it is not "Poor Man's Pudding"; the words themselves have changed meaning because the economic reality has asserted its power over the "poetic" power of Blandmour's optimism. The "pudding" is not pudding, and calling it so has no material effect.[9] Despite the best efforts of the Romantic imagination, transcendent language fails in the absence of financial support; or, as another Melville narrator puts it, "All the world over, the picturesque yields to the pocketesque."[10]

Even more than the direct parodies, "Poor Man's Pudding" may be Melville's harshest attack on the Romantic economics of "Resolution and Independence." However, yet another similarly structured tale, "Jimmy Rose," suggests that his thoughts on this particular dilemma did not confine themselves to ironic criticism of symbolic values. Like "Cock-A-Doodle-Doo!" and "Poor Man's Pudding," "Jimmy Rose" presents an encounter between a narrator of uncertain financial status and a figure who has, at least economically, been "ruined." As in "Resolution and Independence," the narrator draws upon the downtrodden character for a degree of symbolic sustenance, a sort of credit or belief in the sustaining power of human spirit. But unlike Wordsworth's poem, the attitude toward the ruined figure is notably uncertain, and the prevailing tone seems openly troubled by the very notion that genuine suffering might be the source of an illegitimate symbolic wealth.

Born "a man of moderate fortune," Jimmy Rose operates a "large and princely business" that eventually makes him wealthy enough to "entertain on a grand scale" (338). He throws the best parties "in the party-giving city of New York" and has a gift for "saying fine things" to please his guests. Despite his geniality, however, a series of disastrous events and bad decisions leaves him bankrupt.[11] He never recovers his wealth, and yet when the narrator meets him again twenty-five years later, the ruined Jimmy is not "dry, shrunken, meagre, cadaverously fierce with misery and misanthropy..." (342). His bad fortune has not destroyed his essentially "rosy" nature, and he is able to frequent the houses of his former friends and smile in the face of his own misfortune.

Though the roses still bloom in Jimmy's cheeks, however, the narrator, despite all his efforts, fails to follow the Romantic pattern and convert his friend into a symbol of hope. Amazed by the ruined man's attitude, the narrator nevertheless registers a degree of uncertainty about Jimmy's apparently constant smiles:

> But the most touching thing of all were those roses in his cheeks; those ruddy roses in his nipping winter. How they bloomed; whether meal and milk, and tea and toast could keep them flourishing; whether now he painted them; by what strange magic they were made to blossom so; no son of man might tell. But there they bloomed. And besides the roses, Jimmy was rich in smiles. (343)

Rather than lead to a larger expression of the value of faith or hope in the face of financial disaster, the narrator's language suggests that he is simply unable to understand his friend's contradictory condition. He does little more than register his surprise at the incongruity, along with the suspicion that Jimmy's "roses" may be rouge. The hint is fleshed out in a later scene when a charitable young woman brings the dying Jimmy "some little delicacies, and also several books, of such a sort as are sent by serious-minded well-wishers to invalids in a serious crisis" (344):

> . . . as the gentle girl withdrew, Jimmy, with what small remains of strength were his, pitched the books into the furthest corner, murmuring, "Why will she bring me this sad old stuff? Does she take me for a pauper? Thinks she to salve a gentleman's heart with Poor Man's Plaster?" (344)

Though himself an ostensible symbol of Romantic hope, Jimmy here echoes the anti-Romantic argument of the narrator of "Poor Man's Pudding." His denunciation of the charitable young woman's literature also casts doubt on the optimistic reading of his own rosy cheeks and wealth of smiles.[12] The narrator's response—"Poor, poor Jimmy—God guard us all—poor Jimmy Rose!"—does little to suggest that Jimmy represents such hope or that the narrator is able to convert the dying pauper into a symbol for spiritual wealth. In fact, one of the story's primary ironies concerns the fact that Jimmy was ruined by over-extended *credit*, the financial equivalent of the Romantic transformation of poverty into wealth.

There are of course other Melville tales from the middle 1850s that can be said to comment upon the basic structure of "Resolution and Independence." "The Piazza," for instance, turns the encounter with the leech gatherer into an ironically reciprocal attempt to symbolize the distant other. The narrator goes in search of his dream (a distant "spot of radiance" in the mountains) but finds only a poor cabin and a lonely young woman who dreams the same dream about his own distant farm. Similarly, "Bartleby, the Scrivener," the darkest and most famous of the group, gives us a leech gatherer who will not respond, who in fact refuses all attempts at communication and symbolization. His death in the "tombs" of New York leaves the regressive, Romantic narrator at a literal loss for words. Not even the lawyer's sentimental epilogue—in which the scrivener becomes the representative of forlorn humanity—is able to transcend Bartleby's simple refusal to accept either help or meaning. Even here, economics plays a similar role, blinding the affluent narrator to the corrupting relationship between the symbolic structures of money and language; in Wall Street, neither functions well enough to reach or save Bartleby. In fact, among his many refusals we could list the general refusal of credit (both financial and linguistic) through its correlative, the lawyer's attempts at charity.

Taken as a whole these stories represent a significant attempt on Melville's part to redefine the ground upon which Romantic language must rest if it was to have meaning in America during the 1850s. His insistence on the power of money to disturb or alter the symbolic structure of language reveals a growing concern with the transformation of human values into marketable commodities. The difficulty in separating spiritual and economic expressions of faith (the barber's sign on the *Fidèle* reads, "No Trust") thus reflects and intensifies the difficulty of communicating with others. In this context, Wordsworth's encounter with the leech gatherer seems to belong to a different age, one in which the symbolic power of language and the corresponding faith in human connection, despite economic hardship, had yet to fail.

Notes

1. The other significant source of Melville's views on Wordsworth is his annotated copy of Wordsworth's poems described by Thomas Heffernan in "Melville and Wordsworth" *American Literature* 49 (1977): 338-51. Especially relevant to the current discussion is Melville's underscoring of these less hopeful lines from a dedicatory sonnet to William, Earl of Lonsdale: "Gladly would I have waited till my task / Had reached its close; but Life is insecure, / And Hope full oft fallacious as a dream." As Heffernan explains, "The lines cannot help suggesting to an informed reader the unjust and heartless mistreatment of the Wordsworth family by the preceding Earl, Sir James, Lowther, cousin of Lord William. Twenty years the family of the maturing poet lived in poverty and hardship while the Earl's debt went unpaid. Even when Lord William made a prompt settlement on his assumption of the title, £2,000 in interest still not paid. Forty-four years old, indeed, Wordsworth was still the butt of indignities. Melville, when he made the comment, was forty-one" (345).

    Jonathan Hall notes a slight attack on Wordsworth in *White-Jacket*, and considers *Pierre* to be an extended criticism of several aspects of Wordsworth's thought. See "The Non-correspondent Breeze: Melville's Rewriting of Wordsworth in *Pierre*," *ESQ: A Journal of the American Renaissance* 39.1 (1993): 1-19.

2. *The Piazza Tales and Other Prose Pieces, 1839-1860*, vol. 9 of *The Writings of Herman Melville*, eds. Harrison Hayford, Alma A. MacDougall, and G. Thomas Tanselle (Evanston and Chicago: Northwestern UP and the Newberry Library, 1987), 283, 272. All subsequent references to the tales will appear in the text.

3. Fisher calls the narrator "a functioning schizophrenic" and argues that "Wordsworth's *gladness* might . . . be synonymous with Melville's *madness*. . . ." See *Going Under: Melville's Short Fiction and the American 1850s* (Baton Rouge: LSU Press, 1977), 173. See also Hall, who argues that the narrator is not mad but is "a consistent disciple of a Romantic philosophy of perception" (17, n.9).

4. The standard interpretation of the tale, set forth originally in Egbert S. Oliver's "'Cock-A-Doodle-Doo!' and Transcendental Hocus-Pocus," *New England Quarterly* 21 (June 1948): 204-16, establishes the cock as a figure for transcendentalism in general and Emerson and Thoreau in particular. See also

Hershel Parker, "Melville's Satire of Emerson and Thoreau," *American Transcendental Quarterly* 7 (Summer 1970): 61-67 and William Bysshe Stein, "Melville Roasts Thoreau's Cock," *Modern Language Notes* 74 (1959): 218-19.

5. *The Confidence-Man: His Masquerade*, vol. 10 of *The Writings of Herman Melville*, eds. Harrison Hayford, Hershel Parker, and G. Thomas Tanselle (Evanston and Chicago: Northwestern UP and the Newberry Library, 1984), 52-53. Subsequent references will appear in the text.

6. See, for instance, Melville's comments on Goethe in a letter to Hawthorne: "Here is a fellow with a raging toothache. 'My dear boy,' Goethe says to him, 'you are sorely afflicted with that tooth; but you must *live in the all*, and then you will be happy!' As with all great genius, there is an immense deal of flummery in Goethe, and in proportion to my own contact with him, a monstrous deal of it in me." *Correspondence*, vol. 14 of *The Writings of Herman Melville*, ed. Lynn Horth (Evanston and Chicago: Northwestern UP and the Newberry Library, 1993), 193.

7. As Marc Shell argues, following Marx, "credit money (the extreme form of paper money) divorces the name entirely from what it is supposed to represent and so seems to allow an idealist transcendence, or conceptual annihilation, of commodities. In the institution of paper money, sign and substance—paper and gold—are clearly disassociated, much as word is disassociated from meaning in punning." *Money, Language, and Thought: Literary and Philosophical Economies from the Medieval to the Modern Era* (Berkeley: U of California P, 1982), 19. I am indebted to Shell's analysis for this fundamental understanding of the relationship between language and money. See also his *The Economy of Literature* (Baltimore and London: The Johns Hopkins UP, 1978).

8. As Leon Chai notes, Orchis's change of attitude is due in part to his new status as a "Come-Outer," a group devoted to revealing "one's inmost nature." Thus, in yet another irony, an essentially Romantic impulse leads to the expression not of Orchis's love for mankind but of his greed and need for money. See *The Romantic Foundations of the American Renaissance* (Ithaca: Cornell UP, 1987), 97-98.

9. Though Dame Coulter herself calls the dish "our pudding," she does so with a degree of domestic irony, quickly admitting that "it is only rice, milk, and salt boiled together" (172).

10. "I and My Chimney," *The Piazza Tales*, 357.

11. See William B. Dillingham, *Melville's Short Fiction, 1853-1856* (Athens: U of Georgia P, 1977), 302-5 for a discussion of possible connections between Jimmy Rose and Melville's family.

12. Fisher sees Jimmy as a "type of Christ" who in the end "can find no cheer, manage no smile, and muster no faith" (144). Despite his argument that "Melville's emphasis is upon Jimmy's goodness," Richard Harter Fogle suggests a similar undercurrent of despair: ". . . Melville makes us wonder if God has not taken advantage of poor Jimmy's fineness to torture him to the limit. . . ." See *Melville's Shorter Tales* (Norman: U of Oklahoma P, 1960), 61-62.

Romantic and Realist Rubble:
The Foundation for a New National Literature in Dostoevsky's *Poor Folk* and Melville's *Pierre*

Richard Kaplan

At a gathering of eight Nobel laureates in literature in 1995, the 1994 Nobel winner, Oe Kenzaburo, said through an interpreter, "It is the second job of literature to create myth. But its first job is to destroy that myth."[1] Fyodor Dostoevsky and Herman Melville would have agreed. Throughout their careers both routinely and systematically undermined the prevalent myths and literary conventions of the time, and they did not spare Romanticism. This was an era when the novels of Russia and the United States overwhelmingly consisted of slavish imitations of Western European Romantic models, and when calls for a unique national literature regularly sounded in the literary magazines of Russia and the United States. The two nations needed a kind of novel that would speak to them in culturally relevant and comprehensible ways. Dostoevsky and Melville used metafiction to move beyond imitation to writing about subjects their country's citizens could recognize. Once they broke the shackles of subject matter, they could cast off the chains of other conventions as well, and begin to write a new kind of novel for their emerging nations' emerging literatures.

Poor Folk (1846) and *Pierre* (1852) parody or attack Romanticism in many ways. Both ridicule the characteristic rhetoric, intensified sensitivity, and flights of heightened feeling that characterized Romanticism. The excesses of melodrama and sentimental fiction are also exposed to ridicule, as Dostoevsky and Melville routinely remove the feelings, objects, and incidents that typically give rise to rhetoric, leaving the rhetoric like a poorly designed roof with no foundation or walls left to prop it up.

Both works also present stylized versions of Romantic portrayals of women: *Poor Folk*'s Varenka clearly descends from the tradition of "sweet, silent, but passionate . . . pathetically naive and helpless heroines" favored by Russian practitioners of French Romanticism, who especially emulated George Sand—though in the end Varenka proves herself savvy and worldly wise.[2] In Melville's novel *Pierre*, Lucy seems a reconstruction of a character out of early Wordsworth; of her upbringing in the city we are told that she "did not at all love the city and its empty, heartless, ceremonial ways. It was very strange, but most eloquently significant of her own natural angelhood that, though born among brick and mortar in a sea-port, she still pined for unbaked earth and inland grass."[3] These flat, stereotypical parodies of Romantic ideals in William Dillingham's words embody "Melville's recollection of his own early interest in the English Romantic poets and his covert denunciation of their influence."[4]

But it is in their treatment of landscape that Dostoevsky and Melville most significantly undermined Romantic conventions, moving away from the characteristic landscape of glorious nature to an internal landscape of consciousness. In moving the field of action and feeling from glorious nature to the distorting, Romanticizing fancies of their characters, Dostoevsky and Melville both reduced the Romantic conception of landscape into rubble and established the foundations of Modernism. Of course, at the same time they prefigured Modernist myth they also destroyed it.

The setting of *Poor Folk*, though ostensibly urban, is largely the personal world of the main characters Devushkin and Varenka. As he would do later in *Notes from the Underground* (1864), Dostoevsky confines the action to a space the size of a hole, and within that space he operates largely within the psychological dimension. We get Devushkin's subjective, Romanticized, sentimentalized impressions of the city. For example, Devushkin at first speaks glowingly of the spring fragrance in the air and nature coming alive, but quickly switches literary modes (to

Naturalism) and calls his flat "a regular slum."[5] He mentions the dark, the dirt, the blank walls, the disorder. Yet we cannot rely upon him for an accurate description, for as soon as he starts describing the flat he jumps to talking about the people rather than the apartment itself. Of the people he says to Varenka, "I shall describe them satirically, just as they are and in detail" (33). He focuses more on style and the literary impression he makes on Varenka than on objectivity.

Having given this bleak account of his apartment, he then inexplicably concludes, "In short it is all very satisfactory"—and immediately thereafter says that the most wretched room there is more than he can afford. He achieves whatever literary effects he thinks he's achieving at the expense of consistency or consistent sense. And Varenka notices this: "I knew at once from your letter that there was something wrong—too much of paradise, and spring, and fragrance, and singing birds. I was sure there would be poetry too . . . The rest was all there—the tender feelings, the rosy dreams and what not!" (35). She also observes that his room is cramped and uncomfortable, despite his attempt to describe it as roomy. So we have a blatant discrepancy between the way he describes something and the way it (probably) is. And in fact he admits this in his next letter: "What sort of fragrance could there have been when any sort of garbage may lie about in the courtyard under our windows" (37). Then later, in the naturalistic mode: "And the smell is abominable . . . In a word, it isn't nice" (41). His letter of April 12 is as grim and unpleasant as the letter of April 8 was glowing, and in all likelihood neither is accurate.

Devushkin looks at landscape as something to elicit tender feelings. When he finds nature in the city, he sees it only as a reflection of his feelings; depressed, he goes outside and finds "nature was so sad" (115). He commits the pathetic fallacy almost every time he puts pen to paper. Varenka's vivid description of the country is no better, for it is mediated through memory and is a Romanticization, a childhood memory tinged through Romantic lenses.

Robert Louis Jackson wrote of Dostoevsky, "He centers his artistic quest on man in his concrete environment; but Dostoevsky does not, like Zola, ground it there."[6] He grounds it, we might say, in the consciousness of his characters. By presenting to us Devushkin's Romanticized view via inconsistent portrayals, Dostoevsky demonstrates that once one begins to sentimentalize and Romanticize, that then extends to the environment as well, and a rational or approximate view of things as they are is lost. Romanticizing does not stop with the books we read and, indeed, from which we first learned to do it; once practiced, the practice extends to everything.

In Devushkin's case—as in Pierre's—environment functions simply as another subject for him to Romanticize, and that tendency extends to his ability to clearly view the predicaments of those close to him. The shallowness of the books Devushkin reads begins to overtake his view of reality beyond just landscape, with the result that he takes a shallow view of the real events that are troubling Varenka: when she is deeply concerned and seriously considering the offer of governess, he blithely tells her not to even think about it. Well-meaning though he is, he continually refuses to see the true nature of her situation. Woeful naivete and a misplaced faith in the virtues of fiction characterize his response to her troubles: "Come, come, Varenka! Pay no heed to bad advice. You will do better to read your book again and more attentively. It will do you good" (87).

Devushkin has become almost incapable of understanding the import of real problems; when he has a real tale of misfortune to relate, he can't remember any of the details (96). He considers his own actual misfortunes "not really worth reading about" (97) because they seem insufficiently literary. Walter Benjamin wrote, "What distinguishes the novel from the story (or the epic in the narrower sense) is its essential dependence on the book . . . The birthplace of the novel is the solitary individual."[7] If this remains true for the reader as well as for the writer, then losing touch with reality and becoming absorbed in the world of books is only an exacerbation of the tendency which novels inherently encourage. Novels by their very nature pull us into the world of books, and to throw ourselves into the world of novels is to surrender ourselves to that pull.

Countering that pull is the push toward human contact generated by the impulses of charity and human decency. Devushkin and Varenka need companionship, and they provide this for one another through their mutual acts of kindness—a companionship considerably more satisfying than the famous relationship between Akaky Akakievich and his coat in Gogol's tale "The Overcoat" (1842). In fact, *Poor Folk* was written as a polemic against Gogol's "The Overcoat."

So Dostoevsky has more to offer than simply an attack on Romanticism's conventions. Devushkin manages to function as both a warning against the illness of applying Romanticism's conventions to life and as the antidote to that illness. Although his reading has so conditioned his desires that he desperately longs to become the hero in a sentimental love story, he inadvertently demonstrates a different kind of heroism. What he does for Varenka he does "out of sympathy and feeling of kinship" (92). He gives his last twenty kopeks to his friend Gorshkov. And his writing too forms part of his goodness; many of his letters he writes not for idle amusement, but to comfort Varenka. And, when he occasionally forgoes his attempts at style, we can see that his sentimental feelings are often genuine and deep; he very much takes Varenka's plight to heart once he has realized its seriousness. His determination in the face of adversity to do something for Varenka, no matter the cost or the seeming impossibility of it, separates him from those who never go beyond dreaming: "I myself know that I am fit for nothing, but I shall force myself to be fit for something, after all. Nothing will deter me" (104). A well-intentioned burst of Romantic feeling will not help Varenka, but acts of kindness will. As he says at the end, "Good deeds never go unrewarded, and virtue never fails to win the halo of divine justice" (144). And he is rewarded, as she addresses him in her final letter as "my constant and truest friend" (145).

Devushkin says "as everyone knows, Varenka, a poor man is worth less than rubbish and can be respected by no one—no matter what the scribblers say—everything will continue as of old" (98). This defines the basic tension in the story: a Romantic or sentimental literary treatment demands making a hero out of a poor clerk, but in reality nothing can change, and the conventions of genre can change nothing. Readers are "paying for the spectacle of a poor man" (98), not sincerely empathizing with one. And of course, for that reading pleasure to continue, there must continue to be poor men such as he. Devushkin wants simply to be respected as a man, rather than to have stereotypical poor clerks sentimentalized over while he languishes in poverty without anyone caring: "The polish was missing perhaps, and the tone and brilliance too, but I was a man at heart and in mind" (115). This simple statement of dignity gives Devushkin a stature that the greatest poetic celebration could not.

Like *Poor Folk*, *Pierre* functions as a polemic against the dominant literature of its day—and as such it reads as a critique of Romanticism. *Pierre* opens with an idyllic rural setting. Saddle Meadows is described as a dream world under the spell of a "verdant trance" (3). "Wonder smitten with the trance-like aspect of the green and golden world" in which he lives, Pierre enjoys a Romantic filial love with his mother, an uncanny closeness in which they revel in one another's mutual adoration (3, 5). This would appear to be a world of complete felicity, a Romantic Eden. Pierre is nurtured in the loveliest of places, under the care of a loving mother—his father has died—without any strife or conflict. Surely this is utopia according to Romantic ideology.

But utopia proves to be a prison. And even when he leaves it, Pierre has not come to see it for what it is; "Pierre remains blind to the suffering and evil in the country because of his romantic mind and because of his pride,"[8] writes Barbara Smith-Lemeunier. Though hampered by this blindness, Pierre soon comes to feel that this utopia is incomplete; it's utopia minus a sister. Melville has thus begun by planting his hero firmly within a feminine Eden, a rural and domestic paradise, but then driving the hero out because of the smothering presence of women: a demanding and all-consuming mother who wants to play the role not just of mother but also sister and lover, a potential bride whom he does not want, and a real half-sister with whom he cannot fulfill his incestuous desires, especially in this paradise.

Pierre and his mother/sister embody the Romantic ideal, expressed in the poems of Shelley, Keats, and Byron, of complementary souls; added to that is the sentimental ideal of domestic harmony. In their "verdant trance," in "the playfulness of their unclouded love, and with that strange license which a perfect confidence and mutual understanding at all points, had long bred between them, they were wont to call each other brother and sister" (5). But Pierre and his mother are not brother and sister, and do not exhibit the kind of mingling of complementary souls that, say, William and Dorothy Wordsworth represented. If they resemble any Romantic brother-sister relationship, it would more likely be that of the tragically doomed Manfred and Astarte. In other words, the Romantic ideal of the brother and sister who are true soul mates, so frequent a theme in Romantic poetry and so often implied in sentimental fiction, cannot be consummated in the very setting which gives rise to it.

Pierre, Isabel, and Delly depart Saddle Meadows, and it is an unreal, sad departure, so different from the happy sendoff we expect for lovers leaving their quiet village after a grand but simple country wedding. If that departure is a bit unreal, so is the country setting from which they depart: the chief appeal of it to Pierre and his mother had never been its natural beauty but its ability to remind them of the names and patriotic feats of their ancestors. Perhaps because the world of that "verdant trance" was never quite genuine, perhaps because there he was bound by his inherited past and by the conventional morality of the country, the domestic sphere, and the sentimental romance, perhaps because, as Smith-Lemeunier says, the "country is a place to meditate in, but it does not provide the substance for meditation" (104), Pierre must leave the country to seek the city.

Although the focus on the state of Pierre's consciousness acquires its greatest intensity late in the novel, in fact the landscape begins to shift away from the merely physical and into the realm of consciousness well before the shift from country to city. When Pierre returned to the house at the beginning of Book 5, like Nick of Hemingway's story "Big Two-Hearted River" "he firmly gazed abroad upon the charred landscape within him" (86). The landscape he views is no longer the bucolic paradise of Saddle Meadows, but the troubled inferno of his emotions. Although "man can not wholly escape his surroundings" (277), Pierre must learn to look clearly within before he can clearly see the world outside of himself.

He does not gain clarity of vision into either himself or the surrounding world when he encounters the city. Indeed, when Pierre first arrives in the city it seems like Hades itself: "there was no moon and few stars," the street lamps on the road leading toward the "obscure heart of the town" "seemed not so much intended to dispel the general gloom, as to show some dim path leading through it, into some gloom still deeper beyond" (229), and all appears garish, ghastly, nightmarish, dark, monstrous, surreal, and evil, a horrible and perverted natural landscape where the soft grasses of the green sward have been replaced by the punishing pavements of stone and mortar. The monstrous city of *The Waste Land* seems positively benign by comparison. The city lights in *Pierre* even render natural beauty, or what was apparently once natural beauty, horrific:

> Pierre turned; and in the flashing, sinister, evil cross-lights of a druggist's window, his eye caught the person of a wonderfully beautifully-featured girl; scarlet-cheeked, glaringly-arrayed, and of a figure all natural grace but unnatural vivacity. Her whole form, however, was horribly lit by the green and yellow rays from the druggist's. (237)

Compare this with the earlier description of Lucy in Saddle Meadows:

> Her cheeks were tinted with the most delicate white and red, the white predominating. Her eyes some god brought down from heaven; her hair was Danae's, spangled with Jove's shower; her teeth were dived for in the Persian Sea. (24)

In these two portraits, the ideal of pure feminine romance stands juxtaposed against the nightmare of gritty Naturalism. Similarly, the garbage accumulating underneath Devushkin's apartment window parallels Pierre's dark view of the city. Neither Devushkin's nor Pierre's descriptions, however, provide a reliably objective account of reality.

The delusions that Pierre suffers in the city are not new, for his view of the country was equally distorted. As A. Carl Bredahl, Jr. has argued in *Melville's Angles of Vision*, the shifts in physical setting in *Pierre* embody changes in Pierre's psychological perspective; the psychological is simply rendered in physical terms.[9] Just as in *Poor Folk*, descriptions of environment are filtered through the main character's distempered imagination; in analogous fashion the distorted setting reveals the protagonist's distempered mind. The physical environment of the city thus reflects the sense of imprisonment and rigidity that Pierre increasingly feels. And the prison in which Pierre dwells is the prison of his still too conventional imagination, while the rock which falls on him is the rock of convention.

As Kenneth Dauber comments, Pierre's move from country to city simply exchanges one restrictive and false conventional setting for another, for as he abandons the "Spenserian world of Saddle Meadows, Pierre adopts only the Byronic one of the Apostles. There is, indeed, no Pierre, but in one such conventionalized world or another."[10] In a similar manner, the novel ends with Pierre imprisoned for murdering his cousin in a duel, and thus the setting has moved from one extreme to another, from the open meadows of the country to the walls of an enclosed prison. With this ending Melville has brought the Romantic and the Realistic, the bucolic and the urban, into collision. He has taken Romantic ideals, turned them into a nightmare, and then just as completely reified the epitome of the urban nightmare. Neither is what it at first appears: the rural Utopia is badly flawed and severely restrictive; the urban nightmare offers friendship and opportunity. Melville brings these two types into collision without celebrating either. He has thus gone beyond what Donald Fanger describes as Romantic Realism—the fusing of Romanticism and Realism—also fusing with them their generic cousins sentimentalism, sensationalism, the Gothic and the melodrama, only to short-circuit the wiring and destroy each of the component parts in one disastrous explosion at the end.

In fact, a prison seems the only logical place for the clash between generic types to end. If Melville as artist sees them as equally restrictive and false, then it makes sense that he would end by killing off not just his hero but those tropes as well; they expire together in a prison of their own making. Unable to escape the world of conventional fictional texts, a fly caught in the web of his own consciousness's endless metaliterary intertextuality, Pierre expires and in the process illustrates the impoverishment of a consciousness not fed by contact with life outside of fiction. As Michael Paul Rogin suggests in his reading of *Pierre*, the novel finally overtakes its protagonist, who dies within it, unable to escape.[11]

Pierre's Romanticism, like Devushkin's, has removed him from and blinded him to reality. Pierre's desire to have his mother as his sister, for example, springs from the Romantic idealization of the single soul that finds its true mate in its sister, and his blindness to the sometimes savage cruelty of country life springs from the Romantic idealization of unspoiled nature. The course he takes with respect to Lucy and Isabel may be attributed to the fact that he has read too many white lady/dark lady romances. But, of course, it is not just Romanticism or sentimentalism per se that is to blame: the fault rests with the literature from which Pierre has uncritically absorbed these ideas.

Dostoevsky and Melville did not wish to merely restructure Romantic and Realist myths; the constant barrage against nineteenth-century literary conventions that they launched leaves those conventions in a shambles in these two works. Moving the landscape of the novel from a Romantic physical landscape to a Romanticized psychological landscape enabled these two writers to build something new atop that shambles, and to lay down the foundations upon which the edifice of Modernism would be constructed. But they also went further than Modernism, showing that consciousness alone is no better equipped to confront life than a reader who knows nothing but fictions. In fact, consciousness alone is exactly what a reader trapped in the world of reading novels has. Devushkin in his Romantic mode, Dostoevsky's underground man and Pierre all stand as cautionary warnings of what becomes of the person trapped within a world of fictions, unable to reach the world beyond the text.

Looking at the world beyond the text—life, not the manufactured, illusory, distorted world of fictional texts—puts out the blinding, shadowy light that sentimentality and Romanticism cast over the world. *Poor Folk* and *Pierre* suggest that the way out of the isolation of one's own consciousness, and, for that matter, out of the infinitely self-referential world of postmodern intertextuality, is to perform a simple act of human kindness while forgetting about what books would have us do. It is this that Makar Devushkin does at the end of *Poor Folk* and that Lucy and Isabel attempt to do at the end of *Pierre*.

Neither *Poor Folk* nor *Pierre* promises that such acts will be rewarded, and in *The Confidence Man* Melville even suggests that they may be tantamount to conceding to being hoodwinked. But because these texts do not provide any easy answers, they push their readers away from fiction and into the world beyond in order to seek those answers. The reader leaves Dostoevsky and Melville's texts armed with a better sense of the dangers of expecting life to conform to fiction or poetry's conventions, the lies at the heart of fiction, and the dangers of thinking that one's own consciousness is sufficient for greeting the world.

Dostoevsky and Melville can afford to drive readers away from fiction because they know those readers will always come back and will always want to believe; but they also depend upon those readers to return with minds filled with more than just other novels as referents, to return willing to receive lessons in how to read the Europe's literature at the same time they read examples of what the world's two youngest nations can build upon the exhausted foundations erected by the old.

Notes

1. Ronald Smothers, "A Close Encounter of Nobel Laureates," *The New York Times* 26 Apr. 1995: B1.

2. D. S. Mirsky, *A History of Russian Literature from its Beginnings to 1900*, ed. Francis J. Whitfield (New York: Alfred A. Knopf, Inc., 1958), 36.

3. Herman Melville, *Pierre, or The Ambiguities*, eds. Harrison Hayford, Hershel Parker, and G. Thomas Tanselle (Chicago: Northwestern UP and The Newberry Library, 1971), 26.

4. William B. Dillingham, *Melville's Later Novels* (Athens: U of Georgia P, 1986), 193.

5. Fyodor Dostoevsky, *Poor People*, in *Stories*, trans. eds. Olga Shartse and Julius Katzer (Moscow: Progress Publishers, 1971), 33. I have used Shartse and Katzer's

translation, as I feel it is the best available. Note that they use the title *Poor People*; for familiarity's sake I have retained the more commonly used title *Poor Folk*, even when identifying quotations from their edition.

6. Robert Louis Jackson, *Dostoevsky's Quest for Form: A Study of His Philosophy of Art* (New Haven: Yale UP, 1966), 13.

7. Walter Benjamin, "The Storyteller: Reflections on the Works of Nikolai Leskov," in *Illuminations*, trans. Harry Zohn, ed. and intro. Hannah Arendt (1968; New York: Schocken Books, 1969), 87.

8. Barbara Smith-Lemeunier, "'Tis Hell in Both Worlds': Country, City and American Myth in Melville's *Pierre, or, The Ambiguities*," in *Mythes Ruraux et Urbains dans lat Culture Américaine*. Actes du Colloque des 2, 3 et 4 Mars 1990. Avant-propos par Serge Ricard (Aix en Provence: Publications de l'Université de Provence, 1990), 108.

9. A. Carl Bredahl, Jr., *Melville's Angles of Vision* (Gainesville: U of Florida P, 1972), 43.

10. Kenneth Dauber, *The Idea of Authorship in America: Democratic Poetics from Franklin to Melville* (Madison: U of Wisconsin P, 1990), 207.

11. Michael Paul Rogin, *Subversive Genealogy: The Politics and Art of Herman Melville* (Berkeley: U of California P, 1985; c 1979), 179.

From Revolutionary Legends to *The Scarlet Letter*: Casting Characters for Early American Romanticism

Margaret Reid

In American literary history, it's particularly hard to pinpoint the beginnings of Romanticism. No doubt the movement flowered here later than it did in England, France, or Germany, and many scholars have shown the intricate—and pervasive—influences of continental Romanticism on American transcendentalism and its critics. But in this paper, I would like to explore some early stirrings of Romantic thought in America. Though perhaps not fully expressed until half a century later, Romanticism in America gains much energy late in the eighteenth century. Here I base my argument on the symbolic strategies emergent in two of the early republic's most prominent legends of the Revolutionary war. They are legends that mark a fundamental change in the nationalistic use of self-defining narratives in America. While the early public documents of the revolution—the official narratives, coming from above—were eager to represent models of stability and design to the anxious public, these folktales aggressively opened an imagined space for the complexities of lived history that would challenge or defy the known designs of culture. These stories show internal rhetorics directly linked to the later established symbolic methods of Romanticism in America. I use the example of Nathaniel Hawthorne's *The Scarlet Letter* (1850)—one of the central texts of American Romanticism—to argue the importance of the symbolic strategies made available in the popular legends of the revolutionary era.

In *The Scarlet Letter* as in Hawthorne's short stories, history may be imagined as an exile secretly returning to (and then insistently lingering near) a community not yet ready to accommodate its reintegration. The communal attraction for the exile, despite all of the transgressions that figure embodies, becomes a central tension within American Romantic literature and historiography, and an analysis of the use of this motif in revolutionary legend helps delineate one of the primary representative strategies in Hawthorne's work. During the revolutionary era, that strategy is shaped in particular ways: among the most telling clues to an index of the storytelling imagination in America is the fact that—in the two generations between the end of the war and the establishment of a native tradition of historical romance—no heroic figure or successful battle, no legend which justified resistance through appeals to patriotism or sketches of villainy, could match the pervasive power and interest in the separate tragic fates of two young British sympathizers, one an accomplished officer, and one a civilian woman. Major John André and Miss Jane McCrea may be the two most mysterious ghosts left by the war, if not in their personal histories, at least in their imaginative lives within the American cultural imagination. Both André, Benedict Arnold's British liaison, and McCrea, who chose her Tory lover over all social principles, were killed under ambiguous circumstances on the heavily contested grounds of the Hudson River Valley; both of their stories were immediate sensations not only throughout the colonies and Britain but into Europe as well; yet both were, most essentially, Loyalist sympathizers whose chance misfortune left them tragic but incidental human casualties of war.[1]

As Clinton's agent chosen to receive Arnold's West Point intelligence, André was captured "within our lines" (as Washington described him to the trial committee)[2] returning by land to the British encampment at New York. He had assumed a full disguise and was concealing notes concerning Benedict Arnold's plan to gain West Point for the British. He was hung as a spy on October 2, 1780. Even during the ten day interval between his capture and his death, André began to take hold of the sentimental imagination. Pleas for mercy came from all sides, with rapid, impassioned intensity, and in his last days, André's own words and actions fueled the high "Romantic interest" which, as Washington Irving later wrote, "was thrown around his memory."³ There are no last words or records of noble suffering to attend Jane McCrea's memory, nor was anyone there to plead for her life and her honor. But interest in her story too, was immediate, pervasive, and sustained well into the nineteenth century. With little evidence or knowledge, countless writers retold the story of the young girl, who, hoping to meet with her fiancé, the British officer David Jones, was instead brutally murdered in the forests near Fort Edward, New York, late in July of 1777.

These are the types of legends which had been stirring most powerfully in the years leading up to the development of high Romanticism in America, and I would like to suggest that their ambiguity and terror, rather than their traditional appeals to sentiment, make them strong sources of imaginative nourishment for later writers, directly engaged in the inheritance of European Romanticism. The persistent interest in the deeply ambiguous legends of John André and Jane McCrea throughout the nineteenth century attests to direct challenges facing national narrative: the legends emphasize the character of a historical imagination specifically focused on the renegotiation of the boundaries of communal knowledge, and on the pressures placed on these boundaries by the experiences of lived history. From their earliest appearances in literary and historical texts, the legends of André and McCrea spoke not only to the tragic private losses inflicted by the motion of the emergent culture but also to the often hidden power of personal history in the shaping process itself. André's image haunted American forests to suggest the frightening permeability of boundaries and the tremendous authority latent in privately held military secrets; his image later came to invoke both the losses inherent in cultural independence and questions regarding America's future relations with Europe. In her death, Jane McCrea warned of the dangers of British seduction and the savagery of the American wilderness; she later became an emblem of the threats to home, family, and community unleashed through the energies of the Revolution and believed to be all too rampant in the young republic. Both legends highlight the ultimate limits of civil control, and, by extension, the limits of Enlightenment rhetoric. Both represent fragmented life histories, stories of knowledge and experience irrevocably lost yet endlessly productive of cultural imaginings.

The lives of these two people became examples of an extraordinary type of symbol—functional only because it is textually predetermined to lead to the *mis*appropriation of complex identities. With these symbols, the power of the icon rests in those fragments of identity that escape clear representation; these icons wield imaginative power exactly insofar as they resist interpretation, turning their culture back upon itself, to question the workings of their developing stories. This is the symbolic structure that allowed for an American appropriation of the stories of these lost British lives. To thrive in the national imagination as sympathetic figures from the enemy camp, André and McCrea needed the context of knowable plots and freedom from deterministic allegorical readings. Their stories multiplied and deepened because they presented the forever-troubling dilemma of historical materiality without narrative frame. It is the same dilemma that opens *The Scarlet Letter*.

Once found in the attic of the old Salem Custom House, Hawthorne's scarlet A compels storytelling in a uniquely troublesome way: it is an artifact of cultural history, but it has not found a place in a museum or library; it is an emblem of personal experience, but it has not survived within any familiar context, as, for example, a family heirloom. Instead, the place of the A in the Custom House attic suggests that—as an artifact—it hovers just at the outer reaches of the narrator's interpretive responsibility. At once too hot to hold and too oblique to read, the scarlet A is an aggressively material fragment of history that must be understood in its inadequate present context as the trace of something more. It stands for the clear need to transmit a story into a context at once stiflingly familiar and perilously foreign; the need to find (whether through recognition or construction) places in communal memory that can accommodate not only the historical fragment, but also its remote context, its story.

"That scarlet letter, so fantastically embroidered and illuminated upon [Hester's] bosom . . . had the effect of a spell, taking her out of the ordinary relations with humanity, and inclosing her in a sphere by herself" (53-54)[4]; Hester's role, both in 1850 and in her Puritan community, is precisely this—to embody a New World of language, "a sphere by herself"—but as such, also to provide a fundamental link between present and future. Much has been written about Hester's letter as an emblem of sin, but the real power of the "A" within this fiction of early America lies in its positive force: Hester's disapproving society gives her a badge full of cultural potency, not only when she is "Angel" or "Able," but from the start. Like the eerie laughter in "My Kinsman, Major Molineux," the "A" in *The Scarlet Letter* is the means of revelations beyond the language of the community; it is a force (by definition positive) conveying an unnamed negative message into a world where sheer negativity as yet has no codified place. Though given in the impulse of exclusion, the letter, like the laughter, derives a power from the significance of the gesture of "giving": it is through the giving, the abdication of powers unknown to the giver, that new cultural roles evolve which only the recipient can play.

In presenting Hester with an artifact with a material life of its own, the town fathers add to her private share of the community's history and knowledge. The artifact's uncanny survival through the violent discord of two hundred years following its initial entrance into society suggests an exceptional power: given to, and then fully embraced by, Hester Prynne, somehow the A—which she keeps to herself so long after any official interest in her punishment ends—survives her death, to be reclaimed by cultural memory, found in a quiet corner of a public space. In the context of the end of the book, particularly the image of the gravestone carved for Hester and Dimmesdale together, the narrative significance of the discovery of the letter in the Custom House attic takes on an eerie, if not sinister, aspect. "ON A FIELD, SABLE, THE LETTER A, GULES": so reads the tombstone; and yet apart from the bodies, that letter, a symbol so saturated with histories, must have refused to rest. In some clear sense, then, the field of sable becomes the dark historical memory of the life of Puritan Boston—not the darkness of the body, the grave, or the graveyard, but the darkness of the attic which somehow has enabled the inexplicable recurrence of a deeply foreboding sign of primal divisions within a changing American community.

And Hawthorne explores both the privileges and the dangers of the symbolic foundations of American language within a self-consciously devised system of language and irony which allows (or compels) Hester and her scarlet "A" to function within both a dogmatic religious code and a democratic political code.[5] While Hester's town magistrates understand transgression and punishment in traditional, hierarchical terms, Hester's own experience as the transgressor is creative, innovative, and even obliquely prophetic. Hawthorne, then, brings forth Hester in all of her contradiction and ambiguity as an example of the productivity of America—the prototypical modern culture—even (perhaps especially) in its moments of deepest moral crisis.

In *The Scarlet Letter,* Hawthorne directly addresses the foundations of American symbolic language, the "story" within the rhetoric of national narrative. He finds danger in the "theoretical" nature of both Puritan rhetoric and nineteenth century American symbology, and he makes a progressivist's argument for a new infusion of history into theory. Michael Colacurcio describes the unfortunate results of "progressive history" as the "[reduction of] multiplicity to unity, not only in 'explanation' but in 'reality'. What is edited out from the past will not be available soon again."[6] But I would suggest that Hawthorne is both deeply interested in reviving a sense of national unity and too self-aware to fall into a trap of reductionism. I will argue that, within a complex system of irony and language theory, Hawthorne—through the narrative voice of *The Scarlet Letter*—sets as his first priority the task of making available exactly that which progressive historiography had "edited out," and further, that he then uses that material in the service of a revised plan based on similarly progressive sentiments—but now with the added strength of a newly recovered "reality."[7]

The mistakes of rhetoric and historiography are only half the problem: Hawthorne also directly addresses the problems of approaching rhetoric's philosophical antithesis, pure language; these are problems described by Walter Benjamin in "The Task of the Translator":

> In all language and linguistic creations there remains in addition to what can be conveyed something that cannot be communicated; depending on the context in which it appears, it is something that symbolizes or something symbolized. It is the former only in the finite products of language, the latter in the evolving of the languages themselves. And that which seeks to represent, to produce itself in the evolving of languages, is that very nucleus of pure language. Though concealed and fragmentary, it is an active force in life as the symbolized thing itself, whereas it inhabits linguistic creations only in symbolized form.[8]

In one important way, symbols in Hawthorne's fiction appear to be "the finite products of language," divorced from life and clearly referential. Symbols like a scarlet "A" on the breast of a woman with a child born out of wedlock, or a rose set against the grim prison door, look too readable, too conventional to be the markings of a novel meant to question the established literary tradition and to help define the workings of American language. But Hawthorne turns this common logic around. While using the simplest of symbols, he buries them in such a way that conventional reading will not uncover them: the "A," the stigma, is invested with a fundamental linguistic authority which in an orderly world should belong to a town father, perhaps the preacher (thus the symbol comes full circle); the rose has even a macabre quality about it as the narrator slips it into the hand of a reader forced to surrender the superior status of a living, critiquing being upon entering a fiction which will question the foundations of this culture, its verbal and symbolic order. In fact, these buried symbols are so far from being the "finite products" they appear that they explicitly depend upon and participate in "the evolving" of American language; in every way, the symbol in Hawthorne's work is "concealed and fragmentary," "an active force in life," and the "very nucleus of pure language"—as it enters into history.

But the freereigning power of the symbol is not only emblematic of some future promise—a newly evolved language in a Utopian vision—but is also evidence of a presently fragile or threatened social order. When even the simplest symbols are paradoxical, it becomes clear that there is not a sufficiently strong foundation of rational meaning behind those symbols. Specifically, Hawthorne shows that for a scarlet letter to wield the power it does in Puritan Boston, there must be a problem, of fear perhaps, or of hope, in the community's understanding of language; this community displays both a belief in its own future and a fear of its own present by behaving as a linguistically "evolving" structure. Within the narrative, the "A" moves immediately into the realm of symbol, because there is no place for it in language: the language of Puritan Boston makes the mistake of beginning with rhetoric and symbol, without first establishing a firm base of meaning, original to the new culture. With an eye fixed on the future, this community erases the rational and historical moment. Here, language is imposed upon, and so external to, reality; language—as it is used by this community's leaders—is a map laid upon a territory not yet accurately surveyed. But in Hawthorne's fictional version of Puritan history, he contrasts this static and artificial blanket of referential language with the growth of a language as it inheres in reality—living and imaginative—in the fusion of the "A" with its wearer and the resulting new cultural role. Given the elusive nature of the "symbolized" in "evolving" languages, Hawthorne locates the cultural and epistemological origins of national identity within a fusion of language and symbolism. In doing so, his symbolic method warns against an empty rhetoric which ignores its historical moment and re-affirms the promise of the possibilities for an American identity if history and symbol remain firmly bound.

For Hawthorne, the problem with ahistorical symbolism is the problem with all transcendental language. The transcendental symbol, if infused with faith, is omnipotent because it is beyond the analytic faculties, but without this faith, it is entirely meaningless because it lacks grounding in the verifiable realm of history. A mapped design, however false, defines its land as long as consensus allows. But if the faith falters, only history remains—a history which includes memory of the initial impulse toward design, the "situation that produced anxiety, the forcing of which into concealment is brought about and confirmed by [the] very significance" of the willed structure of belief, the rhetoric and the consensus.[9] In this way, an excessive reliance on a system of purely transcendent symbolic self-definition suggests a fear as deep as the attending belief—a fear that America's self-definition was "essentially diverse" from its "incommensurate" historical reality.[10] And if the model of America were to become more than speculative rhetoric, if indeed it were to become life also, and true history, then, Hawthorne recognized, the nineteenth century had to face the crisis of reestablishing a ground for that speculation. Argument, change, conflict, and even social war all had to be parts of American identity in Hawthorne's model, because if these were denied, then America as a nation had little left on which it might agree—too little to define an essentially untranscendental human history.

To prevent, escape, or repair the emptiness of the speculative American identity would be the function of a previously excluded form of language, here the rational and empirical. The infusion of this language would rejoin the map with the territory through more accurate human charting, and this process would replace consensus of faith with experience. And so within Hawthorne's model, for each of the major characters, for Puritan Boston, and for early America, an active creation of language would be the first imperative for the establishment and survival of an identity. The impulse to read and to listen, again, to be a "member" of the congregation, is at odds with the need to speak and to write, to be a founder. But Hawthorne does not want to cast off the rhetorical design of America; he wants a system in which member and founder, map and topography, are one. In true storytelling (to refer to Benjamin again), member and founder, faith and the establishment of knowledge, fuse as one, causing the preserved and (thus) concentrated story to be held so that it "is capable of releasing [its strength] even after a long time." And the story is not trapped in a mystical (transcendental) form; it is both entirely natural, rational, comprehensible, and also full of a mysterious power for growth. A story, like a promise of delayed fulfillment in a culture, "resembles the seeds of grain which have lain for centuries in the chambers of the pyramids shut up air-tight and have retained their germinative power to this day":[11] these are the paradoxical requirements in Hawthorne's version of a language by and for America.

The depth of understanding implied in character, narrator, and society in *The Scarlet Letter* bears a direct correlation to facility with language; and while "understanding" suggests communal participation in a system of codes, facility is actually dependent upon distance, separation from the congregation, an ability for non-rhetorical, truthful but creative, leadership. Despite the narrator's claims of distance, even he has difficulty extricating himself from the paradoxical webs binding the spoken and unspoken. He can no more say "adultery" than the town fathers can. It seems that he has inherited some degree of language deficiency—but in its reduced form, this language deficiency ironically also embodies the promise of a "bright[er] transparency" for future narrators of the culture's history. As the narrative eye passes by a rose-bush at the prison door, the narrator can "hardly do otherwise than pluck one of its flowers and present it to the reader" (48); this is a strange and jarring moment—another startling narrative symbol. No longer is the narrator so clearly removed from his story; neither is the reader safely distant. Narrative, tale-teller, and reader are here linked in an unsettling way: it is a gesture which implicates all three in the linguistic game which Hawthorne has begun to play. It is interesting to note that when Anne W. Abbott in the *North American Review* complained that "the master of such a wizard power over language as Mr. Hawthorne manifests" had wasted his talent on a "revolting subject," it is specifically Hawthorne's most overt symbolism which seems most bothersome: "fine writing [about adultery] seems as inappropriate as fine embroidery [on the scarlet letter]"; "the ugliness of pollution and vice is no more relieved by it than the gloom of prison is by the rose tree at its door."[12]

The rose blossom is, in one sense, as clear and familiar a symbol as is the "A"—either one can be read through context, tradition, and common intuition. But also like the "A," the blossom is left with free-floating meaning, undefined by the narrator and the characters. Both symbols are too close to the storyteller (who touches them) to be explicated, and similarly both are overly accessible to the reader. Hawthorne self-consciously constructs these symbols as historical and imaginative links which preserve both halves of a definition. They are links which put demands on the present moment—demands which are instinctively rejected by visions of history and symbolism which look for the "relief" of "ugliness" and "gloom" by beauty and new life, the cancellation of history through revision. This narrator instead has entered into the historical life of New England Puritanism, even to the extent of recreating the ritual—now in the fulfilled linguistic form of the novel—which placed Hester and her sin before the community.

Through this ritual aspect of his novel, Hawthorne linguistically reenacts a moment of founding. Such a moment is necessarily unspeakable in its original nature but infinitely powerful as well. In order to represent the paradox of the founding moment, Hawthorne cannot have his Puritans give Hester a label reading "Adultery" or "Adulteress." From his own description, it seems clear that if the narrator of "The Custom House" had found a cloth label reading "Adultery," this label would have been too specific and thus reductive: the less concentrated form of language, the word, could not have cast the same imaginative spell; it would not have represented such a "secret" sin. In the "A," this narrator feels the preternatural power of an unspoken story, the "burning heat" as if of a "red-hot iron" (32). Both he, and the seventeenth century players in Hester's drama, feel the danger and the power of an undefined idea—a symbol as opposed to a label—and both intend to communicate meaning through that symbol. But the meaning that Hawthorne, the narrator, and the fictional Puritans communicate is not definition; it is instead a sign of the entrance into the process of creating cultural language. Hester had suddenly embodied a transgression previously invisible to her community, and first efforts at language can acknowledge only importance, difference, and the need for attention—the intention to define later, once competence is achieved.[13]

In these first efforts toward communication, then, the town magistrates reveal their own inability to differentiate between dangerous and powerful functions of language. Though she is the wearer of the symbol, Hester alone is able to think and to function in a non-symbolic realm. Her understanding and her use of language are based on—but not restricted to—the primary rational and empirical function of words.[14] In Hester, Locke's "arbitrariness" of the word or sign is counteracted by what emanates from that sign; the interplay of "sign" and "emanation" are, for Hawthorne, effective cultural symbolism. Hester is only another powerless Puritan woman destroyed by sin without the (ironic) gift of the imposed, dead letter of the law from the magistrates; with this "gift," though, Hester begins to embody some interplay of sign and emanation—she actually revives social order and a dying language by becoming a living letter: again, a letter of the law.

In empiricist terms, Hester indeed comes to embody the "invisible idea" of a defied cultural value. And the "voluntary," and even in some sense arbitrary, imposition of the sign on Hester—and her later re-assumption of the sign—both work to reaffirm Puritan Boston's social norms. But this only occurs through a complex system of irony: it is not the magistrates' mapping of the "A" onto Hester's character which strengthens the society; it is Hester's own acceptance of the transformative power of a symbol, her embodiment of a promise to a future time (and to a future language) which she will never live to know (or to speak).[15] And within all of this is a birth. It is the birth of a child, of course, but also it is the birth of history and language—possible even from the colony's fragile identity. For Hawthorne, Hester's "A" is not simply an imposed restriction; it transforms to signify also the great potential of growth from within: it is the seed and the promise—a binding promise, literally binding symbol to history. And it is an image of delayed fulfillment equally relevant to the Puritans and to Hawthorne's community.

As the latent promise of a second age, Hester's "A" is significantly *unlike* other Puritan forms of linguistic punishment which were based on the principle of restricting language use. In the language of both the fictional Puritans of Hawthorne's story and the historical Puritans of seventeenth century New England, there is the consistent expression of a cultural hope—perhaps even a belief—that "they had captured the whole of reality in the texture of a rational language"; "word, thought, and thing were one" in this equation.[16] If language could be culturally monitored, then through organized education, controlled speech and literacy, the use of metaphors which were consistently referential—which had as their primary text the biblical Word, known to all—the leaders of the colony hoped to blanket the population with a common morality.[17] In the story "Endicott and Red Cross," the "Wanton Gospeller" reflected in Endicott's shield is one of Hawthorne's examples of language used in the service of controlled authority. He is defined, clearly and publicly, so that the community will immediately contextualize any of his "unsanctioned" "interpretations of Holy Writ"[18] as "wanton"; here "definition" ironically depends upon the vagueness necessary to cover a multitude of possible interpretations. This is the trick which escapes those punishing Hester: the Puritans clearly knew that, in order to avoid being reductive, one's definitions must not confine in such a way as to be immediately obsolete. Metaphorical and symbolic language, ways of anticipating challenge, are integral parts of the Puritan program of thought. However, in *The Scarlet Letter*, Hawthorne's critique points out an excessive reliance on the symbolic and the attending danger to the social structure. He shows that although early America could count on importing rituals—of language, religion, or punishment—the interpretation of these rituals within the new context soon moved beyond predictability. And this lost connection between sign and interpretation had eroded the primary function of ritual—social control—in the colony.[19]

But ironically, the ritual nature of American language remained, though control of the ritual function had failed. In this world conscious of language, the letter "A" on Hester's dress would stand for two uncreated sentences: the biblical criminal sentence—death by stoning—waived in favor of the letter, and the sentence within the narrative which would name her sin. But in these first days of the colony, one founded on the belief in a need for a new code of values, there are words for laws, but no words for broken laws. That is to say, there are laws, to restrict activity and belief, but no clear understanding of the persistent existence of deviant behavior; in this context, there is no way to harness *positive potential of deviance*.[20] This leaves one simple reason why it seems as though no one within the story (including the narrator) can give even a capsule summary of Hester's sin: the necessary words—with the deviance they signify—have been suppressed deeply within (if not purged from) the vocabulary of the colony. Words within this society either have been tied too closely to actions, in an excessively rational way, or radically divorced from actions, in an immediately symbolic way. In both cases, words for sin are comprehensible only within the context of the negative imperative, the religious command-ment. By negating potential action, and by making symbolic meaning explicitly referential, the commandment allows sin no existence of its own. Clearly, then, the punishment of sin remains a ritual in structure, but an empty one—it is a ritual without function, without a defined nemesis.

Although this is a community for which "religion and law were almost identical" (50), they were not quite identical: in Hester's world, and then in Hawthorne's, the faith systems of both religion and national identity only coexist—but do not match—with a legal system which must address and work within lived history. But it is true that both Puritanism, specifically, and laws, generally, are essentially reactionary because they begin in restriction and dissent; thus they acknowledge a dangerous power structure beyond themselves. If the conflict between the reactionary culture and the feared alternative identity is simply denied or artificially blanketed with an agreed upon value system, then culture and power will never fuse into a "positive pattern" of social reality.[21] Hawthorne offers America a different approach—a way to harness the easy route to self-definition guaranteed to the defensive party with the large scale "positive pattern" available only to a potent culture which has moved beyond the language of negativity. And he represents all of this—a power of defense, establishment, conflict, and deviance, in the ironically empowering punishment of the scarlet letter.[22] Like Pearl, this letter has as its "principle of being" the "freedom of a broken law" (134).

In this model, Puritan Boston's town fathers are aware only of the ease of defensive self-definition, they are proclaiming communal values by means of contrast or negation. Rather than asserting their power by denying Hester something, such as a home in an established community, her world actually offers her something new—a scarlet letter—a previously unseen and even presently unspoken fragment of language. Hester, then, is not simply branded but decorated, not only damaged but adorned. The paradoxical sense of promise that has been given into Hester's charge is nowhere more evident than in her first emergence from prison. Walking out of the darkness into light, seen as a different person than the one led in there some time ago because she is now a mother and she wears an "A," Hester has been transformed as an image to the community. But instead of that transformation marking an end, it is surrounded with the images of rebirth, the baby, the first letter of the alphabet, the light. The town fathers believe that they can make of Hester what they will—for them that means to make her purely a *symbol* of sin—but in her historical life, and in the empirical life of her fictional character, the important implicit gesture is an assumption that her personal past, including her adultery, is washed away in a ritual gesture of purification. The whole "ceremony," then, which was meant as a purification rite for the town—a transfiguration of the historical Hester into the symbolic Hester—empowers her not so much because she cares for their forgiveness, but because it shows her that she is a presence threatening to her town, one too real to expel and—as yet—too strange to name. Hester thus gains both the freedom and the burden to fuse her life to a symbol.

Wearing only the single letter, Hester is to flower into the grandest form of Puritan language, a "living sermon against sin" (63). As symbol, and as sermon, she is to stand as the embodiment of the negative potential of every resident in her community. Like Dimmesdale's rhetorical assumption of this same role, Hester's involuntary assumption is outside of the realm of common speech. Although in Hester's case there is an assumed understanding of the message she wears, and in Dimmesdale's case there is an assumed misunderstanding of the sermons he delivers, the two are connected in their knowledge of the "truth" and their status as perceived symbols. As symbols in the possession of the community, Hester and Dimmesdale are elusive and malleable: they are sacred and they are sinners, angels and human beings, prophets and mutes; most importantly, they are the holy sermon whose subject is the unspeakable sin.[23]

In this model, Dimmesdale is not only a victim but a failure as culpable as Chillingworth in terms of the community's project of self-empowerment. He fails to take responsibility both for his own sin and for his own language; in fact, Dimmesdale actively avoids such responsibility through his linguistic manipulations. He speaks in abstractions, in contexts that are more "literary" than "natural," where words are not expected to make a "bright transparency of to-day," but are immediately elevated into symbolic thought: he speaks from the pulpit; his confessions are impersonal. There he takes responsibility for the general state of sin, and foremost to the Puritan mind would be adultery, if not in action, at least in thought. But though implicating himself in generic sin, to a generic congregation, Dimmesdale moves no closer to confession of the specific sin, of its place in history. If he could leave behind his support system of the pulpit and the crowd—even if he could say the same words, but to an individual in the town outside of the church context, he would be using language for its fundamental purpose, to establish mutual understanding. Though like Hester, Dimmesdale plays a symbolic role largely controlled by the community, he accrues some of his own guilt and responsibility in his attempts to step outside of his own personal consciousness, to objectify himself as symbol, and then to manipulate that objectified role. Like Chillingworth, Dimmesdale is given the chance to tell a true story. But Dimmesdale's refusal to take on that role is far more complex: Dimmesdale's response is not silence but a careful narrative which, ironically, through the very perfection of its design, becomes as ineffective and as far from truth as simple denial.

The strength of this linguistic trap and its enforcement from such important figures as the doctor and the preacher make it no surprise that the same frame defines the language relations between Hester and her town. Previous to her sin, Hester was a member of her society, which at its inception was a "Utopia of human virtue." But like all such places, this community "invariably recognized it among their earliest practical necessities to allot a portion of the virgin soil as a cemetery, and another portion as the site of a prison" (47). From the start, then, the most idealistic settlement will understand sin and death as part of the common lot: for idealism to thrive, there must be a simple and clear repository for that which does not fit. The problem arises when the sin (or the death, in horror stories) is not final, does not fundamentally transform the person. Then there is a violation which cannot be sealed in a vault, and the whole order of the Utopia stands threatened. Before Hester's time, Puritan Boston's static framework for knowledge and language had been sufficient; but as the task of self-definition grew more complex, the community no longer could assume that sin would be transformative. In fact, Hawthorne suggests that those who insist on living by the rules of the orderly utopia write themselves out of the progress of history: of the two who believed in a future world of freer expression and love, only Hester is left.

But because of the distance necessary to revelation in Hawthorne's model, Hester herself is unable to become a prophetess in any dramatic sense. Just as the "A" is only the smallest step toward a linguistically potent culture, so too is Hester's own life meant only to begin, and to set into motion, a new, active perception of language. With the deaths of Chillingworth and Dimmesdale, the paralyzing bond is broken, and Hester's life itself continues to make the wilderness somehow more domestic, less symbolic:

> Her sin, her ignominy, were the roots which she had struck into the soil. It was as if a new birth, with stronger assimilations than the first, had converted the forest-land, still so uncongenial to every other pi-grim and wanderer, into Hester Prynne's wild and dreary, but life-long home. (80)

As the only one actively breaking down the barriers to effective language in her society, the only one fusing symbol and meaning, Hester ironically is estranged from the common symbolic frame of reference; she makes her own life as she walks through the "moral wilderness" (199). Creating as she goes, Hester is a pioneer who accepts a challenge to make real that which is only empty rhetoric to the others in her society, to infuse lived meaning and historical experience into a cultural symbol. But she has no one, not even her lover, with whom she can discuss her work; the power of Hester's "magic circle" (246) of language both denies her possible consciousness of personal revelation and secures those revelations for Hawthorne's America. All of Hester's storytelling, then, is left to later generations.

To say that Hester is empowered by the "A" is not to say that she enjoys this power, or that it is personally desirable, or even that she knows exactly what the power is. But to return to her town, to live out her life wearing the "A," is to accept a role never before taken in that wilderness Utopia. That role may be seen as a fundamental model of the dynamic life of national symbolism in American Romanticism. From an earlier era, the strength, persistence, and symbolic vitality of the legends of Jane McCrea and John André within the American historical imagination provide a powerful image of the resources of paradox necessary to the development of cultural storytelling. The story of the origins of a new nation could be advanced *only* by a cultural imagination prepared for exactly the sort of ambiguity that the shifting terms of André's life—from British gentleman to Loyalist spy to American martyr—would entail. To generate the Romanticism which would give full scope to symbolic narratives of American identity, the popular imagination would need to be prepared, for example, to figure the relationship between Britain and the colonies not in an easy allegory of oppressive parent and rebellious child but in the complex metaphor of mutual seduction; and it would have to be prepared, above all, to carry into the communal imagination uncharted spaces of private histories, incommunicable experiences, and untold secrets. And there may be no character in the history of American literature more strongly equipped to fulfill that role than Hester Prynne.

In the emerging process of storytelling in America, the deaths of Jane McCrea and John André prefigure characters embodying the complexities of Romanticism in the New World—characters like Cooper's Spy (1821) and Hawthorne's Hester. McCrea and André, like the characters they inspire, stand for a kind of memory quite different from the ordinary monuments of heroism. Instead they invoke all that eludes memorial representation—all that lies outside of community knowledge, all that therefore cannot be narrated in the inherited language of culture. The developing cultural story of America, then, becomes an agent of mediation between the violent and disordered experience of lived history and the highest ideals of the Romantic imagination. The essential dynamic to the development of a potent cultural story in America—the shifting sensibility from the stagnations of classicism to the dangerous freedoms of Romanticism—was imagined through these early legends as a sustained resistance between the secret and known texts of culture; that model is one shaping force in the evolution of the particularly dark Romanticism of mid-nineteenth-century America. Both the legends and Hawthorne's classic novel demonstrate that the language of Romantic symbolism is a process rather than a spiritual transformation. It must be some time before any story is told, because, especially in the formative stages of a society, "it is singular . . . how long a time often passes before words embody things" (224).

Notes

1. I discuss these legends in depth in my dissertation, "The Limits of National Narrative: History's Secrets in Cooper, Hawthorne, and Wister" (1996). In that fuller context, my argument compares and contrasts the versions of each of these two legends and links them first to James Fenimore Cooper's successful historical novel, *The Spy* (1821). There I focus on both the variations and the *limits* to the variations that caught the national imagination. The legends receive attention in a wide range of contexts including official documents (e.g., *Proceedings of a Board of General Officers* [trial documents published by John Carter in Providence, 1780]; *Congressional Report* [1777]); newspapers (e.g., *Pennsylvania Evening Post*, August 12, 1777; *United States Gazette*, September, 1781); early American histories—national, regional, and local (e.g, Paul Allen, *A History of the American Revolution* [1822]; Henry Lee, *Memoirs of the War* [1812]); and early fiction, poetry, and drama (e.g., Hilliard, *Miss McCrea: A Novel of the American Revolution* [1784]; William Dunlap, *André: A Tragedy in Five Acts* [1798]).

2. Letter from George Washington, read at André's trial proceedings, printed in the Appendix to William Dunlap, *André: A Tragedy in Five Acts* (1798), ed. Brander Matthews (New York: Dunlap Society, 1887), 110.

3. Washington Irving, *The Life of George Washington* (New York: G. P. Putnam, 1856), IV, 108.

4. Nathaniel Hawthorne, *The Scarlet Letter*, in Centenary Edition, vol.1, eds. William Charvat, Roy Harvey Pearce, and Claude M. Simpson (Columbus: Ohio State UP, 1962). All quotations are from this edition.

5. In terms helpful to an understanding of this change in cultural self-definition, Victor Turner has distinguished between the functions of the "liminal" and the "liminoid"—the change in the relation of the transitional (or transgressing) character to the status quo. While in traditional culture, the liminal condition is

"demanding" and "compulsory," the "liminoid" (modern culture's version of the liminal) is a condition of will and choice in which "great public stress is laid on the individual innovator, the unique person who dares and opts to create." And, Turner argues, liminality in traditional cultures "secretes the seed of the liminoid, waiting only for major changes in the sociocultural context to set it growing." Hester is clearly and simply liminal. Her status as an outsider is an enforced punishment. But in Hawthorne's representation of Hester's personal history—in the course of her life and in her entrance into 1850—Hester comes to resemble the "liminoid"; she is the harbinger of a modernity fusing new cultural contexts to the seeds which allowed them to grow. (Victor Turner, "Liminal to Liminoid, in Play, Flow, and Ritual: An Essay in Comparative Symbology," *Rice University Studies*, LX [1974], 53-92).

6. Michael Colacurcio, *The Province of Piety: Moral History in Hawthorne's Early Tales* (Cambridge: Harvard UP, 1984), 457.

7. Hawthorne's language theory involves nothing less than the fusion of empiricist and transcendentalist linguistic philosophies within one symbol. He thus asks his reader to make what Feidelson calls an "integral act of perception [which] effectually 'opens' an imaginative reality" (Charles Feidelson, Jr., *Symbolism and American Literature* [Chicago: U of Chicago P, 1953], 9; see also Roy Harvey Pearce, "Romance and the Study of History" in *Hawthorne Centenary Essays* [Columbus: Ohio State UP, 1964], 224-25, 230-32, 243). The empirical side of Hawthorne's cultural and linguistic imagination is based on Locke's *An Essay Concerning Human Understanding*: Hawthorne's theory takes from Locke the emphasis on the importance of the most basic functions of language for the survival and development of society. Locke explains the genesis of verbal communication as originating explicitly in community need (John Locke, *An Essay Concerning Human Understanding* [1690; London: William Tegg and Co., 1879], III, ii: 323). For Hawthorne, it is Hester Prynne who advances "the comfort and advantage of society." She accepts the "voluntary imposition" of a sign, the "mark" of an "invisible idea." But Hester—and Hawthorne—do more than this with language: an "imaginative reality," made up of language and structured by irony, expands to encompass empirical meaning and speculative (transcendental) suggestion.

8. Walter Benjamin, "The Task of the Translator" in *Illuminations: Essays and Reflections*, ed. Hannah Arendt, trans. Harry Zohn (New York: Schocken Books, 1969), 79.

9. Hans Blumenberg, *Work on Myth*, trans. Robert M. Wallace (Cambridge: M.I.T. Press, 1985), 110.

10. In his 1829 "Preliminary Essay" to Coleridge's *Aids to Reflection*, James Marsh could have been describing this rhetorical form which American identity had taken, and which too many—Hawthorne among them—were beginning to fear was "essentially diverse" from their "incommensurate" nineteenth century reality: "Speculative systems of theology indeed have often had little connection with the essential spirit of religion, and are usually little more than schemes resulting from the strivings of the finite understanding to comprehend and exhibit under its own forms and conditions a mode of being and spiritual truths essentially diverse from their proper objects, and with which they are incommensurate." James Marsh, "Preliminary Essay" to Samuel T. Coleridge, *Aids to Reflection*, 2 vols. (London, 1843), ii: xxv.

11. Benjamin, "The Storyteller: Reflections on Nikolai Leskov" in *Illuminations*, pp. 89-90.

12. [Anne W. Abbott], Review, in *The North American Review*, LXXI (1850), 147.

13. In terms helpful to understanding the magistrates' sincere but inadequate use of language, Mary Douglas describes the evolution of cultural roles: "All the attribution of dangers and powers is part of this effort to communicate and thus to create social forms" (*Purity and Danger: An Analysis of the Concepts of Pollution and Taboo* [New York: Ark, 1988], 101).

14. For Hawthorne, of course, purely rational language would be as insufficient as is the purely transcendental. See Philip Gura, *The Wisdom of Words: Language, Theology, and Literature in the New England Renaissance* (Middletown, CT: Wesleyan UP, 1981).

15. Hawthorne has Hester herself suggest her tie to the future, as it has been imposed by the community: "[T]his badge hath taught me,—it daily teaches me,—it is teaching me at this moment,—lessons whereof my child may be the wiser and better, albeit they can profit nothing to myself" (111).

16. Feidelson, *Symbolism and American Literature*, 94.

17. On the religious and educational importance of language to the New England Puritans, see Dennis E. Baron, *Grammar and Good Taste: Reforming the American Language* (New Haven: Yale UP, 1982), especially 119-39.

18. Nathaniel Hawthorne, "Endicott and the Red Cross" in *Twice-Told Tales*, eds. William Charvat, Roy Harvey Pearce, and Claude M. Simpson, Centenary Edition, vol. 9 (Columbus: Ohio State UP, 1962), 435.

19. In *L'éducation morale* (1925), Emile Durkheim describes the inevitable failure of modes of social control which attempt to sanction thought as well as action. Anthony Giddens, ed. and trans., *Emile Durkheim: Selected Writings* (New York: Cambridge UP, 1972), 112-13.

20. For the implications of deviance specifically within Puritan culture, see Kai T. Erikson, *Wayward Puritans: A Study in the Sociology of Deviance* (New York: Macmillan, 1966).

21. Douglas, *Purity and Danger*, 38.

22. In Hawthorne's model this glittering letter might be compared to Endicott's reflective and unlettered breastplate in "Endicott and the Red Cross"; both symbols have the power to reflect the symbolic totality of the Puritan colony—past, present, and future. I am thinking specifically of the argument that Sacvan Bercovitch makes in "Endicott's Breastplate: Symbolism and Typology in 'Endicott and the Red Cross'": he argues that in the breastplate, Hawthorne has created "an historically verifiable and imaginatively liberating 'metaphor' that opens into a consummate symbol of Puritanism" (*Studies in Short Fiction*, IV [Summer, 1967]). In fact, Governor Bellingham's shield, in which the scarlet letter is magnified, neatly brings together these two symbols. Both of the shields, and the letter too, are emblems of the colony's strength in defense; it is no accident that the one Puritan in the colony to join Hester in ornate dress is the governor.

23. Hawthorne makes the connection between Hester and the Puritan sermon as explicit as that between Dimmesdale and the sermons: "If she entered a church, trusting to share the Sabbath smile of the Universal Father, it was often her mishap to find herself the text of the discourse" (85).

The Unexpress'd: Walt Whitman's Late Thoughts on Richard Wagner

Karen Karbiener

> Weia! Waga!
> Wandering waters,
> Lulling our cradle! Wagalaweia!
> Wallala, weilala weia![1]

In his fortieth year, Richard Wagner composed the score of a musical piece that would become known as the "cradle song of the world"[2]: *Das Rheingold*, the first part of *Der Ring der Nibelungen*. Wagner later claimed that he had been inspired while in "a kind of somnolent state, in which I suddenly felt as though I were sinking in swiftly flowing water." As the "rushing sound formed itself in my brain into a musical sound," the composer envisioned the union of music, stage picture, and compositional idea, and "at once recognized the orchestral overture to the Rheingold, which must long have lain latent within me."[3]

Six years later, in his fortieth year, Walt Whitman wrote a poem that would be labelled as "one of Whitman's two greatest artistic achievements": "Out of the Cradle Endlessly Rocking." Though he remained vague as to what inspired the poem, Whitman directed his readers to test this work—as well as his others—with the ear, not the intellect.[4] Is it more than coincidence that several of Whitman's listeners have 'heard' Wagner in "Out of the Cradle Endlessly Rocking" and other poems? "Whitman, as has often been said, is the Wagner of poets," writes Whitman's friend William Sloane Kennedy; in this century, Edward Haviland Miller is among those literary critics who believe the comparison of the two artists is "a point that is still in need of development." Leo Spitzer claims that "Out of the Cradle Endlessly Rocking," like other poems by Whitman, possesses "a Wagnerian musical density of texture," and Denis Donoghue suggests that many Whitman passages sound like program notes to Wagner's operas. The prominent music critic Edward Dannreuther uses quotations from the "Preface" of *Leaves of Grass* in order to define Wagner for English audiences; Wagner and Whitman's "revolt against rigid form" is paralleled by H. R. Haweis, an influential Wagnerite on both sides of the Atlantic. And in his discussion of America's Wagner cult, Joseph Horowitz notes that "Wagner offered an avenue of intense spiritual experience, a surrogate for religion or cocaine, a song of redemption to set beside Emerson or Whitman."[5]

Such remarks, along with the essays from which they were extracted, can hardly be said to offer significant contributions to melopoetics—that is, the developing field of study comparing music and literature. They are simple analogies based more on assumptions and hunches rather than fact or detailed analysis;[6] indeed, the validity of the comparisons can be questioned on the most basic level because of presumptions made about the artists' familiarity and knowledge of each other. Wagner, for example, does not mention Whitman once throughout his extensive writings. Whitman, who was candid concerning his musical illiteracy, admitted to having a limited knowledge of Wagner's music; he claimed that he had only heard "snatches" of Wagnerian operas in his youth.[7] By the time Wagner became all the rage in New York concert halls, Whitman's concert-going days were over. All he knew of the music was gathered from the comments of friends and from the presses. Certainly, Whitman could not have understood, much less transposed to language, Wagner's complex experiments.

And yet, comparing Whitman and Wagner seems intuitively right somehow. If an age can be said to possess a spirit, both men represent the nineteenth century's idea of the controversial, revolutionary Romantic artist. "Sinful, meretricious, unmelodious, and unsufferably long," "strange, original, and somewhat barbaric"—words used to describe Wagner's operas during his day[8]—could just as easily have been applied to Whitman by his contemporaries or himself. Many of Whitman's ideas—like the notion that "the topmost proof of a race is its own born poetry," pronounced in the first sentence of "The Poetry of the Future"[9]—may well have been included in Wagner's famous tract, "The Art-Work of the Future." And Wagner's creation of a new, personal musical language certainly bears at least a superficial resemblance to Whitman's own language experiments. Once recognized, the similarities and parallels between the works and aesthetic philosophies of the two artists are difficult to ignore; indeed, Whitman himself could not ignore them, especially after evaluating Wagner's accomplishments relative to his own mediocre American reception and artistic limitations.

Music was a vital ingredient in Whitman's poetic formula. If the importance Whitman placed upon music is not evident enough in his titles ("Song of Myself," "A Boston Ballad," "Proud Music of the Storm") or descriptions, Whitman carefully explained it himself in his personal writings. "My younger life was so saturated with the emotions, raptures, up-lifts, of such musical experiences that it would be surprising indeed if all my future work had not been colored by them," he told Horace Traubel in 1888. "A real musician running through *Leaves of Grass*—a philosopher musician—could put his finger on this and that anywhere in the text no doubt as indicating the activity of the influences I have spoken of."[10] Whitman often cast himself in this role of "real musician." "My poems when complete should be a unity, in the same sense that the earth is, or that the human body . . . or that a perfect musical composition is," he wrote in an undated manuscript note;[11] in the peremptory note to "Collect" he equates his own writing process with "the musicians' story of a composer up in a garret rushing the middle body and last of his score together, while the fiddlers are playing the first parts down in the concert-room."[12] "Of course my poetry isn't formless," Whitman told William Roscoe Thayer. "Nobody could write in my way unless he had the melody singing in his ears. I don't often contrive to catch the best musical combination nowadays; but in the older pieces I always had a tune before I began to write."[13]

Based on the overwhelming evidence Whitman himself provided, one can see that Whitman the eager young journalist and Whitman the poet had very different agendas. While the journalist was concerned with winning readers in a land of increasing nationalism, the poet could not ignore the overwhelming effect that the opera had on his artistic sensibility. In a review of *Ernani* written for *Life Illustrated* in 1855, Whitman's reader may detect examples of his mental struggle: "You envy Italy, and almost become an enthusiast; you wish an equal art here, and an equal science and style, underlain by a perfect understanding of American realities, and the appropriateness of our national spirit and body also."[14] By 1863, Whitman forgot about the 'refreshing simplicity' of the Cheney family singers in his excitement over the recent performance of Donizetti's *Lucrezia Borgia*. "Such singing and strong rich music always give me the greatest pleasure," he wrote to Lewis K. Brown and other comrades. "So the opera is the only amusement I have gone to, for my own satisfaction, for the last ten years."[15]

Whitman was essentially musically illiterate and his "references to music are of a uniform and magnificent banality."[16] He himself frequently and unabashedly claimed that his enjoyment of opera "was altogether untechnical. I knew nothing about music: simply took it in, enjoyed it, from the human side: had a good natural ear—did not trouble myself to explain or analyze." Music thus remained an intriguing mystery for Whitman—indeed, so much so that he wrote of its "soul-rousing power, its impossibility of statement" even over literature. "Music, the combiner, nothing more spiritual, nothing more sensuous, a god, yet completely human, advances, prevails, holds highest place; supplying in certain wants and quarters what nothing else could supply," he states in "Democratic Vistas." The human voice, too, contained remarkable expressive capabilities. "Beyond all other power and beauty, there is something in the quality and power of the right voice (timbre the schools call it) that touches the soul, the abysms," Whitman wrote in a late note. "It was not for nothing that the Greeks depended, at their highest, on poetry's and wisdom's vocal utterance."[17]

Whitman's claims that he composed in the method of the Italian opera were thus not referring to his technique, but to his emotional and spiritual input. As he heard the music of the Italian opera come alive through the power of the human voice, so he attempted to make his verses "sing." "No one will get at my verses who insists upon viewing them as a literary performance, or attempt at such performance, or as aiming mainly toward art or aestheticism," Whitman told his readers in "A Backward Glance O'er Travel'd Roads."[18] His claim that *Leaves of Grass* was "an attempt, from first to last, to put a Person, a human being . . . freely, fully and truly on record" and was derived from his attempts to put the operatic experience on paper. Long before Roland Barthes formulated his theories concerning music, voice, and language, Whitman sensed the "grain"—the "body in the singing voice"[19]—in the performances of his beloved Italian soloists:

> I hear the trained soprano . . . she convulses me like the
>   climax of my love-grip;
> The orchestra whirls me wider than Uranus flies,
> It wrenches unnamable ardors from my breast,
> It throbs me to gulps of the farthest down horror,
> It sails me . . . I dab with bare feet . . . they are licked
>   by the indolent waves,
> I am exposed . . . cut by bitter and poisoned hail,
> Steeped amid honeyed morphine . . . my windpipe squeezed
>   in the fakes of death,
> Let up again to feel the puzzle of puzzles,
> And that we call Being.[20]

"Badialdi was the superbest of all superb baritones in my time—in my singing years. Oh! those great days! great, great days!" Whitman gushed. "Alboni, Badialdi, in particular: no one can tell, know, even suspect, how much they had to do with the making of *Leaves of Grass*."[21]

Whitman's "singing years" ended as a result of changes in his health, finances, and living situation, not because of a flagging interest. He was an avid opera-goer through the 1850s until he went to the war front, and he remained enthusiastic about the performances he managed to see afterwards. After he suffered from a paralytic stroke in 1873, Whitman attended only one or two more operas, and rarely returned to New York City except to give lectures. He thus remained a distant observer of rather than a participant in the powerful cultural movement known as Wagnerism, peaking in New York in the 1880s and 1890s.

New York audiences were first introduced to Wagner in 1859, when a production of *Tannhäuser* was performed at the Stadt Theater, but it was the conductor Anton Seidl who institutionalized Wagnerian opera at the Metropolitan Opera House. In the five seasons from 1886 to 1891, he conducted 128 Wagnerian performances, and 149 of everything else. Indeed, Wagner played an important part in keeping the Metropolitan Opera House in good financial condition; in the same five-year span, Wagner's dramas yielded $590,021.70, as against $410,332.75 brought in by the entire non-Wagnerian list. The Wagner Society of New York, made up of fans from all walks of life, stimulated and encouraged encore productions of Wagnerian favorites. Translations of his writings were widely available by 1880, and eagerly discussed in the presses and by intellectual circles. Indeed, "the cult of Wagner dominated America's musical high culture, and helped shaped its intellectual life, throughout the closing decades of the century."[22]

Largely confined to his Camden home by the 1880s, Whitman remained a distant observer of the Wagner phenomenon, although he evidently had known of Wagner since at least 1874, when he mentioned the composer's name in an article for the *New York Weekly Graphic*.[23] Additionally, in an autobiographical note Grier dates to the late 1860s or early 1870s, Whitman claims that he "revels untired in the lore of the Valkyrie, Siegfried, Brunhild, and all involved in Wagner's Ring of the Niblung, and the Tannhauser of the same master."[24] Whitman's reference to *Tannhäuser* is noteworthy, considering that he claimed to "have heard [Wagnerian] bits here and there at concerts, from orchestras, bands."[25] And whether or not he was first motivated by Wagner's retelling, Whitman seems to have been especially interested in the Nibelungen legend, calling it "one of the most distinctive poems" and "great literature."[26] In an undated, unpublished booklet bound by Whitman himself entitled "The Nibelungen Lied," Whitman reviewed the saga's authorship and plot, and described some of the characters in detail.[27]

It was by way of the written and spoken word that Whitman first became acquainted with Wagner's music. Whitman's career as a writer began in a newspaper office, and the mature poet remained active both as a contributor to and reader of American periodicals; in approximately the same span of time—from the first American performance of Wagner in 1852, to the turn of the century—Wagner remained a hot topic for many of Whitman's favorite magazines. Whitman was either published or reviewed in the same periodicals in the years Wagner was reviewed. Perhaps, then, in perusing through the October 1888 edition of *Century Illustrated* for his article on "Army Hospitals and Cases," he noticed the advertisement for a new edition of *The Correspondence Between Wagner and Liszt*, and even if he missed the biographical sketch of the great American Wagnerian Leopold Damrosch ten pages after his own article in *The Critic* of May 7, 1881, he could not have overlooked the cover portrait of the conductor.

Another periodical that helped sustain the public's interest in Wagner was the *North American Review*. Whitman appears to have been a dedicated reader of this magazine, which offered strong support of *Leaves of Grass* in 1856, published several pieces by the poet during his later years, and was edited by Whitman's close friend, James Redpath. In addition to printing many important reviews of Wagner's operas, including a 28-page article by the composer John Knowles Paine in 1873, the *North American Review* distinguished itself by publishing Wagner's only address to American readers: a two-part, 37-page article entitled "The Work and Mission of My Life."[28] Though there is no proof that Whitman read Wagner's statement, an article that Whitman published in the same magazine two years later indicates that he was familiar with at least some of Wagner's writings; Whitman's very title—"The Poetry of the Future"—is suggestive of "the music of the future," the label given Wagner's compositions, or "The Artwork of the Future," an important essay mentioned in "The Work and Mission of My Life."

Whitman may have been encouraged to draw comparisons between Wagner and himself by friends in the music business. Among Whitman's acquaintances were two renowned Wagnerites, James Gibbons Huneker and Robert Ingersoll. In *Overtones*, Huneker recounted a conversation he had with Whitman in which the poet confessed his love for Wagner. Ingersoll, a leading orator of the postwar era, who delivered two lectures in Whitman's honor during the poet's lifetime and an elegy at Whitman's funeral, gave several laudatory speeches on Wagner and his American interpreter, Anton Seidl. If Whitman had been aware of Ingersoll's admiration for Wagner, it would have undoubtedly made an impression on the poet.

Even those of Whitman's circle who were not musically astute saw reason to compare the poet with the controversial composer; as Whitman wondered aloud to Horace Traubel, "so many of my friends say Wagner is Leaves of Grass done into music that I begin to suspect there must be something in it." Traubel, Whitman's Boswell of later years, kept the poet informed of the many Wagnerian operas he attended, and offered comparisons of the artists. "He has done for music what you have done for poetry: freed it, disclosed its unity with life, set aside its harassing traditions," he told Whitman in 1889. When Traubel insisted that Wagner "is just the man not to be known through snatches, as you are just the man not to be known through gems," Whitman agreed that Wagner "was here for a solid purpose." "If he was not you are not," Traubel quickly responded. After Traubel's "warmly enthusiastic" review of *Die Walküre*, Whitman exclaimed, "I know! I know! it must be so! must be. You tell it to me just as the Doctor did." The doctor was, of course, Whitman's longtime friend and correspondent Dr. Richard Maurice Bucke. "Dr. Bucke, who don't go much on operas, banks a lot on Wagner," mused Whitman in 1888; the next year, Bucke's description of *Götterdämmerung* had again piqued Whitman's curiosity concerning the composer. "Doctor thought it a revelation—was filled with it for days and days," he told Traubel excitedly.[29] Whitman was clearly flattered and intrigued by comparisons between Wagner's "music of the future" and his own art.

In many remarkable ways, Wagner was indeed "his man." Striking parallels exist between the lives of the two artists. Born nine days and six years apart in the 1810s, they both grew up as part of very large families, composed their great works as they approached middle age, and died in their seventies. Wagner, like Whitman, had a scrappy formal education. For both Whitman and Wagner, becoming an artist was an internal, self-motivated process—one in which choices were made rather than natural talents developed. Just as Whitman had not exhibited any early poetic talent, Wagner "was never a marvel of musical precocity."[30] Instead, both boys explored the artistic possibilities of various forms of expression; while the future composer wrote poetry, the future poet burst out in song on the Brooklyn ferry. And both youths enjoyed exercising what Whitman later called "vocalism": Whitman took pleasure in "declaiming Homer or Shakespeare to the surf and sea-gulls,"[31] and Wagner had a passion for reading aloud to his friends.[32]

Whitman's and Wagner's lifelong fascination with words undoubtedly stemmed from the artists' first love: the theatre. Whitman noted this in "Specimen Days" and "Memoranda" and specifically thanked the singer Marietta Alboni several times for the "deepest and most lasting effect" her singing had on his art, and Wagner, whose earliest recollections were associated with his stepfather (an actor) and the theatre, credits the singer Wilhelmine Shroder-Devrient with his decision to pursue a musical career.[33] As youths, Whitman and Wagner were moved and influenced by the same works, including operas by Carl Maria von Weber and Gioacchino Antonio Rossini; Shakespeare, too, was an enduring passion of Whitman's and Wagner's.

As mature artists, Wagner and Whitman continued to share similar philosophies concerning the function and purpose of their forms of expression. Both sought to confront, manipulate, energize, and activate their audiences by conveying life or a presence instead of simply creating a work of art. Yet both struggled with the inadequacy of their mediums in order to produce such an effect. Wagner saw the limitations of the various disciplines standing in the way of his goal which, like Whitman's, was the "unconditional, direct representation of perfect human nature."[34] The divisions between the arts, unnaturally erected as a result of social particularism and egoism, must be destroyed; music, poetry, dance, architecture, painting, and sculpture—imperfect in and of themselves—must be united once again as a Gesamtkunstwerk. This principle was the foundation for Wagner's elaborate music dramas, which bombarded audiences with multisensual meaning.

Wagner never acknowledged that he knew of Whitman or the "language experiments" that attempted so much of what Wagner had already accomplished on stage. Whitman, on the other hand, was all too aware of the constant comparisons between his art and Wagner's, especially during the 1880s and 1890s. And yet, almost all of Whitman's comments concerning Wagner were spoken, or written in unpublished manuscripts. Despite Whitman's recognition of the commonalities between his own art and Wagner's, and though he was evidently in awe of Wagner's reputation and accomplishments, Wagner remains unmentioned through the body of Whitman's poetry and most of his published prose. This is indeed unusual, considering Whitman wrote steadily through his final years, often mentioning the names of those who impressed or influenced him; Shakespeare, Burns, and Elias Hicks are among those who receive individual attention in "November Boughs" (published in 1888), while other articles such as "The Old Bowery" and "Our Eminent Visitors, Past and Present" explicitly mention several musicians and dramatists.

Why, then, did Whitman maintain a public silence regarding Wagner and his work? Robert Faner, one of the few critics who has addressed this question, downplays Wagner's influence on the poet. In *Walt Whitman and Opera*, he suggests that Whitman may have maintained a respectful admiration of Wagner, but his interest in the operas remained general; the poet "had worked his way to a full appreciation of Italian opera, and during his most active years he had surrendered completely to its charms. He remained loyal to it as long as he lived."[35] Yet Faner overlooks the fact that the Italian singers Whitman so admired and emulated were absent from every poem written after the publication of the 1881 *Leaves of Grass*. The only work in "Sands at Seventy" and "Good-Bye My Fancy" that refers to Italian opera is "The Dead Tenor," written in memory of Pasquale Brignoli. Even late prose references to Italian opera seemed to acknowledge it not as part of the living present, but of the dead past. "And so let us turn off the gas," Whitman concluded "Old Actors, Singers, Shows, Etc. in New York," a part of his "Memoranda." "The season through—walking, gesticulating, singing, reciting his or her part—But then sooner or later inevitably wending to the flies or exit door—vanishing to sight and ear—and never materializing on this earth's stage again!"[36] In 1888, Traubel was surprised by Whitman's comments about his beloved—but "old"—Italian operas: "Their age is gone. We require larger measures in music as in literature, to express this spirit of the age."³⁷ The "larger measure" Whitman remained vague about may well have been Wagner. In one of his few published mentions of the composer, Whitman had included a quotation from another source that described Wagner's art as the "music of the present"; the draft for Whitman's article indicates that Whitman had clipped out and read more about Wagner than would seem.³⁸ While Whitman seemed comfortable singing the praises of dead artists (such as Scott or Byron) or those with whom he shared less in common (like Tennyson or Carlyle), he seemed to be more reticent concerning Wagner, a living artist, who presented him with some real competition. Perhaps, then, what should be examined is not the lack of mention of Wagner in Whitman's latest pieces, but Whitman's motivation for leaving out references to the man who preoccupied his thoughts.

Throughout his career, Whitman had written of the importance of recognizing an independent, American art; as he announced in his "Preface" to *Leaves of Grass*, "The proof of a poet is that his country absorbs him as affectionately as he has absorbed it."³⁹ By the late '60s, however, Whitman realized that his country had failed him. "In my own country, so far, from the organs, the press, and from authoritative sources, I have received but one long tirade of shallow impudence, mockery, and scurrilous jeers," Whitman wrote to Moncure Conway in February, 1868.⁴⁰ In recognition of his European patrons, who pushed for foreign publication of *Leaves of Grass* and who rescued Whitman from financial ruin in 1876, Whitman gradually exchanged his nationalism for internationalism. In an 1876 preface designed for foreign editions of *Leaves of Grass*, Whitman claimed:

> While my pieces, then, were put forth and sounded especially for my own country, and addressed to democratic needs, I cannot evade the conviction that the substances and subtle ties behind them . . . belong equally to all countries. And the ambition to waken within them, and in their key, the latest echoes of every land, I here avow.⁴¹

By 1881, Whitman told his friends that "I think so much of the internationality element (sentiment) which I have intended as one of the leading fibres of my book." As Clifton Furness notes, "Whitman had indeed come a long way from those exclusively 'patriotic' sentiments" of his earlier works.[42]

Whitman had a particular interest in Germany at this time. He was first approached with the idea of translating *Leaves of Grass* in 1881; when *Grashalme* was finally published in 1889, it inspired the powerful German Whitman movement, and "devotion . . . which can only be referred to as a cult."[43] Whitman had been reading Goethe and Schlegel since his thirties, but now eagerly engaged in discussions about Germany and its art. "The German literature, even in translation, is somehow my own: I am at home with it—readily adjust myself to its spirit," he told Traubel in 1889, after poring through one of Wagner's librettos. Musing, he continued, "I miss a lot through not knowing German . . . I am not a scintillator, I am not a fire-worksy man: I take better to quietude, to the inertia of large bodies: the German gives me the ground under my feet."[44] The same year, Whitman happily reiterated one of his German translators' claims, that he was "a German requisite—that they'll adopt me."[45]

Whitman's craving for praise and approval in his later years are signs of his deep-rooted artistic anxiety. His perception of his failure as an American bard was further darkened by the light of others' successes; Wagner, the darling of the press and the favorite of critics, must have seemed larger than life to the insecure and aging poet. And what could Whitman do that would in any way compare with Wagner's idea—and realization—of the Gesamtkunstwerke? As much as Whitman had attempted to transcend words, he necessarily employed them; the poet was thus bound to the one vehicle that set him free. Next to Wagner's productions, which convey meaning not only through language, but through music, drama, dance, and image, Whitman's efforts to reach beyond the printed word seem simplistic, even primitive. Like his contemporaries, Whitman recognized Wagner's work as "the music of the present"; but he also deemed it a "new world," a term that had been closely associated with Whitman's own writings. He recognized Wagner's operas as demanding "a vocalism totally unlike that required for Rossini's splendid roulades, or Bellini's suave melodies"—operas that inspired *Leaves of Grass*.⁴⁶ "The masters keep on coming and coming again: nature can always do better than her best: is prodigal, exhaustless," Whitman concluded in another discussion he had with Traubel about the composer.⁴⁷ Whitman had recognized the artist who picked up where he had left off, and the art which could overshadow and replace his own work. He wrote to Bucke in 1889: "Sun bursting forth as I write—the great long burr of the Philadelphia whistles from factories or shores often and plainly here sounding, and I rather like it (blunt and bass)—some future American Wagner might make something of it."⁴⁸

Though such overt commentary concerning Wagner is confined to Whitman's private jottings and conversations, several of his late essays make subtle allusions to the composer and his work. For example, there are intriguing similarities between Wagner's essay "The Work and Mission of My Life" and Whitman's "The Poetry of the Future," published within two years of each other in the *North American Review*. From the first sentence, Whitman connects race and art as Wagner had in the earlier essay, substituting America for Germany's name in discussions of a nation's artistic and intellectual potential. German words, names and phrases—such as "esthetik," "Miss Bremer," "storm and stress," "Goethe"—are used throughout. The thrust of Whitman's piece is that the "poetry of the future," like the "music of the present, Wagner's, Gounod's, even the later Verdi's" aims at "the free expression of emotion"; though music may currently setting a revolutionary pace, its "born sister" poetry was not far behind. Even Whitman's last sentence—"democracy waits the coming of its bards in silence and in twilight, but 'tis the twilight of the dawn"⁴⁹—sounds like an attempt to comment upon, and perhaps move beyond, Wagner's art, represented by his idea of a "Götterdämmerung."

Some years later, during Wagner's height of popularity in New York, Whitman included a less hopeful, more angry subtext in "A Backward Glance O'er Travel'd Roads"—in many ways, already his late attempt to justify his work in the face of his less than receptive public. The essay, which evolved from four closely related pieces written between 1884 to 1888, depicts Whitman as bitter over the failure and criticism of *Leaves of Grass*. "I have not gain'd the acceptance of my own time, but have fallen back on fond dreams of the future—anticipations," Whitman announced. No longer the confident young man of the 1855 "Preface," he sees the possibility that his own songs would be left unsung in the future, especially considering the wealth of talent presently available.

> Whether my friends claim it for me or not, I know well enough, too, that in respect to pictorial talent, dramatic situations, and especially in verbal melody and all the conventional technique of poetry, not only the divine works that today stand ahead in the world's reading, but dozens more, transcend (some of them immeasurably transcend) all I have done, or could do.[50]

The remarks, their tone, and the time period in which they were written lead to the assumption that these are veiled references to Wagner. Though "A Backward Glance O'er Travel'd Roads" mentions the Nibelungen myth only once—and that in the context of the medieval tales, not Wagner's retelling[51]—Whitman is suspiciously preoccupied with the "ballads of feudalism" and German thinkers. Key Wagnerian terms such as "motif" and "symphony" are also employed. And during the years in which Whitman responded to his friends' praises of *Götterdämmerung*—"is that how you say it? Does it mean, the twilight of the gods?"—he also wrote of the popular old-world ballads that threatened the life of his own verse:

> What a comment it forms, anyhow, on this era of literary fulfillment, with the splendid day-rise of science and resuscitation of history, that our chief religious and poetical works are not our own, nor adapted to our light, but have been furnish'd by far-back ages out of their arriere and darkness, or, at most, twilight dimness! What is there in those works that so imperiously and scornfully dominates all our advanced civilization, and culture?[52]

Whitman may have respected and admired Wagner, and even enjoyed being compared to him, but he felt threatened by the scope and grandeur of the Gesamtkunstwerke, as well as their commercial success in his own Mannahatta. The very lack of mention of the man who preoccupied Whitman's thoughts in the 1880s thus serves as a late, personal commentary on the value and endurance of his art; ironically, this silence also helps Whitman achieve his own small triumph over the composer. By not mentioning Wagner—by not giving him life through the medium of language—Whitman cleverly vindicated himself as an artist, and reaffirmed the potential powers of the word. As he writes in his late poem "The Unexpress'd," there was "still something not yet told in poesy's voice or print"; for Whitman, indeed, "the best" remained "yet unexpress'd and lacking,"[53] whether it was what he could not put into words, or chose not to mention.

Notes

1. These are the first words of *Das Rheingold*, "Prelude" to *Der Ring der Nibelungen*. Richard Wagner, *The Ring of the Nibelung*, trans. Andrew Potter (New York: Norton, 1977), 4.

2. Ulrich Muller and Peter Wapnewski, *The Wagner Handbook* (Cambridge: Harvard UP, 1992), 39.

3. Richard Wagner, *My Life*, vol. 2 (London: Constable, 1911), 603.

4. Gay Wilson Allen, *The Solitary Singer: A Critical Biography of Walt Whitman* (New York: New York UP, 1967), 235.

5. William Sloane Kennedy, *Reminiscences of Walt Whitman* (New York: Haskell House, 1973), 164; Edwin Haviland Miller, introduction, *A Century of Walt Whitman Criticism*, ed. Edwin Haviland Miller (Bloomington: Indiana UP, 1969), xxv; Leo Spitzer, "Walt Whitman," *A Century of Walt Whitman Criticism*, ed. Edwin Haviland Miller (Bloomington: Indiana UP, 1969), 279; Denis Donoghue, "Walt Whitman," *Walt Whitman: A Critical Anthology*, ed. Francis Murphy (Harmondsworth, England: Penguin, 1970), 433; Edward Dannreuther, *Richard Wagner: His Tendencies and Theories* (London: Augener and Company, 1873), 20; Joseph Horowitz, *Wagner Nights: An American History* (Berkeley: U of California P, 1994), 244.

6. For a quick guide to some of the responsibilities and problems involved in the field of melopoetics, see Lawrence Kramer's article, "Dangerous Liaisons: The Literary Text in Musical Criticism," in *Nineteenth Century Music* 13.2 (Fall 1989), 159-67. Examples of more successful musico-literary comparisons involving Wagner can be found in the following books: Raymond Furness, *Wagner and Literature* (Manchester: Manchester University, 1982), and Stoddard Martin, *Wagner to the Wasteland* (Totowa, NJ: Barnes and Noble, 1982).

7. Horace Traubel, *With Walt Whitman in Camden*, vol. IV, ed. Sculley Bradley (Philadelphia: U of Pennsylvania P, 1953), 248.

8. Anne Dzamba Sessa, "At Wagner's Shrine: British and American Wagnerians," *Wagnerism in European Culture and Politics*, eds. David C. Large and William Weber (Ithaca: Cornell UP, 1984), 246.

9. Walt Whitman, "The Poetry of the Future," *North American Review* 291 (Feb 1881): 195.

10. Horace Traubel, *With Walt Whitman in Camden*, vol. II (New York: Rowman and Littlefield, 1961), 174.

11. Walt Whitman, *The Complete Writings of Walt Whitman*, eds. Richard Maurice Bucke, Thomas B. Harned, and Horace Traubel, vol. 9 (New York: G. P. Putnam's Sons, 1902), 3.

12. Walt Whitman, "Collect," *Walt Whitman: Complete Poetry and Collected Prose*, ed. Justin Kaplan (New York: Library of America), 927.

13. William Roscoe Thayer, "Personal Recollections of Walt Whitman," *Scribner's* (June 1919): 685.

14. Walt Whitman, *New York Dissected*, eds. Emory Holloway and Ralph Adimari (New York: Rufus Rockwell Wilson, 1936), 22.

15. Walt Whitman, *Walt Whitman: The Correspondence*, vol. I, ed. Edwin Haviland Miller (New York: New York UP, 1961), 179.

16. Calvin Brown, *Music and Literature* (Athens, GA: U of Georgia P, 1948), 178.

17. Horace Traubel, *With Walt Whitman in Camden*, vol. III (New York: Rowman and Littlefield, 1961), 511; Whitman, "Specimen Days," *Poetry and Prose*, ed. Kaplan, 874; Whitman, "Democratic Vistas," *Poetry and Prose*, ed. Kaplan, 934; Whitman, "Some Laggards Yet," *Poetry and Prose*, ed. Kaplan, 1269.

18. Whitman, "A Backward Glance O'er Travel'd Roads," *Poetry and Prose*, ed. Kaplan, 671.

19. Roland Barthes, *The Responsibility of Forms* (Berkeley: U of California P, 1991), 276.

20. Whitman, "Song of Myself," *Poetry and Prose*, ed. Kaplan, 54-55.

21. Traubel, *With Walt Whitman in Camden*, vol. III, 173.

22. See Raymond Mander and Joe Mitcheson, *The Wagner Companion* (New York, 1977), 2; Henry Edward Krehbiel, *Chapters of Opera: Being Historical and Critical Observations and Records Concerning the Lyric Drama in New York From Its Earliest Days Down to the Present Time* (New York: Henry Holt, 1909), 212-55; and Henry T. Finck, *Wagner and His Works*, vol. II (New York: Haskell House, 1893), 514.

23. Walt Whitman, *Collected Writings: Prose Works*, vol. I, ed. Floyd Stovall (New York: New York UP, 1963), 322.

24. Walt Whitman, *Notebooks and Unpublished Prose Manuscripts*, vol. II, ed. Edward F. Grier (New York: New York UP, 1984), 883.

25. Traubel, *With Walt Whitman in Camden*, vol. II, 116.

26. Whitman, "November Boughs," "Democratic Vistas," *Poetry and Prose*, ed. Kaplan, 1150, 933.

27. Walt Whitman, reel 25, The Feinberg Collection of the Papers of Walt Whitman, Library of Congress, 20-26.

28. Richard Wagner, "The Work and Mission of My Life," *North American Review* 129.23 (Aug 1879): 107-24; 129.24 (Sept 1879): 238-58.

29. Traubel, *With Walt Whitman in Camden*, vol. II, 116, 339, 427-28, 433, 445, 506.

30. Wagner, "The Work and Mission of My Life," *North American Review* 129.23 (Aug 1879): 116.

31. Whitman, "Specimen Days," *Poetry and Prose*, ed. Kaplan, 698.

32. Peter Burbridge, "Richard Wagner: Man and Artist," *The Wagner Companion*, ed. Peter Burbridge and Richard Sutton (New York: Cambridge, 1979), 18.

33. Whitman, "Specimen Days," *Poetry and Prose*, ed. Kaplan, 704; and Wagner, *My Life*, vol. 1, 44.

34. Wagner, "The Art-Work of the Future," qtd. in Muller and Wapnewski, *The Wagner Handbook*, 587.

35. Robert T. Faner, *Walt Whitman and Opera* (Philadelphia: U of Pennsylvania P, 1951), 53.

36. Whitman, "Old Actors, Singers, Shows, &c., in New York," *Poetry and Prose*, ed. Kaplan, 1293.

37. Traubel, *With Walt Whitman in Camden*, vol. I, 106.

38. Whitman, "The Poetry of the Future," *North American Review* 291 (Feb 1881): 202; and reel 22, The Feinberg Collection of the Papers of Walt Whitman, Library of Congress, 27.

39. Whitman, "Preface" to *Leaves of Grass*, *Poetry and Prose*, ed. Kaplan, 26.

40. Whitman, *The Correspondence*, vol. II, ed. Miller, 16.

41. Whitman, *Walt Whitman's Workshop: A Collection of Unpublished Manuscripts*, ed. Clifton Joseph Furness (New York: Russell and Russell, 1964), 164.

42. See Horst Frenz, ed., *Whitman and Rolleston: A Correspondence* (Bloomington: Indiana UP, 1951), 53; and Furness, 162.

43. Frenz, 12.

44. Traubel, *With Walt Whitman in Camden*, vol. IV, 441.

45. Traubel, *With Walt Whitman in Camden*, vol. IV, 7.

46. Whitman, "Collect," *Poetry and Prose*, ed. Kaplan, 1021.

47. Traubel, *With Walt Whitman in Camden*, vol. II, 116.

48. Whitman, *The Correspondence*, vol. IV, ed. Miller, 329.

49. Whitman, "The Poetry of the Future," 195, 198, 206, 210.

50. Whitman, "A Backward Glance O'er Travel'd Roads," *Poetry and Prose*, ed. Kaplan, 656-65.

51. Mention of the ballads of feudalism occurs on pages 663, 664, 667, and 668. As for Whitman's attention to German philosophers, Goethe's thoughts are mentioned within and even close the essay; see pages 661 and 672.

52. Whitman, "A Backward Glance O'er Travel'd Roads," *Poetry and Prose*, ed. Kaplan, 663-69; and Traubel, *With Walt Whitman in Camden*, vol. IV, 427.

53. Whitman, "The Unexpress'd," *Poetry and Prose*, ed. Kaplan, 653.

GENDER

The Female Gothic, Beating Fantasies, and the Civilizing Process

Diane Long Hoeveler

On the dark and stormy night of February 7, 1823, Ann Radcliffe, pious and devoted wife, paragon of domestic virtues, died raving mad. Or so rumor had it.[1] Condemned by the critics of the gothic novel as the original "madwoman in the attic," Radcliffe created what we have come to recognize as the potent, primal versions of the female gothic, only to be consumed in death by its fantasies. Her novels, particularly *The Mysteries of Udolpho* and *The Italian*, established the pattern that has persisted into contemporary female gothics—a persecuted heroine trapped in a house diffused with manic oedipal anxieties and assaulted by the forces of socio-economic power (often disguised as religion) run amok. The fears that haunt Radcliffe's heroines are as real as they are ephemeral; that is, the author manages to create a fictional world where disinheritance is troped as the equivalent of incestuous rape. And if neither threat actually materializes, the reader vicariously experiences both as if they did through the vivid imaginative fantasies of each of the heroines. As her heroines flee from towers to labyrinthine catacombs to rooms with trick locks, they seem to be running in quick sand. The strange stasis—the slow-motion and then sudden flurry, the revolving cycles of inertia and mania—all are characteristics of the long-winded, hysterical prose of the female gothic. But such devices merely encode and proffer the dominant ideology that lies at the heart of the genre, that lies at the heart of the heroines, that lies at the heart of women in patriarchal society: the ideology I have come to recognize as "gothic feminism."

Radcliffe's later novels actually fictionalize the major claims presented by Mary Wollstonecraft's *Vindication of the Rights of Woman* (1792), for if Wollstonecraft condemns the inadequate educations women receive, Radcliffe demonstrates the disastrous effects of such training in her gothic anti-heroines. But it is in the creation of what I have come to recognize as gothic feminism that Wollstonecraft and Radcliffe have the most in common. Both authors conspired (albeit unknowingly) in creating this potent ideology that persists today in myriad forms and undergirds many of the assumptions of what now goes under the name of "victim feminism," the contemporary anti-feminist notion that women earn their superior social and moral rights in society by positioning themselves as innocent victims of a corrupt tyrant and an oppressive patriarchal society.

At this point, however, one realizes that one has once again succumbed to generalizing about the genre, lapsing into that old critical trap—the generic laundry list. The gothic has always lured its critics into that quagmire and managed to elude systematic analysis as a result. The challenge in writing about the female gothic, then, lies initially in defining one's terms. And, unfortunately, analysis of the "gothic" has traditionally been accomplished through what Eugenia DeLamotte has called "the shopping-list approach." Listing devices or conventions as the 1801 *Monthly* did ("unnatural parents, — persecuted lovers, — murders, — haunted apartments, — winding sheets, and winding stair-cases, — subterraneous passages, — lamps that are dim and perverse, and that always go out when they should not, — monasteries, — caves, — monks, tall, thin, and withered, with lank abstemious cheeks, — dreams, — groans, — and spectres") was standard in the critical discourse through the 1960s. But during the past three decades literary critics have turned their attention to defining the genre by addressing questions about the "meaning of the Gothic myth."[2] The female gothic most recently has been subjected to several useful and provocative interpretations; however, all of them privilege the notion of the "female" "self" in ways that ignore the highly ideological nature of both the gothic "myth" and their own critical analyses. But by employing an approach that does not subscribe to the humanist ideology we can come, I think, to some new insights into the discourse systems that formed "gothic feminism."

In other words, I do not indulge the notion that women can ever escape their social, political, and economic conditions and create or preserve some sort of pristine a-historical "self." In a post-structuralist leap of faith, however, I do believe that we can come to some conclusions (albeit tentative) about the female gothic genre and its complicity with the development of "victim feminism" and "professional femininity" as ideologies. Discussions of the female gothic, like analyses of feminism, have, unfortunately, uncritically participated in the very fantasies that the genres have created for their unwary readers. We, like the characters in the novels or proponents of a monolithic feminism, want to find something hidden, mysterious, deep and esoteric behind the black veil, and usually this elusive deep structure is imaged as some sort of sexual or psychic secret. The lure of the gothic has been precisely in this quality, this notion that as readers we have creative or quasi-artistic power by investing empty signifiers with our own self-created meanings. As critics, however, we cannot afford to become participants in the readers' frenzy, caught up like the characters in the manic dance of the gothic.

The voices that emerge from the female gothic novel tradition—and the discourse-systems that emerge from them—have been traditionally recognized as the voices of Sensibility and the sentimental traditions, melodrama and the hyperbolic staging of female suffering and victimization, and finally what is known as gothic and vindication fiction. I would contend, however, that white, bourgeois women writers have not simply been the passive victims of male-created constructions, but rather that they have frequently depicted themselves, as men have, as manipulative, passive-aggressive, masochist, and sadistic. In short, they have created characters who masquerade as women caught up and struggling against the dynamics of the oppressive and controlling masculine *gaze*. Now we recognize these terms as standards ones taken from psychoanalytic ideologies, and I would identify my use of them as informed by my conviction that psychoanalysis has participated, as has literature, in the rather broad cultural project of "diagnosing" and "curing" social and sexual weaknesses and deviancies that it has actually created.[3]

As early as 1769 Elizabeth Montagu's "Essay on the praeternatural beings in Shakespeare" revealed how quickly and thoroughly the gothic had been constructed, according to Harriet Guest, "as the site of a privatized and licensed dissipation" and an articulation of "a gender-specific utopian politics." For Guest, the gothic as constructed by women writers "facilitated the definition of national character in terms that were both wantonly heterogeneous in their embrace of private and diverse individuals, and redeemed in their idealization of chaste and maternal femininity, the sacred power of Britannia." Middle-class women writers of this period were particularly attracted to the female gothic novel because they could explore within its parameters their fantasized overthrow of the public realm, figured as a series of ideologically-constructed masculine "spaces," in favor of the creation of a new privatized, feminized world. As an example of a feminized discourse of political embourgeoisification, the female gothic participates in the paradoxical enterprise of both criminalizing and deifying women, and thus we are presented over and over again with the gothic anti-heroine and the dead/undead gothic mother. The persistence of both constructions suggests the need of women writers to expose and at the same time conceal the uneasy slippages that existed between apparently opposed concepts of women during this period: public and libidinal sexuality poised against private and unimpeachable chastity.[4] The valorization of the private, extrapolitical aspects of the female gothic novel suggests that women writers conspired with their culture to position women securely within the home, propping up the edifice of the patriarchal family, and insuring its continuance through the fetishization of virginity and marital chastity. But at the same time (melo)dramatic and hyperbolic eruptions continue to be depicted in these fictions—wanton sexuality, adultery, murder, and mayhem—all of which figure a political import that is subversive or ambivalent at the very least.

The female gothic was understood pre-1970 as primarily a psychological fiction exploring the fears and guilt attendant on sexual maturation, but these works can more accurately be read as elided representations of the political, socio-economic, and historical complexities of women's lives under the capitalist system. That is, the female gothic became a coded system whereby women authors covertly communicated to other women—their largely female reading audience—their ambivalent rejection and at the same time outward complicity with the dominant sexual ideologies of their culture. Female authors ironically inverted the "separate spheres" ideology by valorizing the private female world of the home and fictively destroying the public/juridical masculine world. In other words, the female gothic novel reified the "separate spheres" ideology in such a way that women were no longer victimized by it, but fictively took control of it, but only up to a certain point. This point can be located at precisely the creation of what I am calling the professionalization or masquerade of femininity: women's supposedly passive acceptance of their newly-proscribed social and educational identities as wives and mothers of the bourgeoisie. The dominant issue was the professionalization, the institutionalization of bourgeois femininity, a code of conduct that spelled out a proper middle-class woman's behavior and responses to not simply her everyday routines, but her possible sojourn in a dank stone cavern in the heart of Sicily.

And whereas the ideology of the Eternal Feminine demanded female submission, economic disenfranchisement of women, and social conformity to their proscribed domestic roles, the female gothic depicted its young female heroines as anything but entrapped, passive, and docile. Or, to be more precise, the novels represent women who ostensibly appear to be conforming to their acceptable roles within the patriarchy, but who actually subvert the father's power at every possible occasion. I have come to recognize this ideology as gothic feminism, a species of a later phenomenon that was labelled "double consciousness" by W. E. B. DuBois and expanded upon by Ralph Ellison, both of whom revealed it as the root of black attitudes toward white hegemony. Although it may seem frivolous to compare the situations of black slaves to white middle-class women, the same enabling strategies and psychic defense mechanism was used by both groups to survive what each group experienced as alienation and objectification.[5]

Writing his *Commentaries on the Laws of England* in 1765, the jurist William Blackstone stated: "The husband and wife are one person in law; that is, the very being or legal existence of the woman is suspended during the marriage, or at least is incorporated and consolidated into that of the husband: under whose total protection and cover, she performs everything." The ideally "covered" woman of the late eighteenth century and early nineteenth century—not unlike a slave—existed only in relation to her male master/husband. But such an identity, said the female gothic author and reader, was a legal and social construct that could be persistently attacked, deconstructed, and dissolved in the female gothic novel. The most common situation in all of these novels concerns an inheritance, a property, or an estate whose entail is in dispute. And although she has all of the considerable forces of the patriarchy aligned against her—you guessed it—our young, innocent, naive heroine manages to gain her rightful inheritance, usually by besting an evil uncle (read: displaced father-figure). And to make matters perfect, our heroine further triumphs over the patriarchy by creating an alternative companionate family, marrying a "feminized" man who promises, if not in word then through his sheer incompetence, to be completely malleable.

The female gothic constitutes what I would call a rival female-created fantasy—"gothic feminism"—a version of "victim feminism," an ideology of female power through pretended weakness. Such an ideology positions women as innocent victims who deserve to be rewarded with the ancestral estate because they were unjustly persecuted by the corrupt patriarch. If the heroines manage inadvertently to cause the deaths of these patriarchs, so much the better. Montoni and Schedoni, the hapless villains of *The Mysteries of Udolpho* (1794) and *The Italian* (1797), both appear to self-destruct through their own misguided arrogance and egoism, but we know better. The gothic feminist always manages to dispose of her enemies without dirtying her dainty little hands. The position that Radcliffe and her followers advocated for other women to adopt throughout the female gothic novel was one of "wise passiveness" or what we might more cynically label passive-aggression.

In its convergence of psychological and socio-political issues the female gothic—from its inception during the Industrial and French Revolutions through 1848—stands as a distinctive artistic form spawned in reaction to the sexual excesses depicted in the writings of the Marquis de Sade and the radical economic, social, and religious dislocations that occurred with the onset of industrialization and the triumph of a capitalist economy. Women for the first time had a chance to express themselves in widely disseminated and cheaply printed novels that became immensely popular with the new reading audience—largely middle-class women enclosed in the newly created and idealized bourgeois home. These women responded to their sudden change in status with an ambivalence that found its expression in one of the dominant ideologies of the female gothic: the fantasy that the weak have power through carefully cultivating the appearance of their very powerlessness. Such an ideology formed not only the message of the female gothic, but it also accounts for the novels' popularity among women readers who covertly wanted to believe that they could challenge or in some way passively subvert their newly inscribed and institutionalized "spaces," identities, and roles as the wives and mothers of the bourgeoisie.

If we consider the female gothic as a highly ideological signifying system, a discourse system, then we must recognize that we have labelled the genre a literary category only out of desperation, only because we do not know what else to call it. Unlike other neat period distinctions, the gothic is both peculiarly full and peculiarly empty at the same time. It cannot be approached through any narrow category of meaning that will explain its many permutations or manifestations. Trying to limit the genre to a particular time period (as Maurice Lévy has done), or trying to define it in terms of "conventions" (as Sedgwick does)—all of these are essentially futile attempts to give shape to the intrinsically shapeless.[6] I would claim instead that the only contours or parameters that can be applied successfully to the gothic are the codified "spaces" and "voices" that emerge from its own fragmented discourse-system. Stated in the simplest possible terms, the voices that emerge from the novels that traditionally have been identified as female gothic are concerned with delineating highly ideological struggles between "reality" (the forces of political power) and "desire" (the forces of libidinal energy). The nature of these struggles—sometimes seen as sexual or psychic, sometimes social, economic, political, or religious—is less important than the fact that female characters are depicted as constantly struggling against powerful forces that they believe are real and that they believe are poised to destroy them. The enemy is not solely within, as is the case with the majority of gothics written by male authors. The real and ideological enemies for women—female gothic authors and readers—are without.[7] Such a distinction is crucial for understanding that there is a genre of novels written by women about females struggling against alien and powerful forces who resort for their own self-defense to using a battery of strategies—"gothic feminism"—that were drawn from the stock situations of popular stage melodramas and sentimental novels.

The typical female gothic novel presents a blameless female heroine triumphing through a variety of passive-aggressive strategies over a male-created system of oppression and corruption, also known as the protection racket we affectionately refer to as the patriarchy. The melodrama that suffuses these works is explicable only if we understand, as Paula Backscheider has recently demonstrated, that a generally hyperbolic Sentimentalism was saturating the literary ambience, informing the gothic melodramas that were such standard fare during the popular theater season. But melodrama, as Peter Brooks has demonstrated, is also characterized by a series of moves or postures that made it particularly attractive to women. Specifically, Brooks lists as crucial to melodrama the tendency toward depicting intense, excessive representations of life that tend to strip away the facade of manners to reveal the essential conflicts at work, leading to moments of intense and highly stylized confrontations. These symbolic dramatizations rely on what Brooks lists as the standard features of melodrama: hyperbolic figures, lurid and grandiose events, masked relationships and disguised identities, abductions, slow-acting poisons, secret societies, mysterious parentage, and other elements from the melodramatic repertory. In short, melodrama is a version of the female gothic and the female gothic provides the undergirding for feminism as a hyperbolic ideology bent on depicting women as the innocent victims of a corrupt and evil patriarchal system. But, as Laura Mulvey has observed, "ideological contradiction is the overt mainspring and specific content of melodrama, not a hidden, unconscious thread to be picked up only by special critical process." The contradiction at the core of the female gothic, at the core of melodrama as a genre, would appear to be the woman's intense ambivalence toward the paternal home and, by extension, the patriarchy. The home as the site of patriarchally-based, rather than emotionally-based relationships, denies women the chance to exercise their subjectivity, and so their only means of rebelling is to escape, to run away from the paternal domicile. The nightmare in the female gothic novel is that women so frequently cannot run toward what they claim to desire, the man they want to marry. They run instead in a large circle that leads them back precisely to the paternal home, but this time the estate has been magically transformed into a maternally-marked abode through the efforts of the heroine's very circuitous journey. In short, the female gothic novel accomplishes the cultural work of fantasy for women; it convinces them that their safely-proscribed rebellion will result in an improved home for both their mothers and themselves. In rebelling against the patriarch they paradoxically reify the power of the home and family to which they will return, all the while justifying their acts of parricide and class warfare by positioning themselves as innocent victims.

According to Brooks, the gothic novel can be most clearly understood as standing in reaction to desacralization and the pretensions of rationalism. Like melodrama, the female gothic represents both the urge toward resacralization and the impossibility of conceiving sacralization other than in personal terms. For the Enlightenment mentality there is no longer a clear transcendent value to which one can be reconciled. There is, rather, a social order to be purged, a set of ethical imperatives to be made clear.[8] And who better equipped to purge the new bourgeois world of all traces of aristocratic corruption than the gothic heroine? Such a woman—professionally feminine, virginal, innocent, and good—assumed virtually religious significance because within the discourse system so much was at stake. Making the world safe for the middle class was the goal inscribed in both female gothic texts and late eighteenth-century bourgeois feminism. But such a task was not without its perils. What I am calling gothic feminism was born when women realized that they had a formidable external enemy—the ravening, lustful, greedy patriarch—in addition to their own worst internal enemy, their consciousness of their sexual difference perceived as weakness rather than strength.

Consider, for instance, the typical gothic husband. In "The Sicilian Romance, or The Apparition of the Cliff," Henry Siddons's 1794 adaptation of Radcliffe's second novel, the frustrated patriarch chains his rejected wife to a stone wall in a cave and feeds her the way one cares for a forsaken pet that refuses to die. We might legitimately ask, what sort of action is required from women to protect and defend themselves against such evil tyranny? Over and over again, the female gothic writer proffers professional femininity—a highly codified form of conduct, a masquerade—as the only force strong enough to tame the ravages of a lustful, raving patriarch gone berserk.

We have arrived—paradoxically as it may seem—at Luce Irigaray's notion of the "feminine feminine" as opposed to the "masculine feminine" woman. According to Irigaray's revision of Lacan, young girls never successfully resolve the Oedipal phase and instead lag behind in the Imaginary realm, a sort of prison-house of illusory images and childhood landscapes. But instead of viewing this entrapment in the nursery drama as completely negative, Irigaray argues that it opens up possibilities for women that men cannot begin to appreciate or experience. Rather than listening only to what men or patriarchal discourse tells women about their sexuality or their fantasy lives, that is, rather than continuing to be "masculine feminine" women, they need to create themselves instead as "feminine feminine." This latter sort of woman has learned to "mime the mime," mimic and thereby explode the gendered constructions that the patriarchy has invented and codified to enslave and dehumanize her. But central to the notion of mimicry for Irigaray is the technique of masquerade, an attempt to play the gender game as if one were in the know, self-consciously, self-referentially, almost mockingly deflating the very role one would appear to be assuming. For Irigaray:

> There is, in an initial phase, perhaps only one "path," the one historically assigned to the feminine: that of *mimicry*. One must assume the feminine role deliberately. Which means already to convert a form of subordination into an affirmation, and thus to begin to thwart it.... To

play with mimesis is thus, for a woman, to try to recover the place of her exploitation by discourse, without allowing herself to be simply reduced to it. It means to resubmit herself—inasmuch as she is on the side of the "perceptible," of "matter"—to "ideas," in particular to ideas about herself, that are elaborated in/by a masculine logic, but so as to make "visible," by an effort of playful repetition, what was supposed to remain invisible: the cover-up of a possible operation of the feminine in language.

For Irigaray, only when women can bring themselves to a new and unmediated position of selfhood, subjectivity, and language—apart from the patriarchy—will they be able to become a "feminine feminine" woman, that is, defined by woman-marked codes, values, and beliefs.

Irigaray's notions of mimicry and masquerade, however, are most suggestive for the female gothic's discourse network. She argues that women can best battle the patriarchy when they mime the mimes that men have imposed on them. If men have positioned women as simply mirrors for a grandiose masculine imaginary, then women can break through that specular appropriation only when they reflect back to men these same images in grotesque, immense proportions. In other words, women can undo the effects of male discourse only when they act out, overdo, and hyperbolize those same codes. To break out of the masculine imaginary that went under the name of the gothic required a new discourse system, the hyperbolic female gothic, a miming of the mime, a mimicry of the gigantic mirror we call Enlightenment or Sensibility culture.

In an analogous manner, Hélène Cixous has observed: "men and women are caught in a network of millennial cultural determinations of a complexity that is practically unanalyzable: we can no more talk about 'woman' than about 'man' without being caught within an ideological theater where the multiplication of representations, images, reflections, myths, identifications constantly transforms, deforms, alters each person's imaginary order and in advance, renders all conceptualization null and void."[9] The female gothic novel captures this sense of living within a series of interlocking and stifling "networks," each of which demanded a certain psychic and linguistic code—the codes we now recognize as psychoanalytic discourse. And in an attempt to control these networks the female gothic heroine resorted to what we would diagnose as "the talking cure"; that is, she attempted to talk herself out of her perception of life as prison, confessional, asylum, maze, or circus. Her talking cure, the "embodied voice" that emerges from the novels, can finally be identified as what Kristeva has labelled "purposely perverse hysteria." And the texts that demonstrate the effectiveness of her "talking cure," that embody the hysteria, are the documents the authors call "novels" or "romances."

When the Marquis de Sade first indulged his eccentric tastes for the whip, he created not simply the phenomenon we have labelled in his honor—sadism—he also reified its opposite—masochism. Now sadism and masochism existed before the Marquis so kindly brought them into relief; masochism certainly existed long before Leopold von Sacher-Masoch (1836-1895) described it in his novels. Moreover, masochism has the dubious distinction of being one of the few characteristics consistently identified by Freud (and his female disciples) as clearly associated with women. Any analysis of the female gothic novel, unfortunately, has to confront the mystique of female masochism. Feminist literary critics would like to reject any notion of women as inherently masochistic, indeed, as inherently prone to any essentialist quality. But more germane to our discussion is the need to recognize the female author's careful manipulation of the masochistic pose. That is, the gothic heroine indulges in what we would recognize as masochistic gestures for effect. But more important for the female gothic novel, what we call masochism became a stock characteristic of the situation for the gothic heroine. These young women not only tolerate all manner of abuse; they actually seem to seek it out.[10] If an event or situation is comfortable, count on the gothic heroine to pursue trouble.

Consider Emily in *The Mysteries of Udolpho*. A virtual prisoner in a desolate Italian castle, Emily finds herself pursued by not one but two potential rapists. Does she stay sensibly in her room at night? Of course not, she is too busy trying to locate her tortured and starving aunt, imprisoned in another tower of the castle. When Emily does find herself in Montoni's chambers, threatened with marriage to the odious and chubby

Morano, we are supposed to believe that this evil has just descended on our unsuspecting heroine, unprovoked. Such a perception is cultivated by the author in order to conceal the fact that masochism, the deliberate seeking out of pain as pleasure, stands as one of the primary devices in the gothic heroine's arsenal of passive-aggressive strategies. By presenting herself as an innocent and suffering victim, the gothic heroine actually positions herself for the assault, shielded, of course, from the charge or even the impression that she is the aggressor. Playing the victim often simply conceals the fact that one is a victimizer: we are once again within the territory of miming the mime. The women who populate female gothic novels clearly and unequivocally triumph in the end—morally and financially—but generally they have caused a good deal of havoc in the process. And do we condemn these heroines? Never. They have managed to win their readers' sympathies through conforming to the carefully delineated construction of innocent victim, what I am calling the professionalization of femininity, or the cultivated pose of femininity. Do Emily and Ellena just happen to triumph over all their enemies? Radcliffe would have us believe that they managed these feats by doing nothing much at all. Passivity, it would seem, or lying in wait for the oppressor to self-destruct, is its own reward.

All of this brings us to Freud's seminal essay "A Child is Being Beaten" (SE XVII: 175-204; 1919), a source for much recent speculation on the contours of the female gothic novelistic tradition. These novels actually encode in almost uncanny precision the three versions of the beating fantasy as Freud has delineated them. For a girl the first and the third psychological positions in the beating fantasy are sadistic and voyeuristic—another child is being beaten and I am witnessing it—while the second position in the fantasy is masochistic, erotic, and repressed—I am the child being beaten by my father. For the boy the psychic transformation is less complex due to the elimination of one stage. For him the first fantasy, "I am loved by my father," becomes the conscious fantasy, "I am being beaten by my mother." According to Freud, both male and female subjects appear to shift continually between these three (or two) positions largely through the conscious and unconscious permutations of incestuous desire for the father and its repression. The struggles we see in Radcliffe's novels, for instance, between her heroines and various other women who actually take the beatings from a variety of father-substitutes suggests the compulsions at work here. The gothic feminist is a deeply conflicted subject who fends off the blows and manages to watch voyeuristically other women get punished for her projected crimes. Consider, for instance, Jane Eyre who watches Bertha beat and get beaten. Or consider (Miss) Victor Frankenstein, who watches every other child in "his" family get "beaten," that is, killed. The beatings that suffuse these novels suggest the ambivalent construction of gender that lies beneath the surface pose of complicity and passivity. Gothic feminists are angry, while their heroines are pointedly controlled and strategically not angry. These heroines are characterized—unlike their creators—by repression and silence, acceptance or at least the pose of complaisancy. The heroines are professionally feminine, while the anger of the authors can be seen in the violence that happens to plague anyone foolish enough to stand in her heroine's way.

Now this outline of just one of the stock strategies of the gothic heroine presupposes a certain psychological and social matrix, a cash/sex nexus, an interrelation between desire and reality that produces ideology. It is necessary, however, to further situate my approach to the female gothic within the methods outlined by the theorists who have grounded any discussions of sexuality and historicity in the nineteenth century. Gilles Deleuze and Félix Guattari in *Anti-Oedipus* and *A Thousand Plateaus*, volumes one and two of their *Capitalism and Schizophrenia* (1972), maintain that society is invested by desire and is the historically determined product of desire, so that libido has no need of any mediation, sublimation, or transformation, in order to invade and invest the relations of production. Desire creates reality and is solely defined by historical process. Ideology is the attempt to shape desire, and the two types of shaping are radically distinguished from one another. Individual fantasy and group fantasy, fantasy as "speaking playing" and fantasy as "daydream," arise from the need to shape desire. In the latter, analogous to the construction of female gothic novels, the fantasizer experiences institutions themselves as mortal because they can be changed according to the articulations of social desire through making the death instinct into institutional creativity. Commenting on this pattern, John Brenkman argues that within a capitalist system, "it is reification, the transformation of the exchanging of human activity into a set of calculable relations between things, that reconstitutes the subject as a separated individual, that converts play into the interiorized fantasies of the ego, that binds the death drive to eros and makes self-preservation an act of aggression."[11] And, we might add, no one is more adept at self-preservation and its concomitant acts of aggression than the gothic heroine.

And although they think they are revising Freud, Deleuze and Guattari are actually only paraphrasing him when they assert that the only escapes from the spiral of desire/energy/reality/ideology are repression or death, because desire desires death. In order to escape the wheels of the capitalist body-politic, the female gothic novelist and her female reader fantasize a reality that culminates in either repression or death. If the novelist employs repression, then we know ourselves to be reading a work in the realm of the "melodramatically comic" female gothic; if she images death as the only escape, then we know ourselves to be reading a work in the "melodramatically tragic" female gothic tradition. In a world that has been radically desacralized, the tragic is no longer possible, hence the invention of melodrama, the dilution of tragedy in a flurry of emotions signifying little. Radcliffe's novels, Austen's *Northanger Abbey*, or *Jane Eyre* stand as archetypal exemplars of what we might call the "melodramatically comic" female gothic, spawning such modern descendants as du Maurier's *Rebecca*, Margaret Atwood's *Lady Oracle*, Angela Carter's *Nights at the Circus*, and Iris Murdoch's "gothic trilogy" (*The Italian Girl*, *The Time of the Angels*, and *A Severed Head*). In contrast, Wollstonecraft's novels, Shelley's *Mathilda* and *Frankenstein*, *Wuthering Heights*, "The Yellow Wallpaper," Jean Rhys's *Wide Sargasso Sea*, or the more recent work of Muriel Spark (*Not to Disturb*, *The Driver's Seat*) and Joyce Carol Oates (*Mysteries of Winterthurn*, *Bellefleur*, and *A Bloodsmoor Romance*) represent what I would call the melodramatically tragic strain in the female gothic.

Central to what I am labelling the comic pattern is the ideological construction of a bucolic family, a sort of static paradise like Radcliffe's *La Vallée* or *Jane Eyre*'s Ferndean, a locus that cannot be described because it can be imagined only in the vaguest terms. Such a static ideal conforms to and, in fact, endorses the ideology of white, middle-class womanhood prevalent in Europe and the United States for the past two centuries. The female economy operating in the "comic" work valorizes the heterosexual compulsion, presenting the sexes as finally complementary rather than oppositional. On the other hand, the female economy operating in the tragic female gothic denies the viability of heterosexuality, exploding the work through the imagery of gendered warfare.

In order to understand the issues at stake in this dialectic, it is necessary to look briefly at writings by women about sexual difference. From the late eighteenth-century writings of Mary Wollstonecraft to the work of contemporary theorists like Nancy Chodorow and Carol Gilligan, female writers have participated in defining the nature of women as "Other" to men. For Wollstonecraft, women's minds were essentially identical to men's, but these minds became more emotional, less reasonable, more prone to excess through the corrupting influences of patriarchal education. And so what was the solution according to Wollstonecraft? She advised that women would be wise to bury their emotions, become, that is, reasonable "honorary men." Such a position, unfortunately, merely reinforced "feminist humanism" and the domestic ideology, the marginalization of women in the home. By valorizing the autonomous subjectivity of the inner life, Wollstonecraft—despite her overt advocacy of economic independence and rational self-fulfillment for women—ironically ended up advocating a sort of imprisonment for the domiciled woman. In a similar manner, Chodorow and Gilligan, presenting themselves as writing within one tradition of contemporary feminism—white, Western, and middle-class—codify a view of women that valorizes similar essentialist qualities (Gilligan: women subscribe to "an ethic of care") that tends to infantilize or trivialize women. Both assert that the maturation process for women in Western culture stands in direct opposition to the process for men. Woman's identity supposedly is rooted not in the realities of psychic separation, but in resigned acceptance of her inherent-teleological destiny as a woman. Both women further call for a transvaluation of values in which qualities that have been regarded as "womanly" and therefore inferior are recognized as superior by the society as a whole.¹² Such ideologies, created by women presumably for female consumption, stand in direct contrast to the angrier, more subversive voices that emerge from the female gothic novel. These voices present the two sides of women's attitudes toward the heterosexual compulsion. On one hand, a woman can accept and survive; on the other hand, she can rage and self-destruct.

But just to be certain that we do not miss the tragedy implicit in the gothic heroine's attempts to reshape what she thinks is her only "reality," she demands, "Kill me." Such a request would be viewed as strange in any other genre than the female gothic, but this imperative constitutes the climax of Muriel Spark's *Driver's Seat* (1970). And in order that her murderer makes no mistake about her intentions, the heroine repeats her demand in four languages and hands him the knife. Handing the murderer the knife and marking the spot—such gestures expose the desperation, the futility, the impossibility of ever escaping from the madness these women recognize as life in the "melodramatically tragic" female gothic novel. But the heroine's evident masochism actually masks a much deeper social malady. Her need is motivated by a desire to destroy not simply herself, but the very social and economic structures that have created the conditions that have led to her desperation. But if the gothic heroine cannot destroy the patriarchy, she can attempt to outsmart it; she can mime it to death. Positioning herself as the deserving and innocent victim of oppression, malice, and fraud, the gothic heroine exchanges her suffering for money and a man, a means of financial support and security. In the melodramatic scheme of things, a victim is always rewarded because Justice always prevails and suffering (particularly if one is young and pretty) becomes a kind of lucre to be exchanged in the strange barter system that women understood (or misunderstood) as the "shadow labor" of gendered capitalism.¹³

The gothic heroine's status as a reified object, a commodity, reifies her economic and social status in a capitalist signifying system that requires her identity as both a use-value and an exchange-value. If the gothic heroine cannot reform the economic system, she has the option of fictionally transforming her role and complicity in it or escaping it altogether through death. The ultimate ideologies to appear in the female gothic novel concern the heroine's ability to destroy and reconstitute the corrupt institutions that hold her and all the male characters in the novel in thrall. In the place of these public spaces the heroine creates a new private domain that valorizes female-constructed fantasies: the companionate family, an idealized locus of pastoral values, the antithesis of the patriarchal bourgeois family that has subjected the heroine to such indignities throughout the novel. And make no mistake: this world is extremely hazy about genital sexuality, about women accepting their roles and destinies as mothers, as the producers of future owners and workers. Further, if the heroine cannot accomplish the formidable task of reforming the family, cannot cast herself as the triumphant Culture Hero(ine), she vows to die in the process.

But in order to discuss the female gothic novelist's impulse to civilize the family and by extension capitalistic society, and to create an alternative fantasy-body, let us briefly examine two works that attempt to explain the invention of the "civilizing process" that bourgeois women, of necessity, experienced: Norbert Elias's *The History of Manners* and Michel Bakhtin's *Rabelais and His World*. Elias's work traces the creation of what he calls *homo clausus* during the eighteenth century, an individual who will make total biological control of himself a private matter. Such an individual experiences the culturally-imposed "rising threshold of shame and embarrassment" about bodily functions as an endorsement of increasing personal restraint, as the institution of "a wall, of something 'inside' man separating him from the outside world" (259). And it was, according to Elias, the newly-created and controlled "public body" that was given validation by society. This "public body" distinguished itself from the lower social classes by its aping of the courtly value of self-control, along with its acceptance of shame as the secret sin at its (bourgeois) heart. What Elias calls "manners"—highly gendered customs, behavior, and fashions—now were diffused from the court to the upper class, and then to the next class down the social ladder until all classes were ultimately affected by the codes of conduct that were being advocated in the books of courtly behavior that were now saturating the newly literate population. According to Elias, it was through the imposition of such "manners" and the use of shame as a disciplinary tool that the modern state could come into existence. Civilizing the urban space meant that education and recreational activities were now controlled by moral censorship, while the new sensibilities made physical violence, duelling, hunting, and public displays of bodily functions all abhorrent behaviors (126-29).

Bakhtin, on the other hand, privileges the "carnivalesque" body of the early modern period. This body enacts its essentially anti-bourgeois values through intense releases of emotion, destroys authoritarian strictures, and challenges and inverts imposed political and religious systems. The lower classes, of course, are freest to indulge in such *charivari*, or communal dances, while the obverse of such "harmless" activity would be the carnage and mob violence of the French Revolution. The struggle between these two bodies—*homo clausus* and the carnivalesque—can be seen as one locus of meaning in the female gothic novel, although ironically the carnivalesque possibility is generally associated in these works not with lower-class women but with aristocratic practitioners of adultery, gossip, slander, and duelling or poisoning as a way of settling one's scores. A woman like Radcliffe's Emily is advised alternately by her father to conform, to conceal, to privatize, while on the other hand the carnivalesque possibility is always open to them, luring her into the history of the rampaging bacchai Signora Laurentini, aka Sister Agnes. These two bodies, and the warfare between them, characterizes the shifting personae of all of the polarized women in Radcliffe's novels, as well as the two Catherines in *Wuthering Heights* or the struggle between the bodies of Jane and Bertha in *Jane Eyre* or Victoria and Lilla in Dacre's *Zofloya*.

The middle-class founded its status—its economic and political power—on the body of the *homo clausus*, the retentive, controlled, concealed body. And such a body was usually coded as male and gained power through its ability to distance others, to refuse engagement, to mimic the scientific values of objectivity and rationality. The female body, on the other hand, was associated in this formula with diffuse energy, subjectivity, and emotionality. As Gary Kelly has shrewdly observed, the construction of both the sentimental and the reasonable woman during the late eighteenth century was part of a larger ideological project, the creation of a professional middle-class discourse system that would supplant the aristocracy at the same time it gained control over the lower classes. "Woman" in this cultural enterprise was crucial as a pawn in the issues of property, children, and inheritance; and finally she constituted a certain technology of the self that we now recognize as "virtue" and "reason."[14]

The female gothic, in other words, assisted in the bourgeois cultural revolution by helping to professionalize gender, by collaborating in the construction of the professionally middle-class woman and the professionally bourgeois pater familias. Women who did not conform to appropriately-coded bourgeois norms—who reminded the reading audience of long discarded and disgraced aristocratic flaws like adultery, passion, gossip, slander, and physical violence—became themselves the targets of savage beatings throughout the works. Men who are coded as aristocratic, like Rochester in *Jane Eyre* or Valancourt in *The Mysteries of Udolpho*, are allowed to survive only after they have subjected to a vicious beating and thereafter effectively renounce their flawed and anachronistic aristocratic tendencies.

There is no doubt that the body that emerges from female gothic textuality is a highly gendered one, the product of that greatest of dualism machines, capitalism. And the writing that emerges from such a machine is gender-specific, characterized by the female author's contradictory desire to both outwardly conform and at the same time to subvert, that is, to be both a body and a machine at odds with itself. In *A Room of One's Own* Virginia Woolf wonders why women increasingly turned to writing novels during the early nineteenth century, leaving poetry a male-dominated preserve, a bastion of masculine privilege. She proposes some fairly straightforward answers, such as the fact that novels emphasize character and event and can be written with less concentration than can poetry, which requires of its composer a higher degree of attention to details in order to ensure the poem's internal coherence. But then Woolf goes on to talk about the deadliness of either manly and womanly styles of writing, and such a notion, seemingly so liberal, fails to account for the inescapability of ideological constructions of gender, not to mention the historical conditions that determined women's complicity and participation in both accepting and overthrowing those historical realities. If the chaos that characterized France from the pre- through the post-Revolutionary period was not to pollute British society, then female writers had to be enlisted in the attempt to spread an ideology that curtailed the spread of such dangerous notions as equality, fraternity, liberty. The marketplace demanded a gendered society in order to protect the very existence of an economy that privileged the middle- and upper-classes. Major eighteenth- and nineteenth-century female novelists like Radcliffe, Austen, Mary Shelley, and the Brontës all exploited in their fiction the appearance of their compliance with traditional female domestic values. But we should not confuse such a facade with their elided purposes. The female gothic novelist attempted nothing less than a re-definition of sexuality and power in a gendered, patriarchal society; she fictively reshaped the family, deconstructing both patrimonialism (inheritance through the male) and patrilineality (naming practices) in the process.[15] In short, she invented her own peculiar form of feminism. And in challenging both codes of masculine privilege she possessed her rightful fictional birthright: access to the untrammeled desire and energy to re-shape her version of "reality"; in the female gothic novel she creates what she thinks are alternative, empowering female-created fantasies. In her triumphant act of self-creation she rejects her subjugation and status as "other"—whether object or absence. She refuses, that is, to subscribe passively to confining male-created ideologies of the "woman as subject." She proffers instead "victim feminism" as a female-created ideology, mixing one part hyperbolic melodrama with one part Christian sentimentalism, and creating a heady brew that promised its readers the ultimate fantasy: their socially and economically weak position could actually be the basis of their strength. The meek shall inherit the gothic earth because they deserve to; evil is always destroyed because it deserves to be.

The buried reality that lies not very far below the surface of the female gothic is the sense that middle-class women can only experience the male-identified patriarchal home as either a prison or an asylum. A woman would be reduced in such a home to the status of an object, decorative or functional depending on one's husband's class. Life in such a home and the identity it conferred on a woman constitutes the nightmare at the core of the female gothic novel and victim feminism. But the home that is created by Emily and Valancourt at the conclusion of *The Mysteries of Udolpho*, for instance, is not a patriarchally-marked home. Valancourt would appear to be living at *La Vallée* on an extremely tenuous basis, having been perceived by Emily and her friends as damaged goods after his disastrous foray in Paris. Acceptably tamed gothic husbands exist on very short leashes, and it is Emily and her sister-heroines who hold the power in these new households. Having traced the ravaging patriarch out of existence, the gothic feminist lives in her new domicile with her ritualistically wounded husband, a quasi-sibling who, like her, has barely survived his brush with the oppressor and emerged chastened and appropriately and professionally gendered. When critics puzzle over the final castrated status of Rochester, blinded in one eye and missing one hand, they reveal that they do not appreciate the long heritage of wounded and feminized gothic heroes that foregrounds Rochester's history. Consider, for instance, the two gunshot wounds Valancourt received, one of them delivered by his beloved's father, the mild St. Aubert. Beating fantasies emerge in the very real wounds that every gothic hero is forced to endure in the female gothic canon, and it is tempting to explain these stabbings or worse, as Bruno Bettelheim has, as "symbolic wounds." But gothic heroes all endure very real beatings and wounds, not merely symbolic ones, and in the receiving of these wounds it is as if they have earned the right to overthrow their fathers and establish a new companionate family and a redeemed class—a bourgeoisie that has learned to tame its excesses and perfectly balance reason and the emotions. I would contend that gothic feminism participates, as do Sentimentality and Romanticism as intellectual movements, in the broad cultural project of Enlightenment ideology—that is, making the world a safe place for feminized men and masculinized women. Foucault has charted his version of this cultural shift, claiming that it was exploitation rather than repression that characterized the prevailing attitude of the upper classes since the late eighteenth century:

> The new procedures of power that were devised during the classical age and employed in the nineteenth century were what caused our societies to go from *a symbolics of blood* to *an analysis of sexuality*. Clearly, noth-

ing was more on the side of the law, death, transgression, the symbolic, and sovereignty than blood; just as sexuality was on the side of the norm, knowledge, life, meaning, the disciplines, and regulations.[16]

For Foucault, the bourgeoisie distinguished itself from both the aristocracy and the working class by making its sexuality and its health a primary source of its hegemony. Whereas "blood" was the source of the aristocracy's power, "sex" and its control and regulation became the predominant characteristic of the middle class, both men and women. According to Foucault, it was Sade and the first eugenists who advanced the transition from "sanguinity" to "sexuality." But Foucault fails to reckon with the female gothic novelists, whose works chart in increasingly graphic detail this very shift from status and class based on blood claims to the superior form of class, the regulation and control of one's sexuality, one's body. When Bertha Mason jumps from the roof of Thornfield we know that we are witnessing an important event in cultural history. In her mad act of suttee Bertha effectively extinguishes privileges based on blood claims and effectively makes way for her rival, the perfectly controlled and professionally feminine Jane Eyre.

Traditionally, critics have claimed that the hermeneutic implex of the female gothic novel is the question, "what does this mean?" As Barthes notes we continue to read a text because we have bought into its "enigmatic code," that is, we are engaged in trying to decipher those parts of the text that are still unresolved for us as readers.[17] But it is fair to say that the lure in the gothic is that the characters experience an "enigmatic code" that becomes mirrored by our reading process. For the female gothic heroine that "enigmatic code" generally clusters around the question of properly gendered behavior, power/property, and the relation of both to sexuality. But it is also important to recognize that the heroines are engaged less in an interpretive struggle than in a gendered and ideological one. What is at stake here is the war between "masculine" and "feminine" ways of shaping desire/bodies, of containing energy, of controlling ideology. When the gothic heroine creates her own self-serving ideology of the companionate family, then she is ready to reject those juridically-created systems, the prison or the asylum, that have ensnared her throughout the novel.

The gothic heroine's goal throughout most of the text is to ascertain the "secret" that the patriarchy has managed to keep from her, either through an elaborate system of walls and locked rooms (the prison and the asylum) or through the power of language to dissemble, to reveal and conceal at the same time (missing marriage licenses or wills). The gothic heroine spends most of the text cultivating the posture of passive-aggression through the two extremes available to her: hiding in a room/silence/repression of her emotions and her body, or moving through space in a sort of manic dance/hysterically acting out her assault on the patriarchy. But if woman finally is to be embodied in the female gothic text as anything other than passive or aggressive, she must create a social reality beyond merely internalizing the prison, the asylum, the confessional; she must redeem those institutions and mark them as "female" controlled and "female" identified. And so each of the male juridical institutions is taken into, incorporated, swallowed up and reconstituted by the heroine as the newly-created female-defined institution.

In commenting on the nature of revolutions in this period, "or perhaps in any period," Ronald Paulson has noted that there are two basic interpretations of the phenomenon: oedipal and oral-anal. As he notes, in the oedipal version the son kills, eats, and internalizes the father, "becoming himself the authority figure, producing a rational sequence of events, although a sequence that might be regarded unsympathetically as prerational," but in which the "effect is sublime or a progression from sublime to beautiful." In the other category, the oral-anal, the revolution is figured as a "regression to earlier stages of being, an ingestion that produces narcissism rather than internalized paternal authority," a sort of descent into the "grotesque, moving toward the undifferentiation of tyrant and oppressed."[18] The female gothic novel clearly exists as a species of cultural group fantasy work that finds its representation and symbolization in repeated dreams of parricide, seduction, and castration. The female gothic heroine, however, ambivalently rewrites the oedipal revolution by positioning herself as the dutiful daughter reluctantly forced to kill her father, while at the same time she is compelled to swallow and ingest the patriarch's institutions so that they can be reformed in a manner acceptable to her and her newly-validated mother.

In her triumphant overthrow of the patriarchy most gothic feminists finally do battle with that ultimate patriarchal family—institutionalized Christianity. The female gothic heroine usually becomes a heroine after she confronts, outwits, and destroys a terrifically corrupt monk or priest. I am thinking here not simply of Jane Eyre's rather tame duel with St. John Rivers, but of the ferocious struggle against Schedoni that occupied both Ellena and her beloved throughout the entire text of *The Italian*. In finally destroying Schedoni and his evil accomplice, Vivaldi's aristocratic mother, Ellena redeems not only her inheritance, her economy, her world, she also creates a home and companionate family that installs her (and her long-lost mother) as female quasi-deities. She invents, that is, the middle-class family.

The female gothic protagonist as cultural heroine has triumphed precisely because she has brought to birth a new class—the bourgeoisie—shorn of the excesses that characterized the aristocracy that made it unfit to preside over a newly industrialized society. But in destroying and supplanting the aristocracy, the gothic feminist accomplishes nothing less than the resacralization of her world. She excavates the buried body of her real or metaphorical mother, and by doing so she reinstates a fictionalized feminist fantasy: the matriarchy. In redeeming her mother, as Ellena does or as Emily manages to do for her long-murdered aunt in *The Mysteries of Udolpho* or as Julia does for the long-imprisoned mother in *A Sicilian Romance*, the gothic heroine reasserts her inheritance in a long-lost female tradition. This act is represented by the rediscovery and magical reanimation of the mother's supposedly dead body. Further, these novels posit the end of the discourse as located in the rediscovery of a sort of female-coded epistemology embodied in the stories that these women tell each other, the lost narratives about mad nuns and bleeding mothers. The biological heritage of suffering and wounded women is transformed through this ideology into a saga of heroic triumph; the gothic feminist text tells us that the world is reborn and purified through the mother's—not the son's—blood. Gothic feminist heroines discover their own bodies and voices only after they redeem their mothers, and they speak in a voice that some contemporary feminists have come to recognize as "victim feminism." But that voice is considerably more complex than has previously been recognized, largely, I would claim, because its origins in gothic and melodramatic texts have not been recognized or studied.

As Elizabeth Bronfen has argued in *Over Her Dead Body: Death, Femininity and the Aesthetic*, psychoanalysis has consistently attempted to foreground the role and importance of the father in the construction of the ego because of an unacknowledged need to root out, displace and marginalize the mother. But the displacement of the mother from both Freud's and Lacan's accounts of ego formation simultaneously aestheticizes the woman's body as an object of death at the same time it charges it with intense and diffuse anxiety.[19] And strange as it may seem, the same sort of "fort-da" game described by Freud in *Beyond the Pleasure Principle* is played out repetitiously in the female gothic. The female gothic author keeps disposing of the mother, only to reel her body magically back into the text for obsessive view over and over again, revealing that within both psychoanalysis and the female gothic tradition the same wound, the same psychic trauma is being fingered. That wound consists, I think, in the loss of the matriarchy, the loss of the mother as a figure of power or even a fantasy of power in a society that values her role and importance. The sons of psychoanalysis and the daughters of the gothic both mourn the passing of the mother's body from view and control, and so they construct over and over again texts that symbolize their fantasized construction and reconstruction of the maternal, aesthetically potent and deadly beautiful body. Somehow the two movements—psychoanalysis and the gothic—find themselves spiralling into and around yet another attempt to salvage the mother's body and by extension her control and power over society—the late eighteenth- and early-nineteenth-century ideology that now goes under the name of "feminism."

Notes

1. Rumors about Radcliffe's sanity began during her own lifetime, and her earliest biographer expended a fair amount of energy trying to disprove the medical

fact that Radcliffe dies of a brain fever. See T. N. Talfourd, "Memoir" to *Gaston de Blondeville* (London, 1826), as well as Clara McIntyre, *Ann R adcliffe* (New Haven: Yale, 1920), and E. B. Murray, *Ann Radcliffe* (New York: Twayne, 1972).

2. See DeLamotte, *Perils of the Night*, 5. The major pre-1960 critics of the gothic include Edith Birkhead, *The Tale of Terror: A Study of the Gothic Romance* (London: Constable, 1921); Eino Railo, *The Haunted Castle: A Study of the Elements of English Romanticism* (1927; rpt. New York: Humanities Press, 1964); J. M. S. Tompkins, *The Popular Novel in England, 1770-1800* (1932; rpt. Westport: Greenwood Press, 1961); Montague Summers, *The Gothic Quest: A History of the Gothic Novel* (1938; rpt. New York: Russell and Russell, 1964); Devendra P. Varma, *The Gothic Flame, Being a History of the Gothic Novel in England: Its Origins, Efflorescence, Disintegration, and Residuary Influences* (1957; rpt. New York: Russell and Russell, 1966); the major post-1960 approaches include Eve Kosofsky Sedgwick, *The Coherence of Gothic Conventions* (New York: Arno, 1980), and "The Character in the Veil: Imagery of the Surface in the Gothic Novel," *PMLA* 96 (1981), 255-70; William Patrick Day, *In the Circles of Fear and Desire: A Study of Gothic Fantasy* (Chicago: U of Chicago P, 1985); George E. Haggerty, *Gothic Fiction/Gothic Form* (University Park: Penn State P, 1989); Coral Ann Howells, *Love, Mystery, and Misery* (London: Athlone, 1978); Elizabeth MacAndrew, *The Gothic Tradition in Fiction* (New York: Columbia UP, 1979); David Punter, *The Literature of Terror* (London: Longmans, 1980) and *The Romantic Unconscious* (New York: New York UP, 1989); Robert Miles, *Gothic Writing, 1750-1820: A Genealogy* (London: Routledge, 1993); and Jacqueline Howard, *Reading Gothic Fiction: A Bakhtinian Approach* (Oxford: Clarendon, 1994).

3. Helpful discussions of feminism's participation in the ideological construction of gender can be found in Judith Butler, *Gender Trouble: Feminism and the Subversion of Identity* (New York: Routledge, 1990); Denise Riley, *Am I That Name?: Feminism and the Category of "Women" in History* (New York: Macmillan, 1988); Sherry B. Ortner and Harriet Whitehead, eds., *Sexual Meanings: The Cultural Construction of Sexuality* (New York: Cambridge UP, 1981); and Elizabeth Meese, *Crossing the Double-Cross: The Practice of Feminist Criticism* (Chapel Hill: U of North Carolina P, 1986).

4. See the provocative discussion of Montagu and early theories of the gothic in Harriet Guest, "The Wanton Muse: Politics and Gender in Gothic Theory After 1760," in *Beyond Romanticism: New Approaches to Texts and Contexts, 1780-1832* (London: Routledge, 1992), 127-38.

5. Gary Kelly claims that the Radcliffe heroines' "disciplined inwardness clearly indicates that they are heroines of a particularly professional middle-class culture and ideology, albeit a culture and ideology coloured by courtly aristocratic literature depicting nobility of sentiment." Such heroines have no public existence; they "are entirely private and domestic beings or they are the means of transferring property and power from one man to another" (see his *English Fiction of the Romantic Period* [London: Longmans, 1989], 53). On the same subject, also see Mary Poovey, "Ideology and *The Mysteries of Udolpho*," *Criticism* 21 (1979), 307-30; and Kate Ellis, *The Contested Castle: Gothic Novels and the Subversion of Domestic Ideology* (Urbana: U of Illinois P, 1989). On the similarity between female gothic novels and slave narratives, see Kari J. Winter, *Subjects of Slavery, Agents of Change: Women and Power in Gothic Novels and Slave Narratives, 1790-1865* (Athens: U of Georgia P, 1992).

6. See Maurice Lévy, *Le Roman "gothique" anglais, 1764-1824* (Toulouse: Association des Publications de la Faculté des Lettres et Sciences Humaines de Toulouse, 1968), and Alastair Fowler, "The Life and Death of Literary Forms," *New Directions in Literary History*, ed. Ralph Cohen (Baltimore: Johns Hopkins UP, 1974), 77-94.

7. One of the most important contributions to the criticism of the gothic has been made by recent feminist critics who have countered the assumption of such critics as Leslie Fiedler and G. R. Thompson, both of whom have argued that the great horror in gothic fiction is the recognition of the evil other as oneself, thereby situating the focus of the gothic in the psychological realm rather than the social or economic. In contrast, DeLamotte, Doody, Poovey, and Russ all situate the horror for female gothic writers in the external world of economic exploitation and patriarchal corruption. My analysis differs from theirs in subscribing to a view of the "self" as shaped by postmodernist assumptions, that is, that what we call the "self" is a series of discursive, shifting postures.

8. See the extremely suggestive discussion of "Gothic Drama and National Crisis" in Paula R. Backsheider, *Spectacular Politics: Theatrical Power and Mass Culture in Early Modern England* (Baltimore: The Johns Hopkins UP, 1993), 149-234. And for the best discussion of the stock tropes of melodrama, see Peter Brooks, *The Melodramatic Imagination* (New Haven: Yale UP, 1976), 3; 16-17; Laura Mulvey, "Notes on Sirk and Melodrama," *Movie* 25 (1977-78), 53.

9. *New French Feminisms*, eds. Elaine Marks and Isabelle de Courtivron (New York: Schocken, 1981), 96.

10. My reading of masochism differs substantially from the position taken recently by Michelle Masse, *In the Name of Love: Women, Masochism, and the Gothic* (Ithaca: Cornell UP, 1992). Whereas Masse sees women as victimized, I have taken a poststructuralist position and seen them as parodically playing with the pose of victimization. I do admire, however, her use of Freud's essay "A Child is Being Beaten" as a theoretical paradigm.

11. Deleuze and Guattari, *Anti-Oedipus: Capitalism and Schizophrenia*, vol. 1, trans. Robert Hurley, Mark Seem, and Helen Lane (Minneapolis: U of Minnesota P, 1983); John Brenkman, *Culture and Domination* (Ithaca: Cornell UP, 1987), 175.

12. For a fuller critique of Wollstonecraft's "betrayal" of women, see Cora Kaplan, *Sea Changes: Culture and Feminism* (London: Verso, 1986), pp. 39, 41, 155. Also see Nancy Chodorow, *The Reproduction of Mothering: Psychoanalysis and the Sociology of Gender* (Berkeley: U of California P, 1978); Carol Gilligan, *In a Different Voice: Psychological Theory and Women's Development* (Cambridge: Harvard UP, 1982).

13. I am indebted to the profoundly suggestive reading of "broken gender and economic sex" in Ivan Illich, *Gender* (Berkeley: Heyday, 1982), 22-66.

14. On *homo clausus*, see Norbert Elias, *The Civilizing Process, vol. 1: The History of Manners*, trans. Edmund Jephcott (New York: Pantheon, 1978), 249-60; and on the carnivalesque body, see Michel Bakhtin, *Rabelais and His World*, trans. Helena Iswolsky (Cambridge: MIT Press, 1968); Gary Kelly, *Women, Writing, and Revolution: 1790-1827* (Oxford: Clarendon, 1993), 3-5. I cannot do justice here to Kelly's important study, but his two theoretical chapters in this volume are in my opinion groundbreaking essays. Also see Edward Shorter, *A History of Women's Bodies* (London: 1982); Dorinda Outram, *The Body and the French Revolution: Sex, Class, and Political Culture* (New Haven: Yale UP, 1989); Lynn Hunt, *Politics, Culture, and Class in the French Revolution* (Berkeley: U of California P, 1984); and Peter Brooks, *Body Work: Objects of Desire in Modern Narrative* (Cambridge: Harvard UP, 1993).

15. For a discussion of how the domesticated family functioned as the "cradle" for a new class culture, see Leonore Davidoff and Catherine Hall, *Family For-*

tunes: Men and Women of the English Middle Class, 1780-1850 (Chicago: U of Chicago P, 1987). They make the observation: "Public was not really public and private not really private despite the potent imagery of 'separate spheres.' Both were ideological constructs with specific meaning which must be understood as products of a particular historical time" (p. 33). And for related arguments on the construction of the domestic ideology, see Nancy Armstrong's *Desire and Domestic Fiction: A Political History of the Novel* (Oxford: Oxford UP, 1987).

16. Michel Foucault, *The History of Sexuality: Volume I: An Introduction*, trans. Robert Hurley (New York: Vintage, 1980), 148. For a related discussion, see Isaac D. Balbus, "Disciplining Women: Michel Foucault and the Power of Feminist Discourse," *Praxis International* 5 (1986), 466-83.

17. See Roland Barthes, *S/Z*, trans. R. Miller (London: Cape, 1975), 19.

18. Ronald Paulson, *Representations of Revolutions: 1789-1820* (New Haven: Yale UP, 1983), 8.

19. See Elizabeth Bronfen, *Over Her Dead Body: Death, Femininity, and the Aesthetic* (Manchester: Manchester UP, 1992), 28; and on the complex issue of whether or not Freud explains the gothic of the gothic explains Freud, see Peter Thorslev, *Romantic Contraries* (New York: Yale UP, 1981); and Terry Castle, "Phantasmagoria: Spectral Technology and the Metaphorics of Modern Reverie," *Critical Inquiry* 15 (1988), 26-61.

The Canon-Maker: Felicia Hemans and Torquato Tasso's Sister

Donelle R. Ruwe

The lead article of the January 1834 *New Monthly Magazine*, "Scenes and Passages from the 'Tasso' of Goethe," places Felicia Hemans's byline, "by Mrs. Hemans," above the title. The editors, capitalizing on Hemans's celebrity, set up an ideological position in this article, by which Goethe's works will be held accountable to Hemans's standards as an authority on domesticity and poetics. Hemans's five page article opens with a quotation by Wordsworth about the importance of art to the private reader, and concludes with an excerpt from Byron's "The Lament of Tasso." Framed by her citations of popular British authors is Hemans's own commentary and translation of Goethe's play, *Torquato Tasso*. The article follows her series of original poems on Tasso begun ten years earlier: "The Release of Tasso" (1823), "Tasso and His Sister" (1826), and "Tasso's Coronation" (1828).[1]

Hemans's examination of Goethe's *Tasso* clarifies what is sometimes less easy to define in the earlier poetry: the methods by which she coopts the texts of others in order to shape her own story of Tasso and his texts. I argue that Hemans, in her series of translations, poems, and criticism about Torquato Tasso, is practicing a kind of contestatory canon formation, and I use the competing canonizations of Tasso the poet and Tasso's poetry in the Romantic era to demonstrate the potential revisionary nature of Hemans's canon-making project. I will argue that when Hemans presents herself as Torquato Tasso's sister, she resurrects the historical Tasso and depicts him as a brother, projecting herself into his life as a happier and more productive sister who has the time to *read* his texts, produce children, and transmit his texts to succeeding generations. By rehistoricizing Tasso, she shifts the construction of the canon from a naturalized father-to-son tradition into a literary tradition that is constructed by the readers and teachers of texts—in Hemans's poetry, this reader is Tasso's sister. By depicting this literary patriarch as a literal brother, and then writing from his sister's point of view, Hemans reinscribes untouchable masters within bourgeois domesticity, thereby projecting herself into the horizon of literary history as a sister who influences and even transforms her brother's literary projects.

In reading Hemans's presentation of Tasso's sister as an act of canon creation, I am setting one traditional model of canonicity as a patriarchal father-to-son tradition against a competing version in which canonicity depends upon institutions of education. In traditional models, such as that delineated by Edward Said in *The World, The Text, and the Critic*, Eurocentric literary history is a patrilineage. Said posits a three-stage model for the way literary canons are depicted and transmitted: filiation, affiliation, and naturalized affiliation. Filiation is a natural, genealogical passing on of tradition from father to son. Affiliation, a cultural compensatory order such as a literary tradition, is created to replace a chromosomal father-to-son inheritance. The third stage naturalizes this affiliation so that it takes on the power of genealogical affiliation. By contrast, John Guillory's *Cultural Capital* argues that canonicity is a function of ideological state apparatuses such as the school: the texts that are taught and transmitted in institutional contexts become canonical. Guillory's depiction of canonicity as an act of textual transmission suggests a way of reading Hemans's poetry of Torquato Tasso as a powerful act of canon-making.

In the late eighteenth century, Torquato Tasso had become a hotly contested figure in biographical and aesthetic writing. Debates about his status as a literary genius exemplify larger debates about the role of the poet in society and the definition of genius. While early biographies had portrayed Tasso as a misunderstood genius (Manso, Layng), a new group of biographies grounded in scholarly archival work and medical debates about insanity, challenged these early, glorified accounts of Tasso's life. In the earlier legendary versions, Tasso is presented as a solitary genius who falls in love with his patron's sister, the Princess Leonora, and then falls victim to political machinations within the Duke of Ferrara's court, which he is too noble and otherworldly to understand. As these stories go, Tasso's unwise love and inability to behave as a sycophantic courtier result in his imprisonment by the Duke—during which imprisonment, the suffering Tasso loses his sanity. By contrast, P. A. Serassi's landmark *Vita di Torquato Tasso* (1785) takes a more critical approach to history and debunks most of the popular Romantic rumors about Tasso. After studying documentary evidence in the ducal archives in Ferrara, Serassi questioned that Tasso had ever been involved with the Princess Leonora, and further suggested that his incarceration by the Duke was caused by Tasso's temperamental behavior and was probably for Tasso's own good. In addition to Serassi's application of strict standards of historical verisimilitude, other Romantic era biographies apply new advances in scientific fields such as medicine to the life of Tasso. The physician Nathan Drake presents Tasso as a clinical case study of the dangers of an unrestrained imagination, *On the Government of the Imagination, on the frenzy of Tasso and Collins*. John Black's *Life of Torquato Tasso with an historical and critical account of his writings* (1810) reflects the early nineteenth-century concern with the treatment of the insane, emphasizing the moral dangers in the lack of restraint in conduct and imagination, presenting Tasso as a cautionary example to "all young persons" who might consider "indiscretion, or want of foresight, as a test of, or constant attendant upon, genius."[2]

By contrast, the canonical authors seem irresistibly drawn to the legendary Tasso, to the pathos of his incarceration and loss of sanity. Byron and Goethe created literary texts envisioning Tasso as a misunderstood (Byronic) genius. Both Byron and Shelley visited the site touted as Tasso's cell and agonized over his imprisonment, and Shelley describes Tasso by using his characteristic revolutionary rhetoric—pitting Tasso's genius against the stupidity of a tyrant. In collecting a piece of wood from Tasso's supposed prison door as if it were a holy relic, Shelley aligns Tasso with the imagery of martyrs and other noble, heroic sufferers—individuals who have died, but whose work lives long after them.

The Romantic era's fascination with Tasso's life—whether this fascination explores the historical, medical, or legendary aspects of Tasso—forms part of a trend that had been building throughout the eighteenth century: readers were increasingly more familiar with Tasso's life than his poetry, and confirmed his genius only partially through his poetry and primarily through accounts of his persecutions. C. P. Brand comments upon this Romantic era trend, noting that although Tasso's poetry had been widely read and appreciated in England in the seventeenth and early eighteenth century, between 1750 and 1850 Tasso's biography began to attract more and more attention. The valorization of Tasso's life over his poetry comes hand-in-hand with Romantic poetic sensibilities in which critical and aesthetic writings focus on the genius of an author and the ways in which poetry is an expression of an author's subjectivity. Tasso's struggle for greatness within the Italian epic tradition, his victimization by court politics and his patron's power games, his fabled passion for the Princess Leonora, and his incarceration in a madhouse inspired Goethe, Byron, and Shelley to create works presenting his life as a symbol of creative endeavor and of the Romantic artist. And part of this fascination with Tasso's life, interestingly enough, involved the feminization of his works, with their ability to manipulate readers' emotions and engender what Leigh Hunt called a tender, effeminate voluptuousness.[3]

In British Romantic constructions of canonicity, Tasso's poetic reputation rests more on his Romanticized life's failures than his verses' success; thus, Romantic representations of Tasso reveal prevalent notions of the relationship between a poet's art and life. Goethe's play *Torquato Tasso* (1807) and Byron's dramatic monologue "The Lament of Tasso" (1817), portray Tasso as an idealized suffering artist struggling against an unsympathetic, politicized and materialist world in order to stage discussions about the nature of aesthetic genius. Less well known are Felicia Hemans's constructions of Tasso which self-consciously refer back to the Tassos of Goethe, Byron, and the translator John Hoole in order to shape a contrasting version of Tasso as the paradigmatic Romantic era artist. Hemans's translations of and commentary on Goethe's *Torquato Tasso*, as well as her commentary on Byron's "Lament" and Hoole's "The Life of Tasso," and her own deeply intertextual series of poems on Tasso's life provide a radical critique of these texts' images of the alienated artistic genius as well as their constructions of canonicity.[4] Hemans feminizes the Tassos of Goethe and Byron, and she makes her own Tasso's canonicity dependent upon his reception and transmission by a feminine audience, not upon his individual genius. In Hemans's version of the male artist and his canonicity, women are the canon-makers.

I am arguing, then, that Hemans is able to translate her characteristic maternal and domestic poetic persona into a strategic position for canon-making rather than a position that retreats from canonicity as Ross, Leighton, and Mellor have suggested.[5] The standard Romantic era estimation of poetic greatness is grounded in a theory of individual imaginative genius—even the poetry itself becomes increasingly subjective and celebratory of the poet's self and his imagination. For Ross, Hemans's domestic persona allows her to escape public notoriety and the fear of being labeled a monstrosity (a public woman), but this domestic persona also removes her from the self-glorification of the poet and his poetic project that defines the great artist—Hemans becomes the "conscience of culture," she does not become its prophet, its quest-hero, or its genius (202). Leighton and Mellor, like Ross, see Hemans's domestic persona as anticipating the Victorian cult of the poetess in which the poetess is a powerful and revered cultural icon of morality and affective authority. When these critics identify Hemans as the matriarch of the Victorian poetess, they also note that her domestic poetic, with its affective authority, comes with an aesthetic cost: in the nineteenth century, the "poetess" label marks works of second-class aesthetic status, for these works depend upon the author's deliberate renunciation of the self as artist, a public refusal of aesthetic ambitions. In an era that defines great works through acknowledging the genius of the author—Tasso's self rather than his texts—, the poetess's denial of herself as possessing extraordinary talent and her concomitant cultivation of the quotidian in both her content and in her subject position would seem fatal to her artistic reputation. By contrast, Guillory's alternative model of canonicity as dependent upon the transmitters of texts provides a more active and more potentially powerful role for Hemans's participation in Romantic era canon creation.[6]

Representations of Tasso's and Hemans's poetic selves would seem to epitomize the gulf between the genius-poet and the poetess at its greatest polarity: Tasso, the poet whose reputation depends upon his life as "the most interesting in the world," and Hemans, who cultivates a reputation as a most ordinary woman. However, it is here, at this moment of absolute discontinuity in constructions of the poet, that Hemans intervenes by reinscribing the Romantic Tasso back into domesticity. She does not feminize Tasso—rather, she stages a reunion between Tasso and his sister in which she has Tasso, the poet, attempt to return to his home and family, to attempt to re-enter the private and domestic realm. Hemans contrasts the anomalous—but happy—life of the sister to Tasso's public misery, and shows how Tasso has sacrificed his private self for his poetry. This contrast between the private and the public, however, exists only in terms of the poet's life—even as the poet sacrifices his privacy for poetry, the longevity of poetry itself depends upon the private. John Guillory's useful locating of canonicity not in inherent qualities of a text but in the transmission of a text explains how Hemans can reconcile two seemingly disparate ideological formations: feminine domesticity and mainstream canon formation. Hemans makes canonicity dependent upon the feminine private sphere. Guillory contends that canonicity is not a function of the author's self-representation but a function of institutionality, and locates this transmission within the institution of the school. Hemans's poetry locates this transmission within home-schooling: a mother educating her children. Hemans constructs canonicity as a function of the audience of readers—often private, female readers— and not as an effect of an author's acknowledged genius. Further, Hemans gains increased control of her own poetry's reception and of literary history by linking her poetry with the domestic sphere over which she, herself, resides.

Hemans's *New Monthly Magazine* review, translation, and critical essay entitled "Scenes and Passages from the 'Tasso' of Goethe," stresses the question of canon construction and artistic genius (both Tasso's and

Goethe's genius). However, in critiquing and translating Goethe's presentation of Tasso, Hemans valorizes the role of women in Tasso's life and returns again and again to particular concerns paradigmatic of women writers in the Romantic era: the importance of emotional moderation and self-control and the prioritization of an "ethic of care" over a solipsistic imagination. Thus, Hemans's commentary praises Goethe for realistically presenting the agonies of the artistic genius, but chides him for not countering these scenes of pain, frustration, and agony with other, more active, scenes in which the audience's emotion is allowed release.[7] At the same time, Hemans reconstructs Goethe's Tasso according to her own standards by selecting for translation only those passages which feature the roles that women play in fostering the creation and transmission of literary texts.

Goethe's play opens with a young, insecure Tasso presenting his newly written *Gerusalemme Liberata* to the Duke of Ferrara and his sister the Princess Leonora. Goethe then follows Tasso through a series of foolish acts caused by his feelings of inadequacy as an artist and as a man: as an author he fears he will never measure up to Virgil or Ariosto; as a man, he is constantly compared unfavorably to the successful, confident, and politically ambitious courtier Antonio. Tasso's increasingly erratic behavior leads to his incarceration. When released, he is determined to return to his sister's home in Sorrento. In the climactic final scene, Tasso attempts to kiss the Princess, and only succeeds in alienating his last supporter. Although Goethe consistently portrays Tasso as a victim of his own insecurity as well as of the machinations of a political and materialist world, Hemans chooses to translate only those passages in which Tasso and art are shown to be dependent upon feminine recognition and support. Similarly, when she reprints limited excerpts from Byron's "The Lament of Tasso," she does so in order to present Tasso as a humble Christian. Further, Hemans will quote Wordsworth in order to switch the criterion for determining aesthetic merit from the celebration of genius to the emotional effect of a work on its audience—an audience that she presents as feminine. Rather than separate high art into an elite group of texts whose worth will be immediately appreciated by a select few, Hemans suggests that great art will be appreciated by anomalous individuals who respond affectively, not intellectually, to poetic texts.

"Scenes and Passages from the 'Tasso' of Goethe" is Hemans's contribution to the *New Monthly Magazine*'s series entitled "German Studies" (January, 1834). Hemans's Germanic study is singularly British: her essay places Goethe's *Tasso* within the context of British Romanticism and, more specifically, within the context of the gendering of art. Hemans's review is less about Goethe's individual work than it is about defining the genius-poet, the "master-mind," and how this genius and his works are received by society. Her article thus opens by affirming the significance of Goethe's work to private readers, and by insisting that the transcendence of the poet is a feminine quality. He cannot linger long from his "better home," for his "gentler and holier" poetic spirit is opposed to the tempestuous spirit of the public (1). To give the sensitive poet a feminine interiority, a gentle and holy nature, is not, in itself, an unusual move. Gender-crossings and the colonizing of feminine sensibility (men's poetry claiming for itself emotional authority and private interiority) are hallmarks of British Romanticism, and have been studied at great length in recent criticism sensitive to the gendering of aesthetics.[8] What makes Hemans's feminization of the poet interesting is that she locates not just the spirit of poetry within feminine non-worldliness, but that the audience of such poetic texts is openly acknowledged and even embraced as feminine. Hemans, as a woman and a wildly popular poet, has no need to scapegoat the mass public as a group of barely educated, silly novel-readers of bourgeois taste.

In insisting that Goethe's play must meet the approval of common readers, she codes her readers as feminine. As a critic, then, she has created a position that allows her to speak from a position of domesticity as well as aesthetic authority: she responds as a representative of the universal feminine reader. Not surprisingly, since she implies that her position is supported by Wordsworth, her essay on Goethe later quotes Wordsworth's sonnet on the incapacitating effects of a troubled world on the interior life and productivity of the poet, "The World is Too Much With Us."[9] This poem becomes part of Hemans's examination of the way in which the world treats the gentler spirits, whose "ethereal natures of love, devotion, and enthusiasm" must confront the "withering breath" of the world.[10]

And when Hemans selects excerpts from Byron to support her commentary on Goethe, she applies this same technique of decontextualization. By lifting portions of a poetic text from their original placement within a poetic narrative, she is able to manipulate the context which shapes our readings. When in the conclusion of "Scenes and Passages," Hemans cites Byron's "The Lament of Tasso," she does so to provide what she calls a more noble version of Tasso: "The majestic lines in which Byron has embodied the thoughts of the captive Tasso will form a fine contrast and relief to the music of despair with which Goethe's work is closed" (5). However, Hemans reprints only a limited portion of Byron's text, singling out Tasso's taking consolation in his Christian epic and in the presence of God. By taking only a selection from the poem, Hemans does not present the Tasso who would become immortal, but the feminine suffer-and-be-still Tasso who takes comfort in Christianity rather than in creating a temple of his own. And so, instead of Byron's final vision of Tasso as independent, self-righteous, and beyond the norms of ordinary society, Hemans brings Byron's poem to premature closure. The Tasso that she contrasts to Goethe is not Byron's Tasso, but her own re-writing of Byron's Tasso.

Even more astounding than Hemans's remaking of Wordsworth and Byron is her revisioning of Goethe's Tasso. Hemans's "Scenes and Passages" all contain selections featuring women. Hemans translates the moment when the Princess crowns Tasso with a poet's laurel; when the Princess argues for a woman-centered golden age of society and of art; when Tasso's final "strain of passionate gratitude and enthusiasm" for the Princess overcomes him; and, the longest of her translated passages, when the Princess reminisces about her first encounter with Tasso. The central figure in these passages is not Tasso but the Princess Leonora (the sister of Tasso's patron), whom Hemans presents as the ideal of self-sacrificing womanhood. Hemans writes that Leonora's feelings for Tasso contain "all the deep devotedness of a woman's heart, with the still purity of a seraphic guardian, taking no part in the passionate dreams of earthly happiness . . . a deep feeling of woman's lot on earth, —the lot of endurance and of sacrifice,—seems ever present to her soul" (3). Certainly the women in Goethe's *Torquato Tasso* are central figures: they mother Tasso, validate his artistic project, act as buffers between Tasso and the other men (who are more powerful physically and politically), and inspire in Tasso excessive demonstrations of emotion. Hemans does not translate any of the passages spoken by Tasso's patron the Duke of Ferrara or by Antonio, Tasso's chief rival. Instead, Hemans focuses on Leonora and on women's role in the artistic process. For example, when Leonora tells Tasso of what she believes is the golden age of literature, she defines that golden age through the reverence given to women:

> When earth has men to reverence female *hearts*,
> To know the treasure of rich Truth and Love,
> Set deep within a high-soul'd woman's breast;—
> When the remembrance of our summer prime
> Keeps brightly in man's heart a holy place;—
> When the keen glance that pierces through so much
> Looks also tenderly through that dim veil
> By Time or Sickness hung 'round drooping forms;
> When the possession, stilling every wish,
> Draws not Desire away to other wealth;—
> A brighter day-spring then for *us* may dawn;
> Then may *we* solemnize our golden age. (3)

Hemans's translation emphasizes the importance of women's hearts and links the recognition of feminine hearts to any age that can be described as golden.[11] Her italicized emphasis of "*we*" and "*us*" attest to her insistence that this golden age be one in which women are reverenced: the italics are not in Goethe's original. Hemans, through Goethe, finds the golden age eternally present so long as men revere women's hearts. Such a depiction of a golden age would appeal to a poet whose defining characteristic for generations of readers and reviewers is her relationship to domesticity—in particular, a domestic poetic that aestheticizes affectivity, that explores sentimentality and its relationship to poetic ambition.[12]

Least obvious, but most subversive of all of Hemans's strategic repositionings of Goethe, is the way in which her translation functions as a socially sanctioned re-writing of Goethe's play. A translation, Lawrence Venuti notes, is frequently a domestication of the foreign text: it brings back the cultural other into the familiar and recognizable. The more fluent or "invisible" the translation, the more likely it is that the translation has carefully masked its own domestic values. By "domesticate," Venuti means the work of adapting a foreign text to the stylistic standards of, in this case, Hanoverian England; he does not mean to adapt a text to domesticity—and yet the term is doubly apt for Hemans. She domesticates Goethe in that she adapts him to British standards, but her particular standards are those of domesticity and sentimentality. According to eighteenth-century standards, Hemans's project of domesticating Goethe is a perfectly appropriate act of translation. Venuti suggests that, by the late eighteenth century, translation had become defined as an act of transcending linguistic and cultural difference through the translator's unifying subjectivity.[13] Alexander Fraser Tytler's *Essay on the Principles of Translation* (1791) is an influential, late eighteenth-century treatise on translation and "a key document in the canonization of fluency," which suggests that what is most important in a translation is the translator's aesthetically "correct taste" and "exquisite feeling," allowing the translator to translate fluently. The standard of fluency further allows the translator, if necessary, to alter the original, correcting careless or inaccurate expressions in the original. In other words, Hemans's sympathy as a reader allows her to correct Goethe and, thus, the text she transmits to her readers is her own domestication of Goethe.

Marlon Ross, in his interpretation of Hemans's translation of Goethe, suggests that she is attempting to rescue the solipsistic poet from his own angst by insisting that the internalized quest—the self-communion and search for poetic identity with its accompanying interiority—be re-envisioned as an external conquest. As Ross suggests, Hemans is like other female Romantics in that she tends to be fascinated by the external quest rather than by the internal quest, which he associates with the major male Romantics: "female writers . . . tend to be fascinated by the immanent conflict between masculine and feminine desire embedded within the form [of the external quest]. . . . Poetic romance is a safe habitat for women writers both to experiment with high poetry and to examine the friction between feminine and masculine desire without overtly placing men and women in adversarial positions."[14] In Ross's reading, Hemans's intertextuality—her use of Wordsworth, Coleridge, Dante, Goethe, Byron, and Tasso himself in her review—is neither an attempt to alter the movement of masculine desire nor an attempt to change what the heroine (such as the Princess Leonora) represents. Rather, Ross reads Hemans's poetry as an overlay of feminine desire onto this pattern. My reading, by contrast, does not ask if Hemans re-inscribes women as objects within the Romantic quest—even if as desiring objects. I suggest that Hemans is engaged in finding a place for women as readers of men's poetry—Princess Leonora who "interprets" Tasso's behavior, Hemans as a translator and as critic, and Hemans as spokeswoman for the mass of private readers who appreciate "the still small music" and whose "female *hearts*" (3) must be reverenced before there can be a golden age.

Hemans's "Scenes and Passages" uses translation and decontextualization of important male authors to create a golden age of literature, one that is centered on feminine and domestic terms. In the earlier series of poems, "The Release of Tasso," "Tasso and His Sister," and "Tasso's Coronation," Hemans also uses Tasso as a trope for literary history: both as an author who records cultural history (as in his epic of the crusades *Gerusalemme Liberata*) and as a part of literary history himself. Hemans, however, takes up Tasso's life precisely where Goethe's play stops—and instead of presenting Tasso as a portrait of herself as does Byron, she presents herself as Tasso's sister. Hemans allows the interaction between the two siblings to highlight the differences between the pursuit of fame and hence canonicity, and the transmission of texts and thus the making of canons. In "Tasso and His Sister," Hemans uses the brother-sister relationship to show how masculine poetry is limiting and, in the end, dependent upon feminine recognition and transmission.[15]

Hemans, in constructing a literary history of women readers who interpret and transmit the texts of men, is making visible the canon-making work of women. Guillory, in *Cultural Capital*, indicates that any educational institution systematically distributes cultural capital through regulating access to the means of both production of literacy and the consumption of texts—how to write, what is acceptable written language, how to read, and how to interpret what is read. Scenes of schooling, such as Hemans's "Tasso and His Sister," can be discussed as scenes about the transmission of texts. Such moments stand against other imaginary images of canonicity, such as the standard Romantic ideology of the alienated genius whose aesthetic greatness does not need the support of institutions to maintain its canonical status.

Guillory, of course, is focusing on the visible and public institution of schools. It would be an error, however, to assume that "the school" is only a formal school. Recall that in the early nineteenth century mothers provided a literary education for their children, selecting texts, introducing them to their children, and telling their children (as well as the adults who would purchase and use her text) which books should be read and for what reasons they should be considered good.[16] Hemans's authority comes from the establishment, from the way in which her poetry seems to glorify widely held sentiments. Her poetry seeks to find a place for women as individuals with the cultural authority to pronounce beyond doubt what is obviously canonical and should be known by any British man or woman. Poems such as "Tasso and His Sister" stage a scene of reading in which the institution reproducing texts and, not coincidentally, reproducing new and educated citizens, is the home. Hemans's poetry suggests that canonical status is inferred upon texts by an unindividuated mass of women readers who transmit a text from one generation to the next.

"Tasso and His Sister" opens on a fragrant evening in Italy in which a mother mesmerizes her children through her rendition of her brother's "words of power," his "proud, undying lay":

> But still and thoughtful, at her knee
> Her children stood that hour,
> Their bursts of song and dancing glee
>   Hushed as by words of power.
> With bright, fixed, wondering eyes that gazed
>   Up to their mother's face;
> . . . .
> Forth from a poet's magic book
>   The glorious numbers read;
> The proud, undying lay, which poured

> Its light on evil years;
> *His* of the gifted Pen and Sword,
> The triumph and the tears. . . .

Hemans stages here a pedagogical scene in which a maternal figure is shown actively transmitting and controlling a received master-work of the canon, Tasso's epic poem of the crusades. The lay, which tells of "Godfrey's deeds, of Tancred's arm, / that slew his Paynim love," is clearly more in line with an active, questing masculine poetry than a feminine poetry of affections. Yet this masculine poetry is narrated through the doubled voices of women: Hemans the poet and Hemans's protagonist, the young mother who is also Tasso's sister. It is clear that Tasso's "words of power" are given life not through Tasso's "triumph and the tears" but through the "meek tears of woman."

In staging this moment of textual transmission, Hemans focuses on the mother's role as the transmitter, or midwife, of culture, the one who passes down texts from generation to generation, thereby creating the canon. I claim that Hemans actually withholds the sister's recognition of the producer of the poem. Hemans never does re-integrate Tasso back into the family. According to Harding, what this scene does do, however, is provide "a different, more humanizing and socializing conception" of the transmission (not only the production) of poetry (147).

Hemans takes the scene of her poem from both Hoole's "The Life of Tasso," and Goethe's *Torquato Tasso* but with significant revisions that have great importance for my reading of this poem as an act of canon formation. In her transformation of these texts, Hemans subtly undercuts the authority of Tasso's literary reputation and, in so doing, she undercuts the authority of constructions of literary history based on an author's genius. By re-introducing the figure of Tasso's sister, who is absent in Goethe's text and of minimal significance in Hoole's "Life," Hemans re-inscribes Tasso the author within the historical Torquato, the absentee brother and uncle. However, this reinscription of Tasso within domesticity is challenged by Hemans herself—for she refuses to allow Torquato Tasso to have a personal identity outside of his identity as an author. Tasso is, in fact, a legend, and the cost of becoming legendary is the loss of the private self. The reunion between Tasso and his sister is a biographical scene which works symbolically to show the collision between the legend and the person, and personal cost of legendary status.

Hoole, Goethe, and Hemans each use the reunion scene between Tasso and his sister to explore the nature of Tasso's famous poetic identity as it contrasts to the simpler life he has left behind, as represented in his sister. In Hoole's accounts of Tasso's reunion, a disguised Tasso tricks his sister in order to make her prove her loyalty to him. Goethe's play suggests that Tasso is not quite so devious, but that he is certainly self-centered. Hemans's "Tasso and His Sister" assumes that the sister is loyal, and switches the loss-of-recognition from Tasso's voluntary choice to one of his involuntary loss. He is not disguised—other than through years—he is himself, and he, as himself, is not recognized. When Goethe's Tasso announces his plan to leave the duke's court and to go to his sister's home, the Princess urges caution, for Tasso has been prohibited from going into Naples. Tasso apparently listens, but continues to build his own plans and dreams of the journey. He hubristically assumes that he will be welcomed and recognized, but the Princess interrupts Tasso's daydream and asks him to recognize the essential selfishness of his actions. Tasso neither acknowledges the danger that he is in nor behaves nobly, for he considers neither his sister's safety nor the emotions of the friends he has decided to leave behind. The Princess takes on a familiar feminine role—urging caution, and begging Tasso to behave according to an ethic of care that attends to the immediate needs of others over the desires of his individual self. She attempts to make Tasso acknowledge the selfishness inherent in his plan to leave the court and to descend, without warning and in disguise, on his sister:

> PRINCESS: . . . Is it a noble thing to speak as you do?
> Noble to think of your own self alone,
> As if you had no friends whose hearts were hurt?
> . . . .
> You choose the black smock and the pilgrim's purse
> And the long staff, and of your own free will
> Go off in poverty . . . (232-33)

The Princess's description of Tasso's plan is less flattering than Tasso's imagination would like: she finds his plan not only selfish but hypocritical. To put on pilgrim's garb and "go off in poverty" makes a mockery of genuine pilgrims and their vows. Hemans also depicts Tasso in pilgrim garb, but suggests that Tasso is engaged in an actual pilgrimage and presents the sister's garden as the shrine that Tasso humbles himself to enter. In Hemans's reunion of Tasso and Cornelia, she shows how Tasso (described as a pilgrim) has been absent too long to be either anticipated or recognized by his family. Indeed, his sister can only recall him through texts—through recognition of Tasso as an author—but what Tasso seeks is not fame but privacy and personal, emotional reintegration into the ordinary life exemplified by his sister and her children. Tasso is a battered, forgotten and impotent pilgrim who begs recognition from his sister, as if she were the shrine, the end of his voyage, and Tasso approaches his sister as a pilgrim would a shrine—she is the end of his Romantic quest, the holy land to his Crusade, the womb he desires to reenter. But, as in so many other quests, the questor who returns home has changed so much that he is no longer recognizable.

If Goethe's scene in which Tasso imagines returning to the home of his sister Cornelia Sersale is unflattering to Tasso, it is at least more flattering than Hoole's history in which Tasso does, indeed, return to his sister in disguise. In Hoole's account, Cornelia is a defenseless widow (her sons are not at home and she is surrounded by female attendants). She is so sorely frightened by the news brought by Tasso-in-disguise that she faints.

Hoole's Tasso stages an epic scene in which he plays an Odysseus disguised who returns to test his ever-faithful Penelope. Hoole's Tasso manipulates the emotions of his sister through his text (the apocryphal letter) and through his feigned tale. While Tasso's words (both written in the false letter and spoken) are unreliable, the sister reveals her truth through her responsive and uncontrolled body, but as a "speaking" subject her emotions are not expressed except through gesture.

Hemans omits Hoole's details of men's manipulation and women's weakness in her version of the tale. Hemans's sister is surrounded not by feminine attendants as in Hoole, but by her own physical progeny and

Tasso's figurative child—the epic *Gerusalemme Liberata*. As Hoole reminds us, Cornelia's children were boys. Thus, Hemans is covertly presenting the sister as not only fertile, but in control of the boys who will be the childless Tasso's heirs, even as she controls Tasso's textual immortality. Further, unlike the sister who faints in Hoole, in Hemans's account it is Tasso who is emotionally distraught. Unlike Tasso, his sister is not an otherworldly and ineffectual figure. She is fertile and educated as well as an educator. It is important to note that his return to the home and his private life interrupts the reading of his own epic—once again Hemans presents the private and public life of an author as disjunctive. Such an interruption figures the revisionary process by which Hemans is resituating Tasso within the domestic sphere.

Significantly, when Tasso's sister cannot identify the strange man in her garden, the memories which Tasso tries to invoke in her are memories of the gender-equality of brothers and sisters as children. But these memories also contain early examples of Tasso's life-long dependence upon women to recognize and support both the man and the artist. Tasso's dependence on women in contrast to the more independent, mature and manly Antonio is a central tension within Goethe's *Tasso*. If Tasso the man is dependent upon women, Hemans's poem suggests that Tasso's art had also always been dependent upon women.

Hemans has Tasso invoke the early equality of the brother and sister, who played "hand in hand" and who prayed and sang as one. She also has Tasso remember a moment in which his sister crowned him with a laurel—a wreath made by her own hands. In the opening scene of Goethe's play, one of the passages that Hemans translates in her *New Monthly Magazine* column, the Princess Leonora and her attendant make wreaths with which they crown busts of Virgil and of Ariosto as they spend time "dreaming back to the golden age of poets" (147). When Goethe's Tasso presents the Princess and her brother the Duke with his completed volume, the Princess removes the laurel from Virgil and bestows it on Tasso. Hemans's poem shifts the scene of Tasso receiving the hand-made wreath from the adult Tasso to Tasso's early childhood, indicating that Tasso's legendary poetic career was first acknowledged by the sister.[17]

Hemans intensifies, though her prioritization, the drama of women's transmission of texts that is present in Goethe.

Hemans questions the insubstantiality of cultural fame by contrasting the historical man, Torquato, with his legendary identity as Tasso. She couples the image of Tasso the great poet who transcends all national and temporal boundaries with a Tasso who has lost his individuality and self-identity. In the center of stanza five, the midpoint of the poem, Tasso returns: a "way worn," "wan," "pale," pilgrim who gushes tears. As a man of feeling, Tasso is touched both by the domestic scene he witnesses and his exclusion from it—for his sister does not recognize him. To become a public name is simultaneously to become nothing in the private realm, for "the bard of gifts divine" and "the proud, undying lay" is also "unknown" and "Forgotten! e'en by thee!"

Hemans continues to transform the nature of the poet-as-questor by presenting the quest—as a method of self-exploration and self-identification writ large on the epic scale—as potentially empty of any such significance. Tasso's epic poetry leads to loss of self-knowledge. Thus, Hemans's text dramatizes the Romantic, literary quest for self-identity as a journey into isolation and sameness—eventually to death. Hemans stands solidly within a domestic aesthetic and pronounces the hollowness of the masculine Romantic trope of the questor. The Romantic questor who attempts to discover what lurks inside the mind of man moves inward into himself but does not move forward with his life. Hemans's depiction of the sister, who requires neither lofty deeds nor goals, provides an alternative way of structuring identity. Rather than presenting women as unable to have a quest, Hemans presents the quest as undesirable and the male questor as impotent. To return home, aged and out of place, after a life of adventures is as ancient a narrative pattern as Homer's Odysseus. Yet this Penelope does not wait at home endlessly weaving and unweaving. In Hemans's version, the woman matures and moves into a new stage of life, motherhood. It is the man—who is culturally allowed more mobility and more scope for ambition and self-definition—whose life has gone nowhere, whose texts retrogress, lead backwards to less than his beginning. At one time, he had a home—now he has only his public texts and his public life. She who was once a daughter is now a mother. He has only textual progeny—and even that depends upon his sister for survival.

Because this poem seems so similar to Hemans's many poems pitting domesticity against masculine values such as war, nationalism, and high art, it is easy to forget that it is actually atypical. She typically describes homes that exist only as nostalgic memory ("The Homes of England") or that have been destroyed by war ("The Sisters of Scio"). However, this poem presents home in the process of being regained. In doing so, Hemans makes the literary world—as represented in Tasso—depend upon recognition by domesticity. Tasso exists only because his sister transmits his text, and "breath[es] her brother's name . . . The weary one, the unknown, / that came, the bitter world to flee, / stranger to his own." In keeping with Hemans's usual ironic approach to domesticity, the potential recognition by his family that Hemans holds out to Tasso is never realized.

I suggest, building on previous scholarship,[18] that "Tasso and His Sister" presents the master canon as existing only as it is mediated, as dependent not upon the transcendent, inherent value of its works, but on the mediators—in this case, the sister. Hemans creates an active place for women within canonical poetics—not as canonical themselves, but as canon mediators and, thus, canon creators. Further, this "scandal" of Tasso and Leonora is the single event in Tasso's life that is most endlessly debated in various biographies. While the better documented histories could find no evidence for Tasso's affair with "Leonora," other histories exploited the romantic possibilities of star-crossed lovers. The very lack of historical documentation for this affair suggests that constructions of history—which are presented as true—are demonstrably contradictory. Hemans's poem, thus, subtly engages competing constructions of biography in presenting her own narration of Tasso's reason for returning to his sister's home in Sorrento.

The scene with Tasso's sister, that Goethe's play foretells and Hemans's poem enacts, occurs at the moment in Hoole's "The Life of Tasso" when Tasso begins losing textual and political control. When Tasso leaves his sister to return to the court at Ferrara, the Duke refuses to return Tasso's manuscripts, believing that he has "lost all of his fire" and is "incapable of producing any thing new, or of correcting his poems" (400). Hoole quotes a letter of Tasso's in which Tasso admits that he cannot be the "master of his own works," but that he would yet refuse to be "a shameful deserter of Parnassus for the gardens of Epicurus, for scenes of pleasures unknown to Virgil, Catullus, Horace, and even Lucretius himself" (400). Hoole's Tasso struggles against the seduction of pleasure, the siren's call that leads the author into feminized gardens of ease, pleasure, and artificiality.

Given the garden's characteristic association with femininity and masculine emasculation, it is not surprising that Hemans further revises literary history by staging the reunion of Tasso and his sister in a garden. In Romance poetry in general, the garden is archetypically a feminine site which, as in the *Romance of the Rose*, exists to be conquered. Thus, *Gerusalemme Liberata* portrays gardens as places of temptation—specifically, sexual temptation. A central moment of *Gerusalemme Liberata* is the hero Rinaldo's dalliance in the garden bower of the sorceress Armida. Like Spenser's Bower of Bliss, Armida's garden is patently artificial if incredibly fruitful: the trees have fruits green, budding, and ripening all on the same branches. It is described as a female womb designed to distract men from their zealous crusades. The entrance to Armida's circular castle is guarded by two naked, bathing women whose exposed bosoms almost defeat the resolute purpose of a group of warriors who have come to "rescue" Rinaldo. They find a blissfully oblivious Rinaldo in the center of the circular garden, holding a mirror for Armida to see her reflection, while he sees his own reflection in her eyes. To break Armida's spell, the warriors show him his reflection as mirrored in his own polished "adamantine shield." Rinaldo sees that "his sword, the only mark of warlike pride, / Estrang'd from fight, hung idly at his side; / and, wreath'd with flowers, seem'd worn for empty show; / No dreadful weapon 'gainst a valiant foe" (Hoole 487). The fertile garden is too feminine, too artificial—it becomes emasculating. While Tasso's hero, Rinaldo, must be saved from the feminine garden and its emasculating effects on his limp sword, Hemans places Tasso within the garden, desiring of the garden, and requiring rescue from the bloody, warrior-like world. In rewriting the Spenserian bower of bliss (which borrows heavily from

Tasso's garden of Armida), Hemans is embedding yet another canonical author within the poem of the sister's garden. Rather than a heroic Rinaldo who must be saved from the garden, Tasso the hero of sword and pen wants to come into the garden that is too idyllic, too beautiful to be anything but art—to return to Jerome McGann's point, a moment of quotation rather than reality.

In arguing for Hemans as a canon-maker, I am not arguing for Hemans as canonical. Indeed, if Hemans's Tasso exists only as a name and legend, his sister is given *no* name at all within the poem. In contrast to Byron's Tasso who finally takes comfort in "immortal names!," Hemans's poem shows the immediate discomfort of immortality to the mortal man. While Hemans insists upon women as mediators and, thus, creators of literary history, she does not present women writing the literature to be canonized. Even the role she does claim for women, history-maker, is undermined by her selection of Tasso as the literary figure whose works and reputation are to be mediated by a woman. It is not Spenser's or Shakespeare's poetry of the British renaissance that requires feminine intervention; their literary centrality is already established beyond the powers of female canon-making. Indeed, while Tasso influenced Spenser, Spenser is considered the greater poet in the literary hierarchies being developed in British literary criticism throughout the eighteenth and nineteenth centuries.

In my interpretation of "Tasso and His Sister," I am attempting to tell a story with a happy ending. It is, perhaps, a reductive version of the Virginia Woolf narrative of Shakespeare's sister—the woman who can find no outlet for her genius and is abandoned by the roadside. Tasso's sister (and Hemans as canon-maker) achieve literary authority, but only because Hemans and her sister-figure do not strive for literary greatness—Hemans assumes less risk and does not have far to fall. Tasso's sister survives, if only because she sets different, and more limited goals. To explore the imagined life of a great writer's sister is a compelling strategy of feminist canonical critiques. Hemans, in imagining Tasso's sister, is not attempting to write herself onto the horizon of literary history as Goethe or Byron did in writing of themselves as refracted through the historical figure of Tasso. Nor is Hemans attempting to discover what barriers might prevent women from becoming writers through imagining the life of Tasso's sister, had Tasso's sister been an artist as great as Tasso himself. Hemans's anomalous and maternal sister is the reader, not the writer, of literature. Hemans dramatizes the services of the women behind the men, valorizing the unacknowledged and unwritten work of such private individuals. Hemans finds a way of uncovering the work done by the transmitters of texts and its relationship to canonicity. Hemans is not asking what prevents women from being artists nor is she writing women into the canon; she is, however, writing women into the production of canonicity, writing of women as the constructors, if not within the constructions, of literary history itself.

In demonstrating that women poets adopt, adapt, or transform masculine poetics—powerful techniques for resisting or subverting the exclusionary practices of male writers—regrettably, I am depicting women's aesthetic position as reactionary literary politics, and am reinscribing women within a patriarchal poetic discourse. Women poets who place patriarchal authority within the trope of a brother can negotiate for a more influential position within poetics—but they are still defining poetry in masculine terms. They do not alter the patriarchal structure of poetry, although they do contend that women should be allowed to position themselves, along with men, within poetic discourse. We must not overvalue the transformative impact of women's challenges to patriarchal Romantic traditions: although these women modify patriarchal poetic discourse, they do not create a new, gynocentric system. Hemans's success depends upon her willingness to compromise with masculine aesthetic paradigms, to work with and against these paradigms, but never in isolation and freedom from them.

Notes

1. "The Release of Tasso," *New Monthly Magazine*, November 1823; "Tasso and His Sister," *Monthly Magazine or British Register*, January 1826; and "Tasso's Coronation," *Blackwood's Edinburgh Magazine*, November 1828. I thank Nanora

Sweet from the University of Missouri, St. Louis for helping me with the original publications of these poems. All citations from Hemans's work come from Felicia Hemans, "Scenes and Passages from the 'Tasso' of Goethe," *New Monthly Magazine*, January 1834, as well as from the three articles listed above.

2. C. P. Brand, *Torquato Tasso: A Study of the Poet and His Contribution to English Literature* (Cambridge: Cambridge UP, 1965), 213.

3. See John Black, *Life of Torquato Tasso with a Historical and Critical Account of His Writings* (Edinburgh, 1810); Roderick Marshall, *Italy in English Literature 1755-1815: Origins of the Romantic Interest in Italy* (New York: Columbia UP, 1934); and Leigh Hunt, *Stories from the Italian Poets* (New York: C. P. Putnam, n. d.).

4. John Anthony Harding suggests that Hemans's "Tasso and His Sister" can be attributed to "a couple of sentences in Germaine de Staël's *Corinne*"; see "Felicia Hemans and the Effacement of Woman" in Feldman and Kelley (146), and endnote 12. Although this attribution is possible, he does not supply corroborating evidence. Later in my discussion of "Tasso and His Sister," I will assign additional sources for this poem: Goethe, Byron, and John Hoole. Hoole's translation was the most widely read translation of Tasso in the late eighteenth and early nineteenth century: it went through ten editions in fifty years after its 1763 first edition ("The Life of Tasso" was added as prefatory material to the translation in 1792).

5. Angela Leighton, *Victorian Women Poets: Writing Against the Heart* (Charlottesville: UP of Virginia, 1992); Anne K. Mellor, *Romanticism and Gender* (New York: Routledge, 1992); and Marlin Ross, *Contours of Masculine Desire: Romanticism and the Rise of Women's Poetry* (New York: Oxford UP, 1989).

6. John Guillory, *Cultural Capital: The Problem of Literary Canon Formation* (Chicago: U of Chicago P, 1993).

7. In demanding a release of emotion within a play, Hemans is following the advice of Joanna Baillie's "Introductory Discourse," which argues for the importance of catharsis in theatre. Baillie suggests that plays that evoke passions should do so in order to allow the audience to experience, in the controlled arena of the theatre, potentially injurious emotions. These emotions are then better understood, recognized, and controlled by each audience member.

8. Keats's renunciation of women's writing in order to define the boundaries of his own poetic is exemplary of a larger masculine pattern of defining poetry as that which is non-feminine. See Alan Richardson, "Romanticism and the Colonization of the Feminine" for a discussion of the ways in which masculine Romanticism "colonizes" a feminine-marked sensibility (in Anne K. Mellor, ed., *Romanticism and Feminism* [Bloomington: Indiana UP, 1988], 13 25).

9. Wordsworth also studies Hoole's translation of *Gerusalemme Liberata*. Wordsworth's juvenile manuscripts from the long vacation of 1788 reflect his study of Tasso's epic which he probably studied in the original as well as in Hoole's translation. In 1787 he donated a copy of Hoole's translation to the Hawkshead School Library.

10. Ironically, Hemans not only appropriates Wordsworth to support her position on the public/private split, she appropriates her own poem, "Tasso and His Sister," which had been published eight years earlier. "Tasso and His Sister" repeats the quote, "superior with the sword and pen," three times within the lyric and uses it, refrain-like, as the concluding line of the poem. Tasso may be doubly masculine in possessing both the phallic sword and the pen, but his poetic identity, even so well equipped, withers before the world's antagonism. "Tasso, recognized by his country as *superior with the sword and the pen to all men*, struggling in so ignoble an arena, and finally overpowered by so unworthy an antagonist. This world is, indeed, too much with us, and but too powerful is often its withering breath upon the ethereal natures of love, devotion, and enthusiasm, which in other regions may bear bright golden flowers, but not in this soil" ("Scenes and Passages" 2).

11. Although this issue is too large to be fully addressed here, Hemans's translation of Goethe's discussion of the decline of art is, perhaps, her confrontation of a crisis in poetry—its decline as a social and political force, its decline as a great art from the golden age to something less.

12. Susan J. Wolfson, "'Domestic Affections' and 'The Spear of Minerva': Felicia Hemans and the Dilemma of Gender," in Carol Shiner Wilson and Joel Haefner, eds., *Re-Visioning Romanticism: British Women Writers 1776-1837* (Philadelphia: U of Pennsylvania P, 1994), 128-66, overviews the way in which the critical reception of Hemans has consistently focused on her presentation of domesticity. Isobel Armstrong, "The Gush of the Feminine: How Can We Read Women's Poetry of the Romantic Period?" in Paula R. Feldman and Theresa M. Kelley,

eds., *Romantic Women Writers: Voices and Countervoices* (Hanover: UP of New England, 1995), 13-32, shows that women writers were centrally engaged in regulating the flow of emotion, and explores how British women writers of the Romantic period engaged political, economic, and aesthetic questions through a tightly-controlled affective language meant to express the physical body as well as the emotions.

13. Lawrence Venuti, *The Translator's Invisibility: A History of Translation* (New York: Routledge, 1995), 40-67.

14. Marlin Ross, *Contours of Masculine Desire: Romanticism and the Rise of Women's Poetry* (New York: Oxford UP, 1989), 271-74.

15. In other poems, brothers are used to show that masculine tropes, such as the Romantic quest, are not only self-destructive but destructive to domesticity as well. For example, Hemans's "The Sisters of Scio" represents two sisters who are forced to leave the smoking ruins of their home—all that is left after their brother's warmaking.

16. For information on women's roles in reproducing aesthetics and constructing canons within the process of home-schooling, see my essay "Benevolent Brothers and Supervising Mothers," *Children's Literature* 25, ed. Francelia Butler, R. H. Dillard, and Elizabeth Lennox Keyser (New Haven: Yale UP, 1997), 87-115.

17. There is yet another laurel moment in Tasso's life—which, unlike the imagined moments between Tasso and other women—involves recognition by that most patriarchal of all authorities, the Pope. When Pope Clement VIII would decide to reward Tasso with the laurel, his acknowledgement comes too late: Tasso falls ill and, before dying, is only able to receive a papal benediction (administered by Cardinal Cynthio). Ironically, then, Tasso never does receive official recognition from masculine hands. Hemans's "Tasso's Coronation" depicts the irony of Tasso's never receiving his papal coronation.

18. Jerome J. McGann, "Literary History, Romanticism, and Felicia Hemans," in Wilson and Haefner, 210-27, suggests that Hemans embeds clichés, quotations, and familiar legends in her poetry, in order to demonstrate that cultural history exists only as it is mediated.

"Ungraspable Phantoms": Keats's Lamia and Melville's Yillah

Debbie Lopez

> The Genius of Poetry must work out its own salvation in a man: It cannot be matured by law & precept . . . That which is creative must create itself—In Endymion, I leaped headlong into the Sea, and thereby have become better acquainted with the Soundings, the quicksands, & the rocks, than if I had stayed upon the green shore, and piped a silly pipe, and took tea & comfortable advice.—I was never afraid of failure; for I would sooner fail than not be among the greatest.
> —John Keats, Letter to J. A. Hessey, 8 October, 1818

> The marriage of Lilith with Samael, also known as the "Angel Satan" or the "Other God," was not allowed to prosper. God was apprehensive lest they fill the world with their demonic brood, and to prevent this he castrated Samael. This mythologem, found in several 17th-century Kabbalistic books, is based on the identification of "Leviathan the Slant Serpent and Leviathan the Tortuous Serpent" with Samael and Lilith, respectively, and on the reinterpretation of the old Talmudic myth according to which God castrated the male Leviathan and killed the female in order to prevent them from coupling and thereby destroying the earth. Leviathan the Tortuous, or crooked, serpent is, to the Kabbalists, Lilith, "who seduces men to follow crooked paths."
> —Raphael Patai, *The Hebrew Goddess*

In "P.'s Correspondence," Nathaniel Hawthorne's deluded narrator relates his imaginary encounters with the various Romantic poets, whom he claims to know first-hand. A monstrously obese Lord Byron, reconciled with his wife and under her influence, "now combines the most rigid tenets of Methodism with the ultra doctrines of the Puseyites" (410).[1] He is busy preparing a new, carefully expurgated collection of his complete works. Shelley, too, has undergone a political conversion and is now reconciled to the Church of England. As for Coleridge, "having been visited with a troublesome affection of the tongue, which has put a period, or some lesser stop, to the life-long discourse that has hitherto been flowing from his lips" (427), he has at long last finished his Lamia poem, *Christabel*. Wordsworth has died without finishing *The Excursion*.

Though presented satirically, P.'s extended description of Keats not only perfectly recreates the image popularized by Shelley and Hazlitt of Keats as a maligned genius, but also renders a composite portrait of the Romantic Artist. According to P., Keats, always ill at ease in the city, is only at home "beneath a natural arch of forest trees, or the Gothic arch of an old cathedral" (422). Because of his acute sensitivity, he has never recovered from the press's savage reviews and will undoubtedly die young, his genius unacknowledged. "He glide[s] about the world like a ghost, sighing a melancholy tone in the ear of here and there a friend, but never sending forth his voice to greet the multitude" (422). His sweetest songs will be those unsung.

Most striking, however, is P.'s fanciful description of Keats's grand poetic project:

> Though for so many years he has given nothing to the world, [Keats] is understood to have devoted himself to the composition of an epic poem. Some passages of it have been communicated to the inner circle of his admirers, and impressed them as the loftiest strains that have been audible on earth since Milton's days. If I can obtain copies of these specimens, I will ask you to present them to James Russell Lowell, who seems to be one of the poet's most fervent and worthiest worshippers. The information took me by surprise. I had supposed that all Keats's poetic incense, without being embodied in human language, floated up to heaven and mingled with the songs of the immortal choristers, who

perhaps, were conscious of an unknown voice among them, and thought their melody the sweeter for it. But it is not so; he has positively written a poem on the subject of Paradise Regained, though in another sense than that which presented itself to the mind of Milton. In compliance, it may be imagined, with the dogma of those who pretend that all epic possibilities in the past history of the world are exhausted, Keats has thrown his poem forward into an indefinitely remote futurity. He pictures mankind amid the closing circumstances of the timelong warfare between good and evil. Our race is on the eve of its final triumph. Man is within the last stride of perfection; Woman, redeemed from the thraldom against which our sibyl uplifts so powerful and so sad a remonstrance, stands equal by his side, or communes for herself with the angels; the Earth, sympathizing with her children's happier state, has clothed herself in such luxuriant and loving beauty as no eye has ever witnessed since our first parents saw the sun rise over dewy Eden. Nor then indeed; for this is the fulfillment of what was then but a golden promise. But the picture has its shadows. There remains to mankind another peril—a last encounter with the evil principle. Should the battle go against us, we sink back into the slime and misery of ages. If we triumph—But it demands a poet's eye to contemplate the splendor of such a consummation and not to be dazzled. (423)

Particularly through *Endymion* and *Lamia* Keats would emerge for Americans as the English poet most obsessed with finding—and losing—paradise on Earth.

It is to the Eden myth that Keats himself turns when offering his famous dictum concerning poetic conception: "I am certain of nothing but of the holiness of the Heart's affections and the truth of the imagination—whether it existed before or not. . . . The imagination may be compared to Adam's dream—he awoke and found it truth." But what if the Adamic Romantic artist discovers that he has misinterpreted the subject of his dream—that, in fact, Eve is a misnomer for Lamia, or worse yet, her Hebraic counterpart Lilith? This dark speculation haunts a large part of Keats's canon, from the otherwise light poetic romance of *Endymion* (1818) with its moon goddess, to the "richer entanglements" of the serpent woman *Lamia* (1820). And notably, those poems are the first two of all the Keats selections in *The Poetical Works of Coleridge, Shelley, and Keats*, the collection which established Keats's reputation in America. American writers who would respond to Keats were thus *introduced* to his work through the juxtaposition of *Endymion* and *Lamia*.

Endymion "guesses at Heaven" (*The Fall of Hyperion* 4), and concludes, however uneasily, that "Poesy alone can tell her dreams,— / With the fine spell of words alone can save / Imagination from the sable chain / And dumb enchantment" (*The Fall of Hyperion* 8-11). Through the poem, Keats would seem to answer affirmatively Wordsworth's query ("Paradise, and groves / Elysian, Fortunate Fields—like those of old / Sought in the Atlantic Main—why should they be / A history only of departed things, / Or a mere fiction of what never was?" [Prospectus to *The Recluse* 47-51]). (Romantic) poetry is indeed capable of envisioning a new paradise on earth, complete with its regenerate Eve, and, in the process, of freeing the poet from the "native hell" of self-absorption. But the abrupt conclusion to *Endymion* suggests that Keats already suspected not only the endurance of the "fine spell of words," but also its very nature. Keats returns to test his "Adam's dream" in a poem which focuses on a heroine who is at once Cynthia and Circe combined: his Lamia.[2]

When American authors incorporate Lamian figures in their own works, they do so precisely to question whether the Romantic Adam's visionary dream might in fact instead prove to be a nightmare. For such authors, Eden is the New World. The new Eve is regenerate, but the spectre of Lilith/Lamia threatens America itself. In *Mardi* and *Pierre*, Melville employs Lamian figures both in responding to Keats in particular, and in inquiring what it means to be, simultaneously, a Romantic and an American artist.

In *Pierre* Melville describes his vulnerable protagonist as attempting "to climb Parnassus with a pile of folios on his back" (321). He could have given no better description of himself writing *Mardi*, Melville's ambitious experimental novel, written in frenzied response to his discovery of literature—and to the birth of his self-conception as a Romantic artist.[3] In his review, "Hawthorne and his Mosses," Melville declares that "it is better to fail in originality than to succeed in imitation. He who has never failed somewhere, that man can not be great. Failure is the true test of greatness" (413). *Mardi* would be that ambitious "failure" that would be the true test of his own potential greatness.

Typically, scholars have viewed *Mardi* and *Pierre* as reflecting antipodal attitudes toward Romantic ideals. *Mardi*'s Taji, bound by his idealized quest for Yillah, is the indefatigable Byronic hero; Pierre, decimated by the dark lady Isabel, is a parody of the Romantic artist. *Mardi* reflects Melville's infatuated engagement with the Romantic muse. *Pierre* captures his disillusioning divorce. But in fact, as I will argue, *Mardi* (1849) implicitly predicts what will in *Pierre* (1852) be agonizingly detailed: Adam's nightmare. Melville's female leviathans, his Liliths, bracket the male threat of Moby-Dick (1851). And haunting both *Mardi* and *Pierre* is the spectre of "Poor Keats." In his critique of Romantic premises, Melville makes strategic use of Keats as epitomizing the sensitive effete male aesthete.

Both Shelley, in *Adonais,* and Hazlitt, in "The Periodical Press," had promoted the notion of Keats as a sensitive plant who had become the victim of hostile reviewers. In the preface to *Adonais*, Shelley relates the specific cause of his death: "The savage criticism on Keats's *Endymion*, which appeared in the Quarterly Review produced the most violent effect on his susceptible mind; the agitation thus originated ended in the rupture of a blood vessel in the lungs; a rapid consumption ensued, and the succeeding acknowledgments from more candid critics of the true greatness of his powers were ineffectual to heal the wound thus wantonly inflicted" (qtd. in Schwartz 326). Thus was Keats, according to Shelley, "hooted from the stage of life" (Schwartz 327). Hazlitt went still further, metaphorically killing the poet off before he had died. As Lewis Schwartz describes, in January of 1821, knowing that Keats was seriously ill and probably dying in Italy, Hazlitt wrote a premature eulogy in which he accused *Blackwood's Edinburgh Review* and the *Quarterly* of having conspired in killing the poet. This image of Keats was largely accepted in both Britain and America even into the early twentieth-century. Before 1829, most Americans formed their conception of Keats from the savage reviews of the *Quarterly* and *Blackwood's* or from eulogies in the periodicals of Leigh Hunt and others (Rollins 5).

By the time Melville and Hawthorne were writing, a great many Americans not only knew Keats by legend; they also knew his works. In the years 1840-42, Melville's own early patron, Evert Duyckinck, published *Arcturus*, a New York magazine which in December, 1841, printed an essay effusively praising Keats's sonnets.[4] "On Chapman's Homer" is compared with sonnets by Shakespeare, Sidney, and Milton, and ranked as surpassing them (Rollins 64). The article goes on, "When we think of Keats, tenderly and sadly, for his early death and wounded spirit, there should be triumph too, in this immortal mind, which can prevail over gloom and disaster, and write its story in imperishable song" (Rollins 64). And in January, 1842, *Arcturus* printed James Russell Lowell's sonnet, "To the Spirit of Keats" (64).[5]

Melville incarnates this spirit of "Poor Keats" in *Mardi*'s legendary poet Lombardo. Leading a "hermit[ed]" existence, Lombardo is impelled to write poetry by his "full heart" (1252). He produces the sublime epic, *Koztanza*, but it is cruelly ridiculed by pedantic critics: "Verbi is said to have detected a superfluous comma; and Batho declared that, with the materials he could have constructed a far better world than Lombardo's" (1257). And in their motivations, these critics resemble those who branded Keats a "Cockney School" poet because of his relatively lowly origins.[6] Lombardo complains: "In their eyes, bindings not brains make books. They criticise my tattered cloak, not my soul, caparisoned like a charger" (1260). Most strikingly, Melville borrows directly from Shelley's preface to *Adonais*; thanks to the careless malignity of his critics, Lombardo is "hooted during life" (1263).

But his work lives on. *Mardi*'s philosopher, Babbalanja, asks rhetorically, "What if [Lombardo] pulled down one gross world, and ransacked the etherial spheres, to build up something of his own—a composite:—what then? Matter and mind, though matching not, are mates; and sundered oft, in his Koztanza they unite" (1258). Yoomi remarks that *Koztanza* has "bettered [his] heart," and Media says, "I have read [the epic] through nine times" (1263). That Melville himself read Keats intently is, however, actually clearer when one compares Keats's actual works with *Mardi* at large. While the parallels between Lombardo and the poet are sympathetic to Keats, Melville actually employs the popularized image of Keats more extensively when questioning Romantic conceptions.

Like Keats's *Endymion*, *Mardi* opens with an alienated protagonist lamenting an enforced communion with mundane companions. Learning of his captain's plan to leave the balmy tropics behind in favor of hunting whales in the Arctic, the narrator accuses him of trying to carry the crew "off to Purgatory" (666). Together with crewmate Jarl, he abandons ship, little suspecting that he is trading a prospective purgatory for what will prove to be his own private hell.

Their first encounter is with two islanders, Samoa and his wife, Annatoo, a crude prefiguration of the Lamian Queen Hautia who will appear at the end of *Mardi*. Like Medusa's myth, Lamia's legend is bifurcated. While in some accounts her beauty enthralls, in others, she stuns through her hideousness. Melville incarnates the two sides of this myth in Hautia, all "sensuous bliss," and Annatoo, "unalleviated ugliness." Regardless of her appearance, Annatoo, like Lilith, loves to gaze at her reflected image—in this case, in the glass of the ship's binnacle—and this seriously detracts from her ability to steer. She is also a snake-woman. She frequently disappears and is found in the hold, coiled away "like a gartersnake under a stone" (793). "Possessed by some scores of devils" (774), she is perpetually incited to mischievous pranks which culminate in her theft of the ship's compass. Her threat is thus death itself; and in this she again anticipates Hautia. For it is the latter who will describe herself as "the vortex that draws all in" (1312), and whose earthly island paradise is surrounded by a dangerous Sargasso sea glutted with wrecked ships (1306). In the last glimpse we are given of Annatoo, she is herself drowning in a swirling vortex.

More complexly, her demise prefigures the fate of Yillah, Taji's seemingly immaculate lover. When Taji discovers Yillah in the evil Aleema's tent, he believes that paradise has overtaken him on earth and that Yillah herself is an angel. She in fact claims to be "more than mortal, a maiden from Oroolia, the Island of Delights, somewhere in the paradisiacal archipelago of the Polynesians" (799). Like Endymion's Cynthia, she has long, golden "Golconda locks" and "blue firmament" eyes (798). She will come to represent Truth, Beauty, Happiness—all that Cynthia vaguely represents to Endymion. The narrator asks her, "Were you not the earthly semblance of that sweet vision, that haunted my earliest thoughts?" (820). He seems to be reiterating Keats's metaphor concerning the workings of the imagination. Yillah is Taji's Adam's dream; he has in some sense awakened to find her true.[7]

But here Melville is in part parodying Keats's idea, in *Endymion*, that whatever the imagination evokes is Truth. Taji's feverish imaginings eventually transform him from the relatively reasonable man who questions Yillah's story concerning her origins, to a man obsessed with abstracting her into the Eve of his personal paradise, into an elusive vehicle of Truth. Yillah fills a gap in the narrator's Romantic text of himself. Like Endymion, through his love object he would be "spiritualized." Eventually, he will even pose as a god, renaming himself, and thus once again reiterating the Romantic claim to dominion over new heavens, new earths.

Like both Cynthia, in the beginning of *Endymion*, and Lamia, at the conclusion of that poem, Yillah disappears. It is in fact her disappearance that initiates Taji's quest and his exploration of the world, Mardi. In other words, whatever else she represents, she is the catalyst of his Romantic *curiositas*. She is also, perhaps more importantly, the reason why he is doomed never to find satisfaction in this world.

But if the novel thus emerges as a story of paradise lost, this resolution may be in large part due to the ambiguities of the woman in whom Taji has invested his trust, Yillah herself. While he envisions himself as championing her innocence, he clearly suspects his own motivations (as Pierre will his own intentions concerning Isabel). After killing Aleema, Taji admits "like lightening I asked myself, whether the death-deed I had done was sprung of a virtuous motive, the rescuing of a captive from thrall; or whether beneath that pretense, I had engaged in this fatal affray for some other, and selfish purpose; the companionship of a beautiful maid. But throttling the thought, I swore to be gay" (796). And while he appreciates Yillah's physical attributes, hearing her recount the mystical story of her origins he considers the possibility that she may in fact be "some beautiful maniac" (799), a notion which, again, Pierre will periodically entertain concerning the more ambiguous Isabel.

Taji eventually concludes that Yillah is angelic, but the more prudent Skyeman, Jarl, sees her as an "ammonite syren" (809). Certainly, she completely spoils Taji for the pleasures of other human companionship. Yillah becomes his "shore and his grove" (806). Like Bulkington, Melville's archetypal hero in *Moby-Dick*, Taji dangerously concludes that it is "better to sink in boundless deeps, than float on vulgar shoals" (1214). Finally, her siren call is to a spiritual if not a physical death. Her repeated attempts to persuade Taji to join her in plunging irrevocably into the ocean prefigure the Narcissus theme which will play such an important role in *Moby-Dick*, particularly in the Mast-Head chapter. From a spiritual standpoint, such immersion in the all-permeating principle of life would result in extinction of self. And though Taji repeatedly denies his obsession with her earthly charms, they lead him on (what Melville describes as) a "Dionysiacal" quest for her "golden Haven" (1214), leading one to suspect that should that haven be reached, his fate might resemble what Ishmael describes as "the delicious death of an Ohio honey-hunter, who seeking honey in the notch of a hollow tree, found such exceeding store of it, that leaning too far over, it sucked him in, so that he died embalmed" (*Moby-Dick* 209). The threat for Taji—as it is for that other Dionysian, Lycius, in the "purple-lined palace of sweet sin"—is one of a physical consummation so intense that it becomes a literal one: Hamlet's "consummation devoutly to be wished."

Finally, Taji's quest for the woman he metonymically describes as his "heaven on earth" lands him in Hautia's bower, a Rappaccini's garden of menacing luxuriousness. Early in the novel, Hautia had appeared disguised as a hooded "Incognito," and throughout, she is defined by her inscrutability. Like Lamia, she is at once both Cynthia, the moon goddess, and Circe, the temptress, darkly commingled. She has a "crescent brow calm as the moon" (1314), but she adorns herself with "Circe flowers." Playing "snake" to Taji's "victim," like Lamia, she seems capable of sucking out his life's essence (1314). She is also a direct descendant of the evil queen responsible for Mardi's initial fall from grace. In Melville's parable, there once were other beings in Mardi besides Mardians: they were "winged beings, of purer minds, and cast in gentler molds, who would fain have dwelt forever with mankind" (1304).

> But the hearts of the Mardians were bitter against them, because of their superior goodness. Yet those beings returned love for malice, and long entreated to virtue and charity. But in the end, all Mardi rose up against them, and hunted them from isle to isle; till at last, they rose up from the woodlands like a flight of birds, and disappeared into the sky. Thereafter, abandoned of such sweet influences, the Mardians fell into all manner of sin and sufferings, becoming the erring things their descendants are now. (1304)

It was Hautia's ancestor who first incited the Mardians to war. In the end, Taji has pursued his new Eden only to find himself, instead, in Melville's version of the old, fallen one.

More frightening, however, is the possibility that in the end is his beginning. Melville entitles Chapter 168 "Concentric, inward, with Mardi's Reef, they leave their Wake around the World," and in so doing reveals that Taji's quest for the ideal, Yillah, is actually a circular journey leading "inward," into the vortex of self. Babbalanja, the Melvillian philosopher in *Mardi*, warns: "Taji! for Yillah thou wilt hunt in vain; she is a phantom that but mocks thee" (1300). And Yillah will in fact prove to have far more in common with Melville's other "ungraspable phantoms" than would at first appear.

Taji's madness results directly from what he learns in Hautia's garden—that in some mysterious way Hautia and Yillah are connected (1305). Taji's rejection of that connection is intense: "Yillah was all beauty, and innocence; my crown of felicity; my heaven below;—and Hautia, my whole heart abhorred. Yillah I sought, Hautia sought me. One, openly beckoned me here; the other dimly allured me there. Yet now was I wildly dreaming to find them together" (1305). Hautia's sirens have lured Taji to the garden by showing him a lily, which in their metaphorical flower language represents Yillah. But while its traditional associations are with purity and innocence, the lily is also "the flower of Lilith . . . and the *lilu* or 'lotus' of her genital magic . . . The underworld gate was a yoni [vulva], and also a lily" (Walker 542). Entrance into the underworld was consequently mythologized as a sexual union (542). And Yillah's name, and that of her bird, *Lil*, are both homonyms for Lilith. Far from being a new Adam, Taji (guilt-ridden over his crime of murdering

Aleema) emerges as being closer to Cain. And not even in Vivenza, Melville's fictionalized version of America, is there a new, regenerate Eve.

Near the conclusion of the novel, Taji gazes down into a whirlpool and sees "something white and vaguely Yillah," and that something white vaguely anticipates the object of quest in Melville's next novel, *Moby-Dick*. Of the latter, Melville will write to Hawthorne: "Let us add *Moby-Dick* to our blessing, and step from that. Leviathan is not the biggest fish;—I have heard of Krakens" (Letter, November 17, 1851). As in Melville's subsequent work, *Pierre*, the "ungraspable phantom" is engendered as the Lamian Isabel, Melville's statement assumes a playful irony: the Lamia is after all, not only a female demon, but also, as the *Oxford English Dictionary* describes, "a fabulous monster; a fish of prey."

Notes

1. All references from "P.'s Correspondence" come from *Mosses from an Old Manse*. Centenary Edition Series, Volume X. (Columbus: Ohio UP, 1974). Relevant scholarship includes Richard Brodhead, *The School of Hawthorne* (New York: Oxford UP, 1986); Anne K. Mellor, *Romanticism and Gender* (New York: Routledge, 1993); Herman Melville, *Mardi: and a Voyage Thither* in *Melville*, ed. G. Thomas Tanselle (New York: Library Classics of the United States, Inc., 1982), 647-1333; and *Pierre Or, The Ambiguities* (Canada: New American Library, 1979); David Perkins, *The Quest for Permanence* (Cambridge: Harvard UP, 1959); Hyder Edward H. Rollins, *Keats' Reputation in America to 1848* (Cambridge: Harvard UP, 1946); Lewis Schwartz, *Keats Reviewed By His Contemporaries* (New Jersey: The Scarecrow Press, Inc., 1973).

2. David Perkins notes that in the latter poem, Keats's moon imagery links Lamia with Cynthia: "But she is also a serpent, which is to say, that Cynthia has now become a serpent" (*The Quest for Permanence* 235). He also points out that Lamia has a "Circean head" (235).

3. In *The School of Hawthorne*, Richard Brodhead comments that "[f]or the first time in *Mardi*, then very strongly thereafter, Melville comes to identify writing with a wholly inward impulse. 'You may think me unwise to have written this

sort of book,' Melville writes his new English publisher in June 1849, but some of us scribblers . . . have a certain something unmanageable in us, that bids us do this or that, and be done it must—hit or miss." . . . "In *Mardi* and its wake Melville is reborn as a literary overreacher: a writer with grand notions of literary greatness" (23).

4. Rollins notes this article without noting the connection between *Arcturus* and Melville (63-64). In fact, Rollins's otherwise comprehensive study of Keats's American reception never studies Melville's debt to Keats.

5. GREAT soul, thou sittest with me in my room,
    Uplifting me with thy vast, quiet eyes,
    On whose full orbs, with kindly lustre, lies
    The twilight warmth of ruddy ember-gloom:
    Thy clear, strong tones will oft bring sudden bloom
    Of hope secure, to him who lonely cries,
    Wresting with the young poet's agonies,
    Neglect and scorn, which seem a certain doom:
    Yes! the few words which, like great thunder-drops,
    Thy large heart down to earth shook doubtfully,
    Thrilled by the inward lightning of its might,
    Serene and pure, like gushing joy of light,
    Shall track the eternal chords of Destiny,
    After the moon-led pulse of ocean stops.

6. Anne K. Mellor notes that the press's characterization of Keats as a lower-class writer also served subtly to feminize him (*Romanticism and Gender* 172). As she points out, the *Oxford English Dictionary* lists, among other entries for "Cockney": "A child that sucketh long," "a nestle-cock, . . . sometimes applied to a squeamish, over-nice, wanton, or affected *woman*" (172). Thus, [w]hen John Gibson Lockhart, in *Blackwood's Edinburgh Magazine* in 1818, assigned Keats to the "Cockney School of Poetry," he was engaging in a politics of both class and gender" (Mellor 172). On the feminization of Keats, see also Susan J. Wolfson, "Feminizing Keats," in *Critical Essays on John Keats*, ed. Hermione de Almeida (Boston: G. K. Hall, 1990), 317-56.

7. Taji will also later Yillah's disappearance through dream imagery: "One morning I found the arbor vacant. Gone! A dream. I closed my eyes, and would have dreamed her back. In vain!" (856).

Aesthetic Discourses and Maternal Subjects: Enlightenment Roots, Schlegelian Revisions

Julie Costello

> Everything in woman is a riddle, and everything in woman hath one solution—it is called pregnancy.
> —Friedrich Nietzsche

Recent studies of gender relations in Western Europe during the late eighteenth and early nineteenth centuries have tended to concentrate on Romantic writers' preoccupations with, and idealizations of motherhood. Despite the fact that the subversive aspects of maternal experience haunted and frustrated many Romantic writers' attempts to celebrate the mother-child bond, critics have largely stressed the ways in which the maternal body figured in the literature and in mainstream philosophical discourses of the period as the source of women's sympathetic natures, and as a site wherein differences, both physical and cognitive, were overcome. Regardless of whether Romantic attitudes about maternity are invoked in support of what Anne Mellor has called (following Carol Gilligan) a feminine "ethic of care," or so as to emphasize the ways in which the maternal body was "colonized" (to invoke Alan Richardson's term) by male writers, scholars have almost uniformly agreed that Romantic representations of maternity are grounded in and supportive of what Terry Eagleton terms the "dream of reconciliation" offered by Enlightenment aesthetic theory.[1]

This article seeks to build upon and extend this growing body of criticism, by attending more specifically to the terrifying and even horrific sublimity so often associated with Romantic motherhood. While the "union" of mother and child was clearly idealized by numerous writers of the period (women as well as men), cultural attitudes regarding the "shared space" of the womb or of the maternal breast were in fact highly contradictory and divided throughout the second half of the eighteenth century, and well into the nineteenth. The intimate proximity between mothers and their children spurred, for example, growing anxieties for moralists, physicians, and educators, who frequently cautioned that maternal sympathies needed to be closely monitored, if not explicitly controlled.[2] Pregnancy, childbirth, and breastfeeding, if seeming to manifest women's natural disposition to give themselves over entirely to their children, demonstrated too for many writers the potential dangers of any individual's sympathetic identification with, or exposure to otherness.

This type of ambivalence, while apparent in the writings of David Hume, Adam Smith, and Immanuel Kant, becomes especially pronounced in the responses of Romanticists like Friedrich Schlegel to their Enlightenment predecessors. Schlegel's reproductive imagery in the fragment collections (1798-1800) and *Lucinde* (1799) indeed reflects acutely the divisiveness associated with maternity and feminine sympathy in Western Europe in the late eighteenth and early nineteenth centuries. But Schlegel also puts an altogether different spin from that of his contemporaries on the concept of maternal sympathy, one which celebrates the radical *sublimity* rather than the beauty of the reproductive process, and the separation rather than the union of mother and child.[3]

A closer look at Schlegel's fascination with the dissonance of the reproductive process helps us to extend the claims of contemporary Romantic-period scholars, who tend to foreground the ways in which the Romanticized maternal body supported an aesthetics of unity or similitude. Situating Schlegel's work within the context of the late eighteenth-century fascination with maternity in Prussia as in England and the colonies, further reveals how preoccupations with the materiality of maternal bonds reflected underlying nationalist concerns, and diverged in striking ways over the face of Romantic Europe. A comparative analysis of the way that gender was inflected differently within the British and German intellectual traditions demonstrates, in other words, not merely how "nature" was invoked during the eighteenth and early nineteenth centuries in the service of culture, politics, and aesthetics, but how naturalized gender categories may mutate in response to culturally specific political agendas (and in fact continue to do so).

The roots of Schlegel's gendered aesthetic lie in eighteenth-century efforts to negotiate an apparent contradiction at the core of Enlightenment theories of the autonomous, self-determining "self" (a contradiction which the mother seemed to embody): What happens to the freedom of subjects when they are confronted, as objects, by other subjects? Early Enlightenment writers attempted to account for this apparent rift between the self and the objectified "other" by representing civil society as a sphere in which the individual is naturally bound to others, who should be treated benevolently in the best interests of everyone. The Irish philosopher Francis Hutcheson, for example, argued that this "law" governing interpersonal relations could be considered moral by virtue of its aesthetic nature. For Hutcheson, we respond to the stimulus of the beautiful deed just as to that of the harmonious object, approving and finding happiness in actions and social structures in which there is "some Tendency to the greater natural Good of others." He refers, for example, to the "natural Affection" parents exhibit toward their children, "notwithstanding all the toil [involved] in educating their young," holding that this behavior is not determined by a biological (or explicitly gendered) instinct, but by a common predilection toward the public good.[4]

Although parental responses within Hutcheson's scheme are not necessarily innate, philosophers in his wake, like David Hume, were far more attuned to the ways in which particular forms of sensibility appeared to be "marked" by the flesh.[5] In defending Hutcheson's benevolence theory against the claim that behind every seemingly disinterested action or impulse lies (at least the trace of) self-interest, Hume insists that the benevolence "hypothesis" is "more conformable" than ego-centered theories of the subject "to the analogy of nature." The analogy Hume provides is of the "fond mother":

> Tenderness to their offspring, in all sensible beings, is commonly able alone to counterbalance the strongest motives of self-love, and has no manner of dependence on that affection. What interest can a fond mother have in view who loses her health by assiduous attendance on her sick child, and afterwards languishes and dies of grief when freed, by its death, from the slavery of that attendance?[6]

The "sensible" mother offers a powerful illustration of disinterested benevolence—not unlike the example Hume gives us of his own widowed mother, "a woman of singular merit, who, though young and handsome, devoted herself *entirely* to the rearing and educating of her children" (emphasis mine).[7] This type of self-sacrificing maternal response ultimately testifies to the utilitarian logic of the benevolence theory, as upon the mother's "assiduous attendance" rests the well-being of the species. Yet Hume's "fond mother" serves too more broadly as an example of the physical "self"-denial which the benevolence theory entails. Indeed, Hume paints a portrait of maternal sympathy which is nothing short of gothic. If as a locus of sympathy, in other words, the loving mother embodies the Enlightenment ideal of an harmonious relationship between the self and another, as an object who inspires pity and terror in Hume's reader, she is thoroughly sublime.

Adam Smith, following Hume, offers us a similar example. Arguing that regardless of an individual's tendency towards selfishness, "there are evidently some principles in his nature, which interest him in the fortune of others," Smith invokes the loving mother:

> What are the pangs of a mother, when she hears the moanings of her infant that during the agony of disease cannot express what it feels? In her idea of what it suffers, she joins, to its real helplessness, her own consciousness of that helplessness, and her own terrors for the unknown consequences of its disorder; and out of these, forms, for her own sorrow, the most complete image of misery and distress. The infant, however, feels only the uneasiness of the present instant, which can never be great.

Smith explains that sympathy is not actually a response to the pain or pleasure of another, but a conception of "what we ourselves should feel in the like situation." He stresses, however (with an image that evokes the condition of pregnancy), that when we place ourselves in the situation of another, "we enter as it were into his body, and become in some measure the same person with him." Only when the agonies of another "are thus brought home to ourselves, when we have thus adopted and made them our own," can they begin to affect us.[8]

Smith prioritizes in this way local, immediate affections over the more strictly utilitarian concept of disinterested benevolence advocated by Hutcheson, suggesting, as Percy Shelley later would in "A Defense of Poetry," that sympathy is based on likeness, and so reflects the aesthetic impulse towards harmony. Yet like Hume, Smith suggestively employs horrific images of maternal suffering in describing the sympathetic connection between mother and child. Responsibility to others obviously carries a painful price, but one held to be absolutely necessary by both Smith and Hume. This sense of responsibility, I would suggest, underscores not only the gendered dimensions, but likewise the underlying nationalist implications of Hume's and Smith's analyses of the function of sympathy. For each, the mother-child bond becomes a model for aestheticized human relations—one which ultimately, perhaps, suggests an idealized re-figuration of the Union of Scotland and England (as discreet "bodies" made one). Yet the self-sacrificial behavior of the benevolent mothers described by Hume and Smith recalls too the explicitly *material* dimensions of forms of national union—serving as a reminder of the immediate responsibilities of governing bodies to nurture and physically care for the bodies of their colonized subjects. Both writers remind us, however, that this type of attention to local concerns, if in one sense more "natural," nevertheless clearly takes its toll, as evidenced by the ultimate self-annihilation of Hume's "fond mother."

German writers of the period would explore these tensions and contradictions still further. The prioritization of (feminized) local interests and sympathies that we find within the Scottish Enlightenment context would be reversed, for example, by Kant, who expressly associates women's spontaneous sympathies with the *dangers* of localized interests. Yet on the surface Kant presents things differently, praising women's reproductive bodies both for their benevolent utility and beauty. Sexual difference, he explains, provides us with a sign of the aestheticized operations of nature: "Why was it necessary for such a pair [man and woman] to exist? The answer is: In this pair we have what first forms an *organizing* whole, though not an organized whole in a single body." Kant is clear on how maternity operates within this system. It is "with a view towards the propagation of their species" that nature has so organized the sexes.[9] This organizational scheme, in turn, confirms a fundamental differences between the sexes: Just as "among the masculine qualities the sublime clearly stands out as the criterion of his kind," so too "all the other merits of a woman should unite solely to enhance the character of the beautiful." Kant explicitly links female beauty, moreover, to woman's "many sympathetic sensations, good heartedness, and compassion." Woman's "philosophy," he concludes, is "not to reason, but to sense."[10]

This distinction helps explain Kant's particular discomfort with his own construction of "feminized" sympathy. Sympathetic identification with another, he claims, is

> beautiful and amiable; for it shows a charitable interest in the lot of other men, to which principles of virtue always lead. But this good-natured passion is nevertheless weak and always blind. For suppose that this feeling stirs you to help a needy person with your expenditure. But you are indebted to another, and doing this makes it impossible for you to fulfill the stern duty of justice.... On the other hand, when universal affection toward the human species has become a principle within you to which you always subordinate your actions, then love toward the needy one still remains, but now, from a higher standpoint, it has been placed in its true relation to your total duty.

This is a standard utilitarian argument directed towards the dangers of excess "giving," but one which reveals the central paradox of Kant's definition of female nature. For if sympathy is at once women's best route to the sphere of morality, it is also for Kant her most dangerous quality. A certain amount of distance from the other seems as necessary to Kant as it is inevitable, lest duty be forgotten in the swell of "fondness for every interest" or "sadness at every stranger's need." When the "motive of the mind does not rest upon a universal principle," he stresses, "it easily takes on changed forms according to whether the objects offer one or the other aspect."[11]

So defining the mutable, inconsistent nature of woman becomes a means for Kant to argue *against* local or privatized sympathies, in favor of a more disinterested "Principle of Coexistence, according to the Law of Reciprocity or Community."[12] Because women follow the dictates of nature, they respond to laws which for Kant are "merely private," and which therefore do not meet the conditions necessary for a truly "international" or "public" law. Kant argues, to this end, that as a "science of right," political duties must be distinguished from sophistic maxims which reduce all duties "to mere benevolence." He offers an example which is evocative of pregnancy but which in fact figuratively reverses the birth process—that of the small state's being "swallowed up in order that a much larger one may thereby approach more nearly to an alleged good for the world as a whole."[13]

Kant's "feminizing" of localized or private sympathies, Eagleton suggests, can be seen as an attempt to deal with the problem of political absolutism in eighteenth-century Prussia, a territory divided into feudal states, "marked by a particularism and idiosyncrasy consequent on its lack of a general culture." State controls on industry and trade, guild-dominated towns, poor systems of communication, and the bourgeoisie's lack of access to ready capital all testified to the potential problems in maintaining exclusively localized interests.[14] In the same manner that regional political sympathies divide, rather than unite the nation, women's ungovernable sympathies threaten for Kant the interests of the many—despite the fact that the physical origin of these sympathies, paradoxically, also evidences the "natural" basis of his system of reciprocal human relations.

It is worth underscoring in this context the ways in which the maternal body so often identified as the source of women's empathetic instincts garnered increasing attention in late-eighteenth-century British and German medical and educational discourses alike. Like their British counterparts, German educators and moralists strongly advocated, for example, the cause of maternal breastfeeding. By 1794, however, with the publication of the Prussian Legal Code, this would become a mandate of the German state. Healthy women were required to breastfeed under the Code, which also assigned to fathers the responsibility for determining when a child should be weaned. In contrast to practices in England, furthermore, wet nurses were licensed in late-eighteenth-century Prussia.[15] This type of explicit jurisdiction of maternal bodies, as Ann Taylor Allen recently notes, contrasted strikingly with German moralists' and educators' prevalent representations of motherhood as an "ineluctable instinct."[16] Institutional forms of control within the German-speaking world in fact enforced the idea that motherhood was more duty than instinct, more a responsibility than a right.[17] While motherhood was thus constructed, in England as in Prussia, as a site wherein public and private interests seem to unite, the German emphasis on maternity as a legislated duty privileged more explicitly the mother's public role in society, and evidenced greater discomfort with the physical and psychic "bonds" of motherhood (and with the sentimentalization of those bonds). Such uneasiness underscores more broadly, however, the variously unstable and contradictory notions of maternity and feminine sympathy which saturate both British and German Enlightenment writings.

In the remainder of this paper I will argue that Friedrich Schlegel—whose representations of gendered "tendencies"[18] can be seen in many ways as an extension of Kant's[19]—radically transformed this sense of discomfort into something *positive*. To be female, Schlegel suggested, was to be a shape-shifter, an individual who experienced the presence of the otherness in herself, and thus who organically signified (at least potentially) the alterity or non self-identity so desired by the Romantic ironist (for whom Schlegel was the most persistent spokesman). To this end, with a move that reworks Kant's suspicions about the processes of the female body, Schlegel genders the ironic posture of the fragment, comparing the creative process of the ironist to that of a fertile woman. "Every idea opens its womb and brings forth innumerable new births" (47), he explains in *Lucinde*. Elsewhere he makes a similar analogy: "Publishing is to thinking as the maternity ward is to the first kiss" (AF 62).

In the *Ideas* Schlegel is perhaps most explicit, invoking Isis, the goddess of fertility, as his Muse (I 1). While we should certainly detect more than a trace of the "colonization" of the female body in Schlegel's scheme, we should note too that Isis is not here a representative of synthesis or unity. Her creative fertility signifies an aesthetic "solution" of a different order, one which is unstable, uncentered (and potentially terrifying): "It's time to tear away the veil of Isis and reveal the mystery," Schlegel rallies. "Whoever can't endure the sight of the goddess, let him flee or perish" (I 1). Schlegel concedes, in other words (like Kant), that the political ramifications of his maternalized aesthetic are somewhat monstrous: "You marvel at the age, at the ferment of its gigantic power, at its violent convulsions, and don't know what new births to expect" (I 5). In so far as the "birth" of the idea implies an irrevocable division of self from other, it portends a loss of control over the creation. Yet because Schlegel figures creative activity as a gestative process, he can affirm that this loss is both natural and absolutely necessary.

Schlegel hints at this doubled relationship to his own fragmentary progeny early in the "Ideas":

> The mind understands something only in so far as it absorbs it like a seed into itself, nurtures it, and lets it grow into blossom and fruit. Therefore scatter holy seed into the soil of the spirit, without affectation and any added superfluities. (I 5)

The gestational language of this fragment can be read (as is generally the case with Schlegel) in two ways. The feminized spirit, on the one hand, must for Schlegel be "penetrated" by masculinized "seed" before it can bear "fruit." Alan Richardson finds this dynamic to be central to the work of many canonical Romantic writers, who could not otherwise claim "emotional intensity and sympathy as male prerogatives."[20] Yet Schlegel's "idea" also offers an alternative reading which revises this masculinized model. His phrasing suggests that the mind "works" in ways which are feminine as well as masculine, both spilling seed and receiving it. This "reconciliation" of subject and object is not to be understood, moreover, as a process tending toward synthesis or fusion (as Hegel, for example, would later suggest[21]), but rather as a dynamic process of endless self-creation and self-destruction. As August Wilhelm Schlegel writes of "a young philosopher,"

[H]e has a theory ovarium in the brain and, like a hen, lays a theory every day; and that's his only possible time of rest in his continual movement of self-creation and self-destruction—which could be a tiresome maneuver. (AF 269)

Appropriating a "maternalized" critical model—i.e., comparing the function of the brain to that of the ovaries—allowed the Schlegels to locate themselves squarely within the Enlightenment naturalist tradition, while critiquing what they found to be its essentially unfruitful (and explicitly masculinized) philosophical methodology: "To *penetrate ever deeper*," Friedrich notes,

> and to *climb ever higher* are what philosophers like to do most. . . . Moving forward is, however, a rather slow process for them. They compete especially in respect to height, outbidding each other remarkably, like two agents at an auction who have unlimited authority to continue the bidding. (AF 303, emphasis mine)

Schlegel associates this type of Lilliputian philosophical acrobatics not only with intellectual sterility, but with bad business. The problem is inherent, he implies, in the method, which pits competitively one thinker against another, and so renders ideas objects of conquest. Schlegel's poeticized approach to philosophy depends rather upon the circulation and distribution of ideas. Poetry is itself "republican speech: a speech which is its own law and end unto itself, and in which all the parts are free citizens and have the right to vote" (CF 65). Women, moreover, embody for Schlegel this democratic impulse; they "have less need for the poetry of poets, because their very essence is poetry" (*Ideas* 127).

Like his Enlightened predecessors, Schlegel ultimately falls back upon this type of appeal to women's "essence." Yet in contrast to the totalizing (and ultimately dangerous) connection between mother and child that we find in Hume, Smith, and Kant, in Schlegel's case the reproductive body works poetically because it acts democratically—it furthers the autonomy of its creation, grants it free citizenship, so to speak. "Just as a child is only a thing which wants to become a human being," he points out, "so a poem is only a product of nature which wants to become a work of art" (CF 21). Like the poet, the mother labors so as to let go, and this, for Schlegel, is the labor of love. Like Kant, he in fact consistently describes woman's "temperament" as her "capacity to love" (I 116). Schlegel does not, however, share Kant's anxieties that this capacity for love might prove disruptive. His aesthetic rather depends upon disruptions, just as the state of physical union experienced during pregnancy tends ultimately towards separation, differentiation. Julius explains in Schlegel's novella *Lucinde* that it is love that "separates living creatures and shapes the world . . . Only in the answer of its 'you' can every 'I' feel its boundless unity" (L 106).

Schlegel reorients in this way Kant's understanding of feminine sympathy. "Real sympathy," he explains, "concerns itself with furthering the freedom of others, not with the satisfaction of animal pleasures" (AF 86). This distinction becomes especially apparent in *Lucinde*, largely via Julius's (Schlegel's protagonist, and an alter-ego figure) developing recognition of the narcissism that drives his desire for total union with Lucinde (whom he initially describes as his "mirror"). When Lucinde becomes pregnant, Julius comes to recognize that his understanding of love as "indivisible," a "total union" without "the slightest taint of restless striving" (L 106) has been misleading. In pregnancy, he expresses in a letter to Lucinde, nature manifests its "endless succession of new forms" (L 107)—not its indivisibility. He suggests further that women must loose a degree of "self"-control during pregnancy, and cautions Lucinde:

> Remember that you're now beginning a new order of things. Up to now I always thought your frivolity was beautiful . . . [b]ut now something else exists which you'll always have to take into consideration, around which your whole world will turn. Now you'll gradually have to adapt yourself to housekeeping—in an allegorical sense, of course. (L 112)

Despite the closing disclaimer, Julius stresses that Lucinde's gestation of an "other" involves a radical decentering of her "self," and that such a revolution in being is inevitably marked by conflict, not harmony. The physical and psychic conditions associated with motherhood in fact render acute the differences, divisions, and misunderstandings which

Julius now recognizes are fundamental to any productive relationship. He henceforth admits that "misunderstandings are good too," and that "discords arise . . . because of our common insatiability in giving love and being loved[.] Without this insatiability there is no love." Love, he realizes, "shouldn't avoid conflict" (L 110).

Schlegel's critique of Julius's drive to possess an elusive feminized ideal serves in this respect as an indictment of the quest of writers like Hume and Smith to represent women's experience as a reflection of their own desires. Yet *Lucinde* seems too as much an objectification of a "new" feminine ideal as a challenge to the philosophical methods which promote such objectifications. Composed chiefly as a (one-sided) series of letters written by Julius, the novella has been treated by most critics as a standard (if unconventional) narrative of personal (masculine) development. Scholars have found Lucinde's function within the text to be, correspondingly, wholly symbolic.[22] One is tempted to suggest that in so rendering his title character the object of Julius's analysis, Schlegel shows himself more the conformist than the revolutionary. His idealized feminine subject is all-but silent in the text that bears her name, still "read" through the totalizing (if fragmented) lens of the male narrator's gaze. Lucinde's (almost complete) withdrawal from the text is of course, in this sense, *Lucinde*'s greatest irony.

Yet it is arguable that such an obvious irony would not have escaped Schlegel. While Lucinde's "absence" from *Lucinde* seems, on the one hand, yet another erasure of the feminine, her retreat from the appropriative gaze of the author (and reader) also seems perfectly consistent with Schlegel's tendency to acknowledge and even insist upon woman's "incomprehensibility." "Mysteries are female," he explains in the *Ideas*. "They like to veil themselves, but still want to be seen and discovered" (I 128). He persistently associates women's "textuality" in this way with that of the fragments themselves, wherein "everything should be . . . guilelessly open and deeply hidden" (CF 108). Acknowledging his own desire to read "woman" like a text, and laying claim to the apparent self-evidence of "femaleness" (the legibility, for example, of women's maternity), Schlegel concedes nevertheless the futility of any attempt to mine the depths of women's nature. Julius makes the same point in *Lucinde*:

> in feminine love there are no levels and stages of development; nothing general at all, but only so many individuals, so many particular types. No Linnaeus can classify and spoil for us all these beautiful growths and plants in the great garden of life. . . . [A]nd no wise man has ever plumbed the depths of femininity. (60)

Classifying women's experiences so as to lend order to human relationships, Schlegel repeatedly insists, becomes a mechanism of control, in literature as in the social world: "Women are treated as unjustly in poetry as in life," he laments. "If they're feminine, they're not ideal, and if ideal, not feminine" (AF 49). This type of logic imprisons women within categories which Schlegel considers "unified and monotonous," preventing them from achieving what they "should and must achieve: namely the recreation and integration of the most beautiful chaos of sublime harmonies and fascinating pleasures" (L 45). Women become "simply types . . . one like the other, without originality and without love" (L 61).

In the vein of contemporary French feminists like Luce Irigaray, Schlegel associates the processes of the female body with diffusion, fluidity, and multiplicity so as to combat this type of analytic assault. If, however, his incomprehensible "woman" escapes uniform masculine categories, Schlegel's reading of feminine otherness also anticipates some of the more problematic aspects of recent appeals to a pluralized, endlessly decentered feminine subject. The radically unstable subject that we find in Irigaray (e.g. "This Sex Which Is Not One"), has no position from which to articulate her "difference," and so must construct an alternative system of discourse or be silenced (like Lucinde).[23] As Toril Moi points out, attempts like Irigaray's (or, correspondingly, like Schlegel's) to rethink the "feminine" as plural, multiple, etc., reproduce idealist categories, enshrine patriarchal power as totalitarian and uniform, and are ultimately undercut by the attempt to *name* the feminine (148).[24]

If, however, *Lucinde* reveals (ironically) the way textual representations of femininity depend upon the objectification (and silencing) of women, clearly Schlegel elsewhere vigorously worked to expose, rather than further, the silencing of women's voices—without as well as within the text. As Sara Friedrichsmeyer notes, Schlegel was in fact an influential early advocate of women's rights and of their participation in all aspects of the socio-political world.[25] In the vein of many German women writers of the period, Schlegel strongly advocated women's right to education (AF 102, AF 173, I 115). He repeatedly critiqued, moreover, those social conventions which restrict women's range of experience. The "fear of ridicule," he insisted, breeds conditions conducive to the "servitude of women and many another cancer of mankind" (CF 106). Schlegel especially disdained—as an acute example of such servitude—the constrictions of marriage, noting that "when the state tries to keep even unsuccessful trial-marriages together by force . . . it impedes the possibility of marriage itself, which might be helped by means of new and possibly more successful experiments" (AF 34). Arguing that the state is an ineffectual mediator of human relations, that forms of governmental control in fact corrupt the nature of true relationship, Schlegel maintains that social structures are lawful only in so far as they are maintained through free consensus and encourage cooperative experimentation and personal growth. His is an explicitly feminized community, an "unfinished" and hence uncentered collage of fragments—much like the German State itself.

Schlegel's representations of Germany in fact foreground the decentralization and fragmentedness in which lies the nation's potential (AF 26) (CF 38). As a subject for criticism, Germany constitutes an artistic "project," which Schlegel defines (in explicitly maternalized terms) as the "subjective embryo of a developing object" (AF 22). Like the "romantic kind of poetry," we might suggest, Germany is for Schlegel "still in a state of becoming"; it can "never be perfected" or "fully analyzed" (AF 116). Nationalism is equated in this way with the impulses behind the fragments themselves, with a collapse of boundaries, or more precisely, with an endless re-fashioning of territories and (as with maternity) an embrace of successive new forms. Schlegel's aesthetic anticipates the demise of the individual state in the service of global community, the sacrifice of one united Germany to diffuse "Germanism" (a term coined by Novalis in one of his contributions to the Athenaeum Fragments to denote "genuine popularity" that occasions "perfect universality" [AF 291]). Whereas Kant saw political rebirth as an act of ingestion, a unification of variety in the interests of the totality, for Schlegel the birth of community works as an expulsion, a dispersion of national identities within a "free market" of fledgling nationalisms. This impulse to defer authority and accept difference lies at the core of Schlegel's vision of civil society: "Decorum would develop," he explains, "wherever everybody expressed themselves openly or cheerfully, and felt the value of others completely" (I 143).

Civil society depends upon women not as models, in other words, but as spokespersons—a role which Schlegel reveals in *Lucinde* he is ultimately unequipped to play. If Schlegel in the end falls into traps which we are ourselves only just beginning to come to terms with and negotiate, his early work nonetheless certainly complicates our current understanding of applications of gender paradigms to Romantic modes of thought, and challenges our assumptions about the ways gender operates across national and genre boundaries. Linking the divisive, rather than the harmonizing energies of the female body to his own revolutionary politics, while using irony to critique this "appropriation" of female difference, Schlegel in fact provides us with a far more comprehensive analysis of the gendered dynamics of language games than hitherto has been acknowledged—one which reflects acutely the divisiveness and ambivalence associated with maternity and feminine sympathy in Western Europe during the late eighteenth and early nineteenth centuries, and which celebrates that which so many of his contemporaries sought to contain.

Notes

1. Terry Eagleton, *The Ideology of the Aesthetic* (Oxford: Basil Blackwell, 1990), 24-25. See also Ann Taylor Allen, *Feminism and Motherhood in Germany, 1800-*

1914 (New Brunswick: Rutgers UP, 1994); Barbara Charlesworth Gelpi, *Shelley's Goddess: Maternity, Language, Subjectivity* (New York: Oxford UP, 1992), and "Significant Exposure: The Turn-of-the-Century Breast," *Nineteenth-Century Contexts* 20.2; Carol Gilligan, *In A Different Voice* (Cambridge: Harvard UP, 1982); Diane Long Hoeveler, *Romantic Androgyny: The Woman Within* (University Park: The Pennsylvania State P, 1990), 25-75; Anne Mellor, *Romanticism and Gender* (New York: Routledge, 1993); Jerome McGann, *The Poetics of Sensibility. A Revolution in Literary Style* (Oxford: Clarendon P, 1996), 66-72; Alan Richardson, "Romanticism and the Colonization of the Feminine," in *Romanticism and Feminism*, ed. Anne Mellor (Bloomington: Indiana UP, 1988), 13-25; Marlon Ross, *The Contours of Masculine Desire: Romanticism and the Rise of Women's Poetry* (Oxford: Oxford UP, 1989), especially 112-54.

2. See, for example, Dr. William Cadogan's remarks in his influential *An Essay Upon Nursing and the Management of Children from Their Birth to Three Years of Age* 10th edition (London, 1772); and Jean-Jacques Rousseau's *Emile*, trans. Barbara Foxley (London: J.M. Dent, 1993), 5-47.

3. Little attention has been paid by Anglo-American scholars to these feminist undercurrents in Schlegel's work. For Phillipe Lacoue-Labarthe and Jean-Luc Nancy, for example, "sexual difference is [for Schlegel] relatively secondary: it is the human in general alone that is divine" (73). See *The Literary Absolute: The Theory of Literature in German Romanticism*, trans. Philip Barnard and Cheryl Lester (Albany: State U of New York, 1988). See also Sara Friedrichsmeyer, *The Androgyne in Early German Romanticism* (Bern: Peter Lang, 1983), for a similar viewpoint. Friedrichsmeyer does argue that Schlegel's feminism is more radical than has been generally acknowledged. Julie Ellison reads Schlegel's authorial stance, alternatively, as decidedly masculinist, especially in relation to Friedrich Schleiermacher's "feminized" hermeneutics of divination. See *Delicate Subjects: Romanticism, Gender, and the Ethics of Understanding* (Ithaca: Cornell UP, 1990).

4. Francis Hutcheson, "An Inquiry Concerning Moral Good and Evil" in *An Inquiry into the Original of Our Ideas of Beauty and Virtue*, 2nd ed. (New York: Garland, 1971), 204-6. See Seamus Deane, *The French Revolution and the Enlightenment in England 1789-1832* (Cambridge: Harvard UP, 1988), on Hutcheson's influence on Burke, and on the influence of the concept of "local affections" on eighteenth century aesthetic discourses. See also Terry Eagleton's chapter on Hutcheson in *Heathcliff and the Great Hunger: Studies in Irish Culture* (London: Verso, 1995), 104-23.

5. Roy Porter and Leslie Hall stress that Enlightenment writers attempted to "set conduct upon a sounder footing, [by] developing a sexual psychology grounded in a proper science of human nature" *The Facts of Life: The Creation of Sexual Knowledge in Britain 1650-1950* (New Haven: Yale UP 1995), 18.

6. David Hume, "On Self-Love" in *An Inquiry Concerning the Principles of Morals* (Indianapolis: Bobbs-Merrill, 1957), 117.

7. David Hume, "My Own Life" in *Dialogues Concerning Natural Religion*, ed. Norman Kemp Smith (New York: MacMillan, 1947), 3.

8. Adam Smith, *Theory of Moral Sentiment* (Oxford: Clarendon, 1976), 9-12.

9. Immanuel Kant, *Critique of Judgement* in *Philosophical Writings*, ed. Ernst Behler (New York: Continuum, 1986), 87.

10. Immanuel Kant, *Observations on the Feeling of the Beautiful and Sublime*, trans. John T. Goldthwaite (Berkeley: U of California P, 1960), 76-79.

11. *Observations* 58, 63.

12. "All substances, so far as they can be perceived as co-existent in space, are always affecting each other reciprocally." *Critique of Pure Reason* in *Philosophical Writings*, 166.

13. Immanuel Kant, *Perpetual Peace*, ed. Lewis White Beck (Indianapolis: Bobbs-Merrill, 1957), 51-52.

14. Eagleton, *The Ideology of the Aesthetic*, 14-15.

15. See Allen; Mary Lindemann, "Love for Hire: The Regulation of the Wet-Nursing Business in Eighteenth-Century Hamburg," *Journal of Family History* 6 (Winter 1981), 379-95; and Ute Frevert, *Women in German History: From Bourgeois Emancipation to Sexual Liberation*, trans. Stuart McKinnon-Evans (Oxford: Oxford UP, 1988), 46-47.

16. Allen, 20.

17. Allen stresses that the central purpose of the Prussian State's increased intervention in child-rearing practices was to this end "not the empowerment of

mothers, but their exploitation as docile servants of family and state" (22). She emphasizes, however, that women educators in late-eighteenth century Prussia utilized the available interest in maternity as a route into the public arena.

18. The term is Schlegel's. In "On Incomprehensibility" he argues that "everything now is only a tendency . . . the age is the Age of Tendencies" (264). All references to Schlegel are taken from Firchow's edition of *Friedrich Schlegel's Lucinde and the Fragments*, ed. and trans. Peter Firchow (Minneapolis: U of Minnesota P, 1971) and will be cited parenthetically in the text as follows: CF (Critical Fragments), AF (Athenaeum Fragments), I (Ideas), L (*Lucinde*). Page references are cited for *Lucinde*, but all other references refer to fragment numbers.

19. Schlegel critiques Kant's understanding of duty (AF 10), and explicitly differentiates their projects (AF 3). Yet clearly Schlegel sees himself as indebted to, inspired by, and in dialogue with the Critiques.

20. Richardson, 15.

21. Like his contemporaries, Hegel aestheticized the maternal body, invoking the process of reproduction (a movement of "unity, separated opposites, reunion") so as to illustrate the dialectical relationship between the single consciousness and the universal "mind." *Early Philosophical Writings*, ed. and trans. T. M. Knox (Chicago: U of Chicago P, 1948), 307.

22. Thus for Peter Firchow, for example, "[W]oman is for Julius (and Schlegel) the most important symbol and manifestation of nature's principle of passivity" (*Lucinde*, "Introduction" 25).

23. See Luce Irigaray, "This Sex Which Is Not One," in *This Sex Which Is Not One*, trans. Catherine Porter with Carolyn Burke (Ithaca: Cornell UP, 1985), 23-33.

24. Toril Moi, *Sexual/Textual Politics: Feminist Literary Theory* (London: Methuen, 1985), 148. See also Judith Butler, *Gender Trouble* (London: Routledge, 1990), especially 25-31, for a similar viewpoint.

25. Friedrichsmeyer, 110.

SUBJECTIVITY

Pushkin's Use of the Term *Romantizm*

Larry H. Peer

In 1825 Pushkin's *Boris Godunov*, with its attempt to poetically portray the turning point in Russian history, was published. The structure of the work represents an attack on the "unities" of time and place, an attack that put Pushkin at the forefront of the Romantic debate about the nature of drama and, indeed, the nature of literature itself. Several months earlier, in May (*Boris Godunov* was published in November), he had astutely remarked in a letter:

> I have read what you wrote on (the German poet and translator Voss') *The Monk*; you did your heartfelt duty by it. This poem, of course, is loaded with feeling and is *more intelligent* than (Kozlov's) *Voynarovsky*; but Ryleev's style has greater flamboyance or sweep. He has an executioner in it with rolled-up sleeves for which I would give much. On the other hand, his *Dumy* are trash and the title must come from the German *dumm* rather than from the Polish, as it seemed at first glance . . . I am still waiting for you to write on Byron . . . I believe you like Casimir, and I do not. Of course he is a poet, but he is definitely not Voltaire or Goethe . . . there is a great difference between a snipe and an eagle! The first genius *there* will be a Romantic and will turn French heads in who knows what direction. Incidentally, I have noticed that everybody here (even you) has the most hazy notion of what Romanticism actually is. We shall have to talk about that at leisure.[1]

This was not the only time Pushkin had remarked that nobody in Russia understood Romanticism. Pushkin's wide reading had acquainted him with the German and English poets and theorists of the new movement and he habitually contrasted them with both the neoclassical and contemporary French poets that he had been reading since childhood (the Pushkin household language had been French). He insists from the first of his theoretical pronouncements that no Romanticism had yet appeared in France and that it was to Germany one would have to turn to find the authentic new poetry.

By the end of 1825 Pushkin is working on an essay devoted to the clarification of the difference between classicism and Romanticism, keying on matters of history and form at the base of *Boris Godunov*. During the next ten years he was to speak of Romanticism many times and in an amazingly consistent manner. Significantly, he insisted from the completion of *Boris Godunov* that he was a Romantic. Yet, recent critics[2] generally ignore his understanding of the term "romantizm" and its meaning for his literary theory, and there has been no attempt to place Pushkin's view in the context of European Romanticism.

The debate over the meaning of the Romantic movement had been current in Russia since the 1790's when Karamzin's *Letters of a Russian Traveler* appeared in Moscow. Most learned Russians considered themselves the heirs and preservers of the poetic greatness of eighteenth-century Russian literature that had been formed by acquaintance with the French neoclassical tradition; therefore, they valorized older, traditional literary ideals. Furthermore, Romanticism was seen by many influential individuals as, among other things, an English import, an attempt to make Samuel Richardson and the mere sentimentalists equal with the great neoclassical authors. The debate over the meaning of the movement did not concern aesthetic doctrines and mythological constructs but nontechnical generalizations, in which the identification of Romanticism with British sentimentalism was of prime importance.

In his reports on the new literature of Western Europe, Karamzin favored the word "Romanticism" to indicate a quality of heart having an excessive, even unhealthy reaction to the picturesque. This quality was adapted from the major English and French sentimentalist novels, and Karamzin claimed that he had had enough of mere "romanticizing" (*romanichestvovat'*) in Russian prose. Karamzin was aware that the idea of

Romanticism was somehow connected to the novel (*roman*) as a genre, a connection that solidified for him the use of the term *romanicheskii* to mean the merely picturesque and sentimental prose narratives opposed to the historical narratives he preferred.

Gradually, however, in the months and years that led to 1825, the larger issues of the debate over the term began to take hold of a few thinkers in Russia. For example, Shalikov, in the now forgotten *Journey to Kronstadt 1805*, uses the term *romanicheskii* to mean simply "like a romance or novel," with no negative connotations. Here the idea of the novel is not treated with contempt, so that anything "novellike" (Romantic) is not to be rejected out-of-hand. There is also here a recognition that the novel deals with an old aesthetic problem in a new way, that problem being how to maintain a sense of reality within an obvious fiction. This is the essential problem of any narrative and, since the novel is the most popular form of narrative, it exemplifies the central aesthetic problem best.

In 1820 Pushkin's *Ruslan and Ludmila* appeared and immediately sparked a debate over the novelty of the work: was its uniqueness to be called *romanicheskii* (sentimental) or *romanticheskii* (modern)? The former term was preferred by Karamzin and had been derived from its root-connection to the novel (in Karamzin's mind, the sentimental novel). The latter term, current in Russian since about 1810, had come to be *both* a synonym for the former term *and* an aesthetic term for whatever ineffable qualities lurked in modern (that is, non-neoclassical) literature. Thus, *romanticheskii* meant both "sentimental" and "modern," even in those cases where "modern" meant "non- sentimental." This confusion accounts for the critical explosion triggered by Pushkin's verse tale, an explosion out of proportion to the importance he gave his own little work. It also points to the reason that Pushkin, in the next five years, began to treat the topic of Romanticism's meaning and its relationship to *Boris Godunov*, a work he considered not only far superior to anything he had ever written, but important in the whole development of Russian literature.

But before Pushkin's 1825 statement on *Boris Godunov* and Romanticism essentially settled the confusion, a critical treatise appeared on the scene. Prince Vyazemsky's famous essay on Romanticism (1822) was important for two reasons: first of all, Vyazemsky was taken seriously by his significant contemporaries, enough that his treatise was regarded as programmatic for any poet who wanted to write a Romantic work, and enough that a revised version appeared in 1824. Secondly, Vyazemsky provided a clear distinction between the uses of the two popular terms for "Romantic." Pushkin noted immediately that this distinction is basic to a definition of Romanticism as an aesthetic and literary phenomenon. Vyazemsky claimed that for most Russians Romanticism was a very dangerous name, implying literary and even political anarchy, and signalling the end of everything proven over the centuries to be enduring and sacred. But Romanticism had other connotations, due to its importation into Russian from Western Europe. It means "like nature" and "like history": like nature in that Romanticism has what we now call "organic form," and like history in that it tends toward a spirit of specific historical moments and peoples rather than toward the generic spirit of neoclassicism.

Romantizm has come to mean, according to Vyazemsky, both that which is *romanicheskii* and that which is *romanticheskii*. Put another way, Romanticism has come to mean both "sentimental and picturesque" and "organic and historical." For those who use the term to mean "organic and historical" Romanticism does not mean "sentimental." For them, a poem may be merely sentimental or it may be Romantic, but never both, since these are mutually-exclusive terms. Vyazemsky understands clearly that by observing the two distinct origins of *Romantizm* we see that Romanticism is not necessarily a squabble over non-technical generalizations.

Pushkin, too, insists very early in his writings that Romanticism had nothing to do with the merely sentimental and picturesque. Significantly, he sees another flaw in the use of the term for non-technical debates: namely, that Romanticism has nothing to do with the squabble over external poetic rules, even though that is the way the term is used in the France of his day. As early as November, 1823, in the draft of a letter to Vyazemsky, Pushkin makes this clear (*Works*, X, 57-58). Pushkin claims that it was with the French Revolution that French poetic style changed and the term Romanticism became enmeshed in political ideas. Chenier's poetry is a good example of this change. A true Romantic would not just change his style but everything else: he would exude a new spirit from every poetic pore. In other words, some who call themselves Romantics are only following a style that rejects classical rules. Such a rejection does not constitute Romanticism, because Romanticism is a complete regeneration of poetry. In other words, the new movement is not just a debate about rules and their political implications.

In the 1825 draft paper on classicism and Romanticism Pushkin observes:

> Our critics have not yet decided upon a clear definition of the real difference between classical and Romantic literary types. We have French journalists to thank for this confusion, for they usually assign to Romanticism everything that seems marked with the stamp of visionary idealism and (what they think is) German ideology, or what is based upon popular superstition and legend, which is a very inaccurate definition. A poem can display all these characteristics and still be classical. What forms of poetry are to be assigned to Romanticism, then? All those which were not known to the ancients and those early forms which have undergone change or been replaced by others . . . (French) neoclassical poetry, born in the lobby and never having gotten beyond the drawing-room, could not shed its innate habits, and we see in it all the affectations of Romanticism, tricked out in strict classical forms. (*Works*, VII, 24-26)

Clearly, it is the French who have corrupted Russia's understanding of the new movement in that they tend to assign everything a sentimental meaning based upon the popular legends of Romanticism. Pushkin points out that a poem can exhibit both these qualities (and others as well) and still be classical. Poetry, as seen from the Romantic point of view, can be classified neither according to external rules or characteristics nor to a rejection of certain rules and characteristics. Romanticism is not the opposite of Classicism. Romanticism is a matter of a new spirit in literature, a spirit that is linked to forms unknown to classical regulations. What usually happens, according to Pushkin, is that poets will think of themselves as Romantics, but their poetry is tricked out to display the external characteristics of Romanticism without the spirit of the new movement, or their poetry represents an attack on Classicism: in neither case are they Romantics.

The acid test, then, of whether this new spirit is present in a literary work is its form. If a poet follows the forms invented by the ancients (epic, tragedy, elegy, etc.) he reveals the spirit of classicism. If, on the other hand, he finds that the spirit of his work transcends the forms of the ancients, takes entirely new forms, combines ancient forms, or transmutes ancient forms, then he works according to the spirit of Romanticism. Romanticism is the spirit of individually-realized creative form.

So how does Pushkin see the history of Romanticism's development? He says that medieval troubadours, by the nature of their vocation, played the game of variation on set patterns that in turn opened the door to the acceptance, in the common man's world, of forms hitherto unknown. The influence of the Moors came next. Then, especially following the inventiveness of the Renaissance, great geniuses arrived on the scene, and Dante, Calderón, and Shakespeare flourished. The crucial thing for these and similar poets was that they took inspiration alone as their guide, thus freeing themselves from slavish imitation of the forms of the ancients. Part of the effectiveness of this native inspiration is linked to the use of their own languages. Classicism is found in Latin and Greek writers as well as in those post-classical writers who, although using a modern tongue, write in the spirit of ancient languages. Romantic writers use their native languages as common men use those languages. Romanticism, then, is neither attached to classical form, nor is it attached to overweening emotionality. It partakes of the robust, the inspired, the inventive. The first great exemplar of this spirit was Shakespeare, in whose work we find a non-classical spirit and freedom of form fused together. This is just what Friedrich Schlegel had said in the *Athenäum* fragments of the 1790's.

Pushkin has in mind accomplishing for his national and linguistic tradition what Shakespeare had done for the English tradition, thus exemplifying real Romanticism for the first time in Russia. In his Romantic manifesto, which takes the form of the preface to *Boris Godunov* (the work intended to exemplify Pushkin's theory), he insists that the literary conscience is governed by the imagination rather than rules, by the artist's genius rather than traditional forms, by powerful and realistic emotions rather than melancholy (*Works*, VII, 112-16). The unfinished and open-ended quality of Romanticism, the strength of its spirit, the necessity to use native and historical materials to create poetry: these are the matters that concern Pushkin most and those that he wished to foster in his own historical drama.

It is a commonplace to say that Pushkin mocks formal restrictions (because they lead to hypocrisy) and fights against external restraints for the cause of freedom and liberty (Mersereau). Pushkin's understanding of the need for freedom goes beyond that, however. We must remember that German Romantic philosophy had begun to take hold among the intellectual elite in Russia at just the time Pushkin saw the weaknesses in the French tradition. This general philosophical outlook, formed particularly by reference to the circulating works of Schelling and Hegel, wiped away the exaggerated claims of the Enlightenment's scientific materialism while extolling the virtues of an organic view of reality. Applied to literature, this meant that poetic form must be organic to be valid. Schelling, whose views on the artistic imagination were well-known, taught that if a poet needed to make a beautiful poem he would not be served by copying the ancients, only by receiving inspiration. Such inspiration is open-ended, never complete. It "moves" and no literary work is ever settled or frozen into a final form. This is the aesthetic sense we feel in Pushkin's work. This is why the French version of Romanticism, at least as Pushkin understands it, is not really about the movement's basic concerns. Romanticism is about radically original aesthetic values, not external poetic characteristics applied for shock value or political reasons.

Thus we see that for Pushkin the term *Romantizm* maintained a cluster of meanings that were the opposite of sentimentality, picturesqueness, or anti-classicism. It is probably for this reason his definition of Romanticism has caused some critics to question whether or not he belongs to the pan-European movement at all. His understanding that Romanticism is about something other than the exploitation of external qualities for new purposes is crucial and aligns him with Friedrich Schlegel, Hegel, and Manzoni. His stature in the history of Western literary theory should no longer be ignored by either Slavicists or generalists.

Notes

1. Alexander Sergeevich Pushkin, *Polnoe Sobranie Sochinenii* (Moscow: Akademia Nauk SSSR, 1979), X, 117. All translations are mine, and references in this essay refer to this edition as "Works."

2. John Bayley, *Pushkin: A Comparative Commentary* (London: Cambridge UP, 1971); A. D. P. Briggs, *Alexander Pushkin: A Critical Study* (London: Croom Helm, 1983); Monika Greenleaf, *Pushkin and Romantic Fashion* (Stanford: Stanford UP, 1994); B. S. Meilakh, *Pushkin i russky romantizm* (Moscow: n.p., 1937); John Mersereau, Jr., "Pushkin's Concept of Romanticism," *Studies in Romanticism* III (1963), 24-41; I. M. Nusinov, *Pushkin i mirovaya literatura* (Moscow: n.p., 1941); and V. M. Zhirmunsky, *Byron i Pushkin: Iz istorii romanticheskoi poemii* (Leningrad: Nauka, 1978).

Romantic Poetry and Civic Space in the Wordsworthian Cave

Fred V. Randel

Wordsworth ended the first decade of the nineteenth century with a narrative poem that, among other things, reviewed the central cave experiences of his major poetry. These were years of profound personal, political, and religious change for the poet, and *The White Doe of Rylstone* is a composition of a more conservative Wordsworth than the author of "Tintern Abbey." But the late poem provides a synoptic view of a structure of images that Wordsworth had long relied upon: a contrast between a cave of protected independence and a cave of renewed interconnectedness. The first is womb-like in its isolation and security, but as it is described in *The White Doe* by an elderly friend of a father and sons threatened with death for their Catholic militancy in late sixteenth-century England, it is neither life-negating nor regressive, but rather a guarantor of hope:

> "Hope," said the Sufferer's zealous Friend,
> "Must not forsake us till the end.—
> In Craven's wilds is many a den,
> To shelter persecuted Men:
> Far underground is many a cave,
> Where they might lie as in the grave,
> Until this storm hath ceased to rave...."
>   (ll. 1097-101)[1]

In a time of fierce ideological embattlement, the way to survival and hope, in this view, is to seek a space of separation from the struggling factions and defense of potential for the future. The speaker here is the poem's only human character who is not identified by his sectarian affiliation. Like the caves which he describes, he represents an unregimented option that is obscured by the drama of conflict. The "persecuted Men" are put to death despite his strenuous humanitarianism, but Emily, who hears these lines, puts into practice a still more interiorized version of his strategy. Religious conflict butchers her family, leaving her a wandering isolate, but she has her own protective inner space: "carrying inward a serene / And perfect sway" (ll. 1612-13).

Eventually a white doe, once a captured possession of her family but now a wild creature again, renews her linkage with a physical world:

> Fair Vision! when it crossed the Maid
> Within some rocky cavern laid,
> The dark cave's portal gliding by
> White as the whitest cloud on high,
> Floating through the azure sky.
> (ll. 1757-61)

Independence, from this vantage point, though good, is insufficient for a fully human life. Emily's sighting of the doe liberates her from a cave of limited consciousness as surely as the Platonic inhabitant of *The Republic*'s cave is liberated by the sight of sunlight. But Wordsworth insists on the materiality, sentience, and possible divine provenance of the newly apprehended reality. Moreover, he avoids the Platonic reductivism of earth, caves, and non-rational responses. He celebrates the possibility of building on the interior space of a guarded selfhood a renewal of "tender fancies" (l. 1779), an affective "intercourse" (l. 1748) with physical exteriority.

In this coda to the Great Decade, a characteristically Wordsworthian structure of contrasted caves combines with the poet's recently kindled Burkean commitment to the Church of England. "A deep distress hath humanized my Soul," he announced in "Elegiac Stanzas,"[2] which, like *The White Doe of Rylstone*, bears witness to his obsession with surviving the sudden and premature loss of a beloved brother. In this personal context of grief and newly aroused identification with traditional institutional structures, Wordsworth constructs a poetical affirmation of an Anglican middle way between what he sees as Catholic overestimation of the potency of images and Protestant negation of externals. Neither the elder Norton, with his belief in the invincibility of a banner picturing the wounds of Christ, nor his Protestant son Francis, with his systematic rejection of props and embodiments, has a credible world picture, as Wordsworth constructs the poem. Emily's inner resistance and reconnectedness and the caves which represent them cooperatively point to what the poem deems wisdom.

Wordsworth's continuing fascination with caves can be misread as a flight from history. In fact, caves are central to his poems from the period of his early radicalism through his poetry of disenchantment to the major poems of the Great Decade and then to the poems of Burkean attachment to institutional structures. During these years, his analysis of history changes, and caves are important tools in the process of rethinking his relationship to it. In his own grapplings with history, he ponders the traditional associations of caves and their usefulness to his own historical moment. As he develops his own structure of contrasted caves, two components of the cave tradition assume a central role: the eremitical cave of the monastic tradition, and the Virgilian cave of possible political and social interrelatedness. *The Prelude* develops both into an original recipe for constructive political intervention. But it was in 1797 and especially 1798 that his poetry first focused upon the two options, and the seminal poems are "Peter Bell" and "Tintern Abbey."

Wordsworth would eventually translate parts of *The Aeneid* into an English verse closely imitative of Virgilian rhetoric and diction.[3] Already in "Peter Bell," despite Byron's dig that allusions to ancient literature were "too classic for his vulgar brain,"[4] Wordsworth was adapting and reworking the sixth book of Virgil's epic for his own purposes. A boy searching for his missing (and, as the reader knows, dead) father happens upon a frightening landscape:

> A cavern high among the hills,
> A rough, it is, a dismal place. . . .
>   (ll. 746-47)

He carries with him a natural and commonplace Wordsworthian counterpart to the magical golden bough that serves as Aeneas's safe-conduct pass when he enters the underworld to meet with his dead father (*Aeneid* 6.136-48, 201-11):[5]

> A branch of hawthorn's in his hand,
> The haws they are both ripe and red,
> And now towards the cave he creeps
> And now into its mouth he peeps
> And then draws back in fear and dread.
>   (ll. 751-55)

Aeneas overcame his fear and found his father in that place, but young Robin in *Peter Bell* does neither. Instead of regretting a modern failure to measure up to Virgil's heroic ideal, however, Wordsworth sets his own values against the Roman poet's. The words from Anchises' lips cement Aeneas's single-minded commitment to a life of military valor and political astuteness, but Wordsworth's cave episode produces an arguably more salutary mouthful. It comes from a child, not an old man, because this is a poem about the rejuvenation of a culture as well as a potter. The boy's "cry of lamentable sort" (l. 707) upon leaving the cave helps stir the hard-shelled Peter Bell toward fear, introspection, guilt, and increased sensitivity.

Peter's progress is measured in part by his recapitulation of ingredients in *The Aeneid*. At the start of the narrative Peter is almost as crude as the barbarians who killed Palinurus as he struggled to the rough cliffs in Italy after almost drowning. They thought him a prize (*praedam*) (6.361) and put him to the sword. When Peter sees an ass standing by a stream, he gives no thought to how it came to be there or who owns it, but only wants to "take" (l. 385) it, beating it brutally when it stays where it is. The 1819 edition makes the connection with the Palinurus story more explicit: the ass is "my lawful *prize*" (l.410; italics added).[6] The animal turns out to be watching over its dead master in the stream, and Peter, after much resistance, ends up grudgingly riding the creature to its home so that he can arrange for the man's burial. The need for proper interment is precisely the reason Palinurus, in the underworld, tells Aeneas the story of his death: he wants Aeneas to bury him so that he can be ferried across the river Styx (6.337-83). The same issue is interwoven by *The Aeneid* with the quest for the golden bough: the Sibyl insists that, before entering the cave at Avernus, Aeneas not only find the magical branch but also bury the drowned Misenus. The funeral ceremonies are interrupted by a chance to find the bough, and after its discovery, Misenus's burial ceremony is completed (6. 149-235). For Virgil the effects of proper or improper burial of the dead are fundamental to the importance of the issue, but for Wordsworth's poem a concern with appropriate burial, regardless of its effects upon the dead, is a mark of sensitivity among the living. Peter Bell's reactions to a drowned, unburied man and his loyal animal and to a branch-carrying son by a cave adapt components of *The Aeneid*'s central cave episode to a world view based on the assumption that "The heart of man's a holy thing" (l. 1312).

The cave into which Robin fearfully peeks is a metaphor for the rugged mind and heart of Peter Bell. The flow of influence is from the filial visitant to the off-putting cavity, not, as in the sixth book of *The Aeneid*, the other way around. (A later Wordsworthian analogue is the doe's effect, in *The White Doe of Rylstone*, on the isolated consciousness of Emily in her cave.) The boy's cry in *Peter Bell* helps Peter's growth process away from the rock-like hardness implicit in his name. It contributes toward making a stone—Latin "petra"—bleed. Peter gets transfixed, as if gazing into his own heart, when he glimpses "a drop of blood upon a stone" (l. 845). In the underworld reached through a cave, Aeneas learns to stop worrying about the woman he left; Peter learns to start worrying about the women he mistreated. Aeneas begins to focus on future greatness, not past calamities; Peter learns to remember.

Instead of fitting the hero, as in Virgil, for conquest, this process fits Wordsworth's hero for weeping (l. 1364) and for life as "a good and honest man" (l. 1380). Virgil's central cave episode lent the authority of the supernatural to a series of hierarchies: Romans over other peoples, men over women, rulers over ruled. Progress, on the basis of this model, means increasing dominance. Wordsworth's egalitarian revision of *The Aeneid* made a bold claim: progress occurs when people—including the crudest among them—become more sensitized, and intervention by political leaders, whether Roman, French, or English, is at best irrelevant. (The 1790s, in Wordsworth's view, had provided ample evidence of what such intervention could do at its worst.) Poets can help spread the progress of sensitization, but only if they articulate the potential already latent in the ruggedest of caves and the most pitiful of cries. *The Aeneid* is Wordsworth's prototype for a poetry of interconnectedness, and he relies upon it for broad aspirations toward societal inclusiveness, as well as for images and narrative components, but he rejects its political and doctrinal solutions in favor of his own.

A second decisive moment in the evolution of Wordsworth's poetics of the cave occurs in July 1798 when he turns to another facet of tradition and inserts into "Tintern Abbey" his first poetic treatment of the cave-dwelling hermit:

> and wreathes of smoke
> Sent up, in silence, from among the trees,
> With some uncertain notice, as might seem,
> Of vagrant dwellers in the houseless woods,
> Or of some hermit's cave, where by his fire
> The hermit sits alone. (ll.18-23)

At first glance, an unpassable cultural gulf seems to separate the enlightened and skeptical speaker, with his talk of uncertainty and seeming, from the hermit's fire-imaged intensity of commitment. Only a generation earlier Gibbon had eloquently constructed such a barrier in the thirty-seventh chapter of his *History of the Decline and Fall of the Roman Empire* (1776-88), with its witty sneers at the early monks' "habits of credulity and submission," the ancient hermits' "unsocial, independent fanaticism," and their allegedly sub-human or bestial habit of taking up residence in caves:

They often usurped the den of some wild beast whom they affected to resemble; they buried themselves in some gloomy cavern, which art or nature had scooped out of the rock; and the marble quarries of Thebais are still inscribed with the monuments of their penance. The most perfect Hermits are supposed to have passed many days without food, many nights without sleep, and many years, without speaking; and glorious was the *man* (I abuse that name) who contrived any cell, or seat, of a peculiar construction, which might expose him, in the most inconvenient posture, to the inclemency of the seasons.[7]

In Wordsworth's passage, by contrast, the rising smoke hovers ambiguously between materialistic and spiritual perspectives: suggesting physical necessity—a source of bodily warmth and cooking heat—but also the contemplative thoughts and prayers "Sent up" to God by a religious hermit. The poem as a whole likewise mediates between the perspectives which, for Gibbon, were antithetical, implicitly turning the cave of credulous fanaticism into a cave of potentially imitable independence.

The best-known modern commentaries on the hermit of Wordsworth's "Tintern Abbey" have reenacted an earlier cultural sequence, begun by early Christian writers such as St. Jerome and completed by Gibbon, of at first celebrating religious hermits as models of spirituality and then scorning them for their repudiation of social and material reality. The hermit of this poem is the hero of Geoffrey Hartman's chapter on Wordsworth in *The Unmediated Vision*: he is a "relic of eternity" and prophet of transcendence, a pure contemplative whose vision has been "freed . . . from the forms of the external world."[8] Hartman's phrasing in his later book on Wordsworth is more secular and psychological but equally devoid of links with people and places: the hermit now is a figure of "shadowy exploration" or descent into the "sole self."[9] In Marjorie Levinson's materialistic and social critique of the poem (1986), by contrast, the hermit exemplifies Wordsworth at his most escapist: "Hermits are in flight from a dreaded reality, a social way of life felt to oppose interiority."[10] And they facilitate the poet's cover-up of the impoverished vagrants who really live in the woods (43). Yet the metaphysical gulf which divides the two critics conceals a deeper intellectual kinship: both assume, like Gibbon, that hermits blind themselves utterly to the physical and social world. What is at issue between them is the ontological question whether *reality* lies in what hermits shut out or in what they envision.

The hermit of Wordsworth's poem, however, is an historical and prophetic, as well as visionary presence. Not only were hermits a socially sanctioned feature of eighteenth-century landscapes, but Wordsworth absorbs a long-range historical framework which addresses a basic interpretative problem: why does the poem juxtapose a cave-dwelling hermit to a ruined Cistercian monastery? Hartman and Levinson offer only generalized remarks about a hermit's indifference to his material environment, but Gibbon resuscitates an ancient and specifically pertinent distinction between "Coenobites," who lived in a monastic community, and "Anachorets" or "Hermits," who lived alone (426-27). The hermits were admired—though not by Gibbon—for their heroic sanctity and asceticism, but defenders of monastic institutions warned against the "abuse and danger" of their separation from authority. Wordsworth later explicitly drew upon the well-established historical contrast between the two types of monasticism. In a passage from "The Tuft of Primroses" of 1808 (later adapted to the third book of the 1814 *Excursion*),[11] he posed symmetrically parallel questions:

> What impulse drove the Hermit to his Cell
> And what detain'd him there his whole life long
> Fast anchored in the desert?. . . .
> What other yearning was the master tie
> Of the monastic brotherhood, upon rock
> Aerial or in green secluded vale,
> One after one collected from afar,
> An undissolving fellowship? (ll. 280-301)[12]

Here, as in "Tintern Abbey," Wordsworth is distinguishing between the hermit and the cenobite. In "The Tuft of Primroses" Wordsworth connects the two roles both chronologically and causally: St. Basil, he tells us, left the cosmopolitan life of an urban scholar to live as a hermit in "delicious Pontic solitude" (l. 317) in a cell on a mountain; eventually many others joined him in a "common life" (l. 463) of contemplation and piety. The hermit, in the tradition remembered by Wordsworth, is, in the long run, the founder of a new society.

The medieval cenobitic monastic institution of Tintern Abbey is a ruin in the eighteenth century, and it is kept on the periphery of Wordsworth's poem, where only the title mentions it. Its contemporary reference is to Burkean notions of institutional religious and political tradition. Burke's comparable architectural image, celebrated in *A Letter to a Noble Lord*, was "the proud Keep of Windsor" viewed as sacred and still vital, embodying the principal British institutions of church and state.[13] Wordsworth's metaphor of institutional credibility undermines such confidence: nothing is left but an abandoned ruin. Yet an earlier phase in the history of monasticism—the individual cave-dwelling hermit—retains, for Wordsworth, considerable attractiveness despite his own participation in a skeptical post-Enlightenment culture.

The poet's fascination with the hermit is based on analogies with his own situation. Both seek freedom from what they perceive as moribund socio-cultural establishments. For Wordsworth in July 1798, the British church and state had discredited themselves by warring and supporting war against revolutionary France, while choking off dissent at home.[14] The French revolutionary government, on the other hand, had guillotined those who disagreed with it and, just a few months before, invaded Switzerland, prompting Coleridge to write "The Recantation: An Ode," with its pointed claim that France was engaging in betrayal.[15] Wordsworth's contemptuous account in *The Prelude* of the behavior of both governments is anticipated by his attempt in "Tintern Abbey" to imagine a way of life that depends upon and commits itself to neither of them.[16] Later in "The Tuft of Primroses" St. Basil would recommend the hermit's cell on the similar grounds that it is "unscarred/ By civil faction, by religious broils / Unplagu'd" (ll. 374-76). The analogue in *The White Doe of Rylstone* is the "den" or "cave" which secures independence "Until this storm hath ceased to rave."

For Wordsworth and the ancient monk, the hermit's cell sidesteps ideological fury. Secondly, both the Wordsworth of 1798 and the hermit—in contrast to the domesticated Coleridge of the Nether Stowey period—have turned away from sexuality and marriage for a rigorously cerebral form of creativity, which may include, as it does for Wordsworth in this poem, a sublimated or metaphorical "warmer" and "holier love" (ll. 155-56). Thirdly, both the poet of Tintern Abbey and the contemplative solitaries of the monastic tradition seek outside the walls of established institutions a numinous experience of "something far more deeply interfused" (l. 97). Finally, what the eremites did in isolation bore fruit for the social groups that succeeded and imitated them. Wordsworth hoped that his own political, intellectual, and poetic independence would have a comparable social effect. His use of a setting near the ruins of a large cenobitic community in order to focus instead on a hermit and on the poet's own unregimented movements of mind asserts the deadness of established structures of power and the need, as in late antiquity, for a new socio-cultural beginning.

It also helps clarify the relationship between the miserable beggars observed at Tintern Abbey by William Gilpin and Wordsworth's transmutation of them into merely "notional" or fancied vagrants who "might seem" (l. 20) to be hidden in the trees in the poem's first verse paragraph.[17] Marjorie Levinson has indicted Wordsworth for suppressing the facts of visible poverty and then pretending—in the sequence moving from the "vagrant dwellers in the houseless woods" to a "hermit's cave" (ll. 21-23)—that victims who suffer poverty are equivalent to a zealot who chooses it (43). But in light of the poem's contrast between cenobites and eremites, a very different reading becomes available. The homeless—whether the literal or metaphorical kind, the latter of which would include all those who can no longer be at home within the institutions that Burke celebrated—are symptoms of a society in need of fundamental change. The cave-dwelling hermit, on the other hand, is a potent, though easily overlooked, agent of change. The atmosphere of veiling that surrounds Wordsworth's presentation of both of them suits his injection of prophecy into description. What the hoped for societal transformation will bring is left open in many respects. But "Tintern Abbey," especially when read alongside "Peter Bell," makes clear that the desired future will bring an increase in personal liberty accompanied by an increase in the recognition of human equality, the "still, sad music of humanity" (l. 92).

Any attempt to secure one of these values by denying the other is rejected entirely. An implied politics, with high standards for governments and political advocates or critics, radiates from the Wordsworthian cave.

Notes

1. William Wordsworth, *The White Doe of Rylstone; or The Fate of the Nortons*, ed. Kristine Dugas (Ithaca: Cornell UP, 1988), 118.

2. *The Oxford Authors: William Wordsworth*, ed. Stephen Gill (Oxford: Oxford UP, 1984), 327 (l. 36). All citations to Wordsworth will be to this edition unless otherwise noted.

3. Bruce E. Graver, "Wordsworth and the Language of Epic: The Translation of the *Aeneid*," *Studies in Philology* 83 (1986): 261-85.

4. Lord Byron, *Don Juan* (3.99.885) in *Complete Poetical Works*, ed. Jerome J. McGann, vol. 5 (Oxford: Clarendon, 1986), 196.

5. Virgil, *Eclogues, Georgics, Aeneid I-VI*, ed. and with trans. by H. Rushton Fairclough, rev. ed. (Cambridge: Harvard UP, 1967), 516, 520.

6. William Wordsworth, *Peter Bell*, ed. John E. Jordan (Ithaca: Cornell UP, 1985), 77.

7. Edward Gibbon, *The History of the Decline and Fall of the Roman Empire*, ed. David Womersley (London: Penguin, 1994), 2: 411-29, esp. 419, 426-27.

8. Geoffrey H. Hartman, *The Unmediated Vision* (1954; rpt. New York: Harcourt, Brace and World, 1966), 3-45, esp. 31-35.

9. *Wordsworth's Poetry 1787-1814* (New Haven: Yale UP, 1964), 28.

10. Marjorie Levinson, *Wordsworth's Great Period Poems* (Cambridge: Cambridge UP, 1986), 34.

11. William Wordsworth, *The Excursion, Being a Portion of The Recluse, A Poem* (London: Longman, et. al., 1814), 112-13.

12. William Wordsworth, *The Tuft of Primroses with Other Late Poems for The Recluse*, ed. Joseph F. Kishel (Ithaca: Cornell UP, 1986), 47.

13. Edmund Burke, *Further Reflections on the Revolution in France*, ed. Daniel E. Ritchie (Indianapolis: Liberty Fund, 1992), 277-326, esp. 310.

14. William Wordsworth, *The Prelude 1799, 1805, 1850*, eds. Jonathan Wordsworth, M. H. Abrams, and Stephen Gill (New York: W. W. Norton & Co., 1979), 1805 version: 10.229-41, 645-56.

15. *The Morning Post*, No. 9133 April 16, 1798: 2. *The Prelude* 10.791-96 makes the same point, while 10.309-60 remembers the crimes of the Terror.

16. For a fuller account of "Tintern Abbey"'s critique of the competing ideologies in the Revolution Debate, see Fred V. Randel, "The Betrayals of 'Tintern Abbey,'" *Studies in Romanticism* 32 (1993): 379-97.

17. William Gilpin, *Observations on the River Wye 1782* (Oxford: Woodstock Books, 1991), 35-36. Levinson censures the "strictly notional being" of Wordsworth's vagrants (43).

Atala's Body: Girodet and the Representation of Chateaubriand's Romantic Christianity

Michael J. Call

Anne-Louis Girodet-Trioson's representation of the burial scene from Chateaubriand's *Atala* may be one of the most successful transpositions of text to painting found in the history of art. Chateaubriand had intended to demonstrate through his new "Christian epic" the harmony of Christian and humanistic ideals. *Atala*, however, unravels the traditional Christian hierarchy of spirit over fallen flesh through its celebration of human passion and sexuality. In the same way, Girodet's painting, while drawing upon traditional Christian iconography, conveys, through its use of multiple oppositions and eroticism, the fundamental deconstruction at work in Chateaubriand's text.

In his preface to the 1805 edition of *Atala*, the fifth reprinting of the text, Chateaubriand explained why he was once more publishing his Indian tale as an extract, separate from the *Génie du Christianisme,* the multi-volume essay in which *Atala* was to have served as an example of a modern Christian epic. Chateaubriand revealed that, in publishing *Atala* apart from the *Génie*, he was yielding to a request made by those responsible for educating the youth of the Church—no doubt the clergy charged with instruction of the catechism—to remove *Atala* from future editions of the *Génie*. This request, coming from Church officials, suggests that the narrative was considered problematic and that it somehow did not fit into an otherwise useful and persuasive defense of the faith.[1] The irony of this situation has been at the core of much of Chateaubriand criticism ever since. Many scholars have interpreted this as proof that Chateaubriand's conversion to Christianity was at best superficial and at worst simply a marketing ploy to get himself published.[2] But I would argue that *Atala*, though certainly not the kind of text Catholic clergy could use to teach the dogma of the Church to young people, nevertheless portrayed a brand of Christianity much like the main character herself, a half-breed engendered by Chateaubriand that suited him and, judging from its popularity, many of his contemporary readers.

To better understand the objective Chateaubriand set out to achieve with *Atala* and consequently the background for Girodet's work, we need to look first at the *Génie* as a whole. In the preface to the first edition, Chateaubriand claimed that his conversion to Christianity had occurred in 1798 in London where, while living the difficult life of an aristocratic émigré, he received the news of his mother's death. Her last words, he was told, had been a plea for her son's return to the faith in which he had been raised. In describing his conversion, he said: "I admit that I did not yield to any great supernatural emanations: my conviction sprang from the heart; I wept and believed."[3] His first book, the *Essai sur les révolutions*, had just been published; it was, he said, the work of an eighteenth-century skeptic. Now, he decided to produce the antidote to his previous work, another essay but this time filled with certainty, a book he described as a mausoleum erected in honor of his dead mother.[4]

Chateaubriand explained that he intended the *Génie* to be a direct counterattack on those who had ridiculed Christianity, claiming it was a cult born of barbarism, absurd in its doctrines, ridiculous in its rituals, an enemy of the arts and letters, of reason and of beauty; a cult which had done nothing but spill blood, enslave men and retard the happiness and enlightenment of the human race. He felt that the Christian writer of the late eighteenth century had to counter each of these claims specifically: "one had to try to prove on the contrary that of all the religions which have existed the christian religion is the most poetic, the most humane, the most favorable to liberty, to the arts and letters; . . . all the enchantments of the imagination and all the interests of the heart needed to be called upon to assist this very religion which they had been warned against."[5]

Anne-Louis Girodet-Trioson, *The Entombment of Atala* (1808).

From the beginning, Chateaubriand considered *Atala* as "the honey on the lip of the cup," one of two entertaining "episodes" included in the *Génie*—the other being *René*—specifically as a "lure" or "bait" to catch the man of the world, "a lure prepared for the kind of reader for whom the work was especially written. Did the author misjudge the human heart, when he set this innocent trap for unbelievers? And isn't it probable that such a reader would never have opened the Génie if he hadn't been looking for René and Atala?"[6] A theological treatise, that is, a discussion of Christian doctrine or dogma, Chateaubriand believed, would not convince the people of his time (*Génie, Oeuvres*, II, 9); the Enlightenment had left its mark and so his reader would have to be shown Christianity's merits in purely human terms. In describing the overall strategy for the *Génie*, he argued for a "milk before meat" approach:

> Persuade the youth that an upright man can be a Christian without being an idiot, eliminate from their minds the thought that only capucines and imbeciles can believe in religion, and you will soon win your cause: then the time will be right, to seal your victory, to talk about theology, but *start by getting people to read you*. What you need first is a religious work which can be popular. You want to take your sick person directly to the top of a steep mountain and he can hardly walk! Show him instead at each step pleasant new things; allow him to stop to gather the flowers along the path, and from one pleasant stop to the next, he will arrive at the summit.[7]

Atala and *René* were also meant to function as proofs of the theory he had previously argued, that is, of Christianity's power to inspire superior works of art. Poets must teach the way Christianity does, by embellishing our lives, correcting our passions without eliminating them, making all subjects more interesting under its light. Christian doctrine and practice mingle marvelously with the heart's emotions and with nature, and religion is our greatest resource when faced with the calamities of life: the poet must prove rather than simply say these things.

The episode *Atala* appeared in the third part of the *Génie*, at the end of a section speculating on the various sites chosen for the placement of monasteries and of ruins and their effect on the human imagination, and close to another section devoted to a review of popular superstitions and the veneration of Christian images situated in nature. *Atala* was meant to illustrate that Christianity and human passion could be reconciled, that the traditional Christian view of the world as fallen and of the flesh as degraded could be made to coexist peacefully with the Indian model of a life lived in harmony with nature, recognizing the beauty of natural human emotions and passions. The opposition of these two ideological positions provides the plot interest of *Atala*.

The attempt to harmonize opposites in fact structures the text on several levels. In terms of genre, it is a kind of poem, half descriptive, half dramatic. Although dealing with Christian themes, it relies on pagan forms. As for the characterization, the author claims that Atala is an example of the contrary impulses of the human heart and the result of original sin. His heroine is half Indian, half Spanish: living with an Indian tribe when she meets Chactas for the first time, she is nevertheless a Christian. Her story is supposed to incorporate everything that is grand and mysterious in man and his history.

On the narrative level, too, Chateaubriand has created an interesting mélange. The telling of the story is turned over to Chactas whose name means "harmonizing voice." Chactas's language is meant to be a blend: half-civilized from his experience in Europe and his years living with Lopez, he speaks the languages of both continents, expressing himself in a mixed style, suitable to the line which he walks between society and nature.

Like the main character herself, then, the text is a half-breed, trying to maintain a happy medium on several levels. But its alleged ecumenism in accommodating divergent ideological paradigms, its attempt to portray them as compatible competitors in the marketplace of thought, would, in spite of all Chateaubriand's professed intentions, disintegrate in the narrative world of *Atala*.

The entire first half of the novel is devoted to a celebration of the fertility of the American wilderness and of the native inhabitants who imitate nature's drive to procreate. As the two lovers, Chactas and Atala, wander together in the wilds of the New Eden, they overhear a young Indian brave singing a fertility song as he runs to his lover's bed, and

Chactas, the pagan, pressures his Christian half-breed lover to yield to his passions but without success; Atala resists for reasons that are left undisclosed to both Chactas and the reader. The text reaches a crescendo of eroticism, however, when Chactas and Atala seek shelter from a storm so savage as to resemble the Inferno itself. At this crucial moment, the discovery of their kinship through a shared adoptive father drives the two even more powerfully toward the consummation of their love but with Wagnerian-like chromaticism, Chateaubriand defers the delicious moment, freezing it in the imperfect: "This fraternal friendship which had come to visit us and join itself to our love was too much for our hearts. Henceforth Atala's resistance would become useless: I felt her place a hand on her breast and make a strange motion but in vain; already I had drunk all the magic of love from her lips . . . Atala was only resisting weakly now; I was on the very brink of happiness. . . ."[8]

The consummation of passion is denied, however, by the sudden appearance of a Catholic missionary on the scene, his intervention accompanied by a bolt of lightning, seemingly sanctioned by the heavens. This missionary, Father Aubrey, has defeated his passions through virtue and the love of God and men, and in him are represented the higher laws of celibacy, denial of the flesh, self-sacrifice and devotion to God; having tamed his passions, he lives a life totally devoted to the welfare of others. Aubrey's voice, much like Christ's, is powerful enough to control both human passion and the very elements of nature.

The movement of the protagonists from chaos, storm, and cacophony to the ascent of a high mountain, led by a spiritual guide, parallels Dante's epic journey in textual structure. And the kind of harmony Dante discovers both in Purgatory and in Paradise is evident in the Christian community Aubrey has instituted in the middle of the wilderness. Aubrey instructs Chactas about Christian life; the savage observes the priest as he conducts Christian rituals for the converts he has assembled in his community which is founded on communally owned property and material equality. Chactas the pagan is duly impressed by what he sees: "I admired Christianity's victory over the savage life; I saw the Indian becoming civilized through the voice of religion; . . . I recognized the superiority of this stable and industrious life over the errant and indolent life of the savage."⁹ Chactas is even led to speculate how wonderful it would be to marry Atala and live in Aubrey's healthy and happy Christian community.

But Christianity's negative side is soon uncovered by the narrative. Unbeknownst to Chactas, Atala has pledged to her dying mother that she will remain a virgin all her life, sworn to follow the higher road traced by Aubrey and the other celibates in devotion to God alone. Celibacy, however, can be nothing short of lethal for a creature such as Atala, a woman whose passion makes her so powerful, says Chactas, that either you have to love her or to hate her. But she has foreseen her weakness and, to avoid breaking her pledge and consequently sending her mother to hell, she poisons herself.

The long death scene which follows opposes dialectically the discourses of Atala and Aubrey, the first a discourse full of the intensity of human passion and the second, a discourse of negativity and denial. Here, the conflict between the two poles is made painfully clear as the priest denigrates human emotion and lauds the celibate life. The text, however, by its powerful appeal to our senses and the sympathy we feel for its frustrated young lovers, has already given the lie to such a notion. The dying Atala reaches the limit of passion when she feels that a divinity was keeping her back from her terrible wishes, and she wanted that divinity to be destroyed so that in the embrace of her lover she would roll through infinity in the debris that had been God and the world. Aubrey chastises her immediately for this kind of thinking.

Atala has, however, already subverted the priest's discourse. Atala wins by affirming, not denying passion. Father Aubrey loses because, in attempting to belittle human love as an illusion or vanity, he belittles everything Atala represents. She, as well as the reader, rejects his sophistry with her last words to Chactas: "My friend, . . . you have made me very happy, and if I had my life to live over again, I would prefer the happiness of having loved you for a few moments while living in exile, to a whole life lived peacefully in my homeland."¹⁰

The last thing Chactas sees of Atala as he is burying her is her breast, rising above the ground like a white lily rises above the dark earth. The image is striking because it appears to condense the oppositions the text has played out. Our final vision of Atala is not a spiritual one; her passion and fertility are reemphasized as even in death her breast attracts her lover.

It is no wonder that the Catholic hierarchy of Chateaubriand's day felt uncomfortable with his so-called modern "Christian epic." Instead of creating a new center of balance for the various oppositions Chateaubriand claimed the novel was intended to resolve, his text tips the scale powerfully in favor of the flesh over the spirit, of sexuality over celibacy. And as a result, like most "half-breeds," even those with good intentions, it found itself marginalized, judged impure, and suspect.

Interestingly enough, Girodet's painting, *Atala au tombeau*, ingeniously captures the subversive nature of Chateaubriand's epic in visual terms. Like the text, the painting is organized around oppositions. In the best of academic traditions, Girodet has taken great care to create a visual balance in the painting. The balance so carefully worked out in the visual space implies the achievement of harmony between these oppositions. However, upon further reflection, it is possible to see in the painting the means by which this implied harmony is simultaneously unraveled.

Spatially, two figures hold opposite ends of a body stretched out between them while two legs of a natural stone arch bifurcate the space directly behind the human figures. Girodet's representation of the dead Atala takes most of its cues from the description given of the body in Chateaubriand's text. Chactas tells his listener, René, that the priest had wrapped Atala in linen woven by the priest's own mother and intended for his own burial, with her feet, her head, her shoulders, and a part of her breast left uncovered. In further describing the body, Chactas's gaze sees the lips that seem to smile, the veins in the pure white cheeks, the white hands clasping a crucifix close to the breast, and the scapulary hung around the neck. Chactas reads her body as that of one who is sleeping or who has been bewitched but this, he admits, is only a product of his own wishes; no sound emanates from the immobile breast and there will be no awakening from this sleep.

Girodet has incorporated in his painting—with one significant exception that will be discussed below—almost all of the textual details given of the dead Atala. The figure on the right dressed in a monk's habit with cowl raised represents Father Aubrey, the Christian missionary. Here again, the text had provided some guidance for the painter as to Aubrey's physical appearance. Girodet, however, did not have the luxury of any such description of Chactas, the young American Indian, and so, left to his own imagination and the precedents set by painters before him, he represents Chactas with a bright red loincloth, long black and braided hair, earrings, and a supremely muscular body.

The appearance of the two male figures sets up a visual opposition, the one clothed and the other almost nude, the one old and the other youthful. Opposing ideological positions are also suggested by their demeanor: the Indian, non-Christian, and man of the flesh, is curled over in his despair while the priest, Christian, and man of the spirit, stands stoically ramrod straight. The gripping fingers of the priest and the taught horizontal lines of the pulled drapery under his fingers emphasize the tension between the two forces holding Atala, as if the two males are in a tug of war over the female body.

Contrasting light values and colors reinforce the oppositional placement of the figures. The upper left corner of the work carries the same dark values as the lower right corner; the lighter values also echo one another symmetrically as well across the canvas. The left portion of the natural rock arch painted in dark tones provides a strong contrast with the body of Chactas, illuminated along the back and handled in generally light flesh tones. The right section of the arch is much lighter, presumably because of the direction from which the light falls; again, this light background provides an excellent contrast with the dark brown habit of the priest, whose flesh is almost entirely hidden. The bright red of Chactas's loincloth and the brilliant greens in the Edenic landscape behind him contrast with the right side's preponderant earth tones.

The aridity of the foreground dominated by the grave and rock formation is contrasted with the fertile and burgeoning landscape on the other side of the arch; the opening in the rock functions as a portal to another world. The viewer's eye is drawn through the opening, toward the light and the cross at the apex of the portal's triangle. The placement of the cross on the horizon, backlit by bright sunlight, suggests the spiritual beyond and the hope of the resurrection and rebirth which awaits believers such as Atala. The Indian is placed in front of the fertile green landscape of the New World behind him while the celibate priest, clothed in brown robes, is visually connected with the brown rock behind him, on which are carved the words: "I have passed away like the flower, I have dried up like the grass in the fields." Taken from the book of Job, these very words had been quoted by Aubrey over Atala's body in Chateaubriand's narrative. Embedded in the sterile rock face, they refer to drought and death; interestingly enough, the priest's brown habit, his hooded and aged face, and his own avowed sterility connect him more directly with these themes than the dead half-breed girl herself.

Two forms of bridging, however, suggest a resolution of these evident oppositions. The rock bridge itself forms the upper half of a visual circle, while Atala's body functions as the lower half of the circle. The bridge she forms implies an attempt at resolution of the multiple oppositions represented in the Indian holding her feet and the Christian monk holding her shoulders. And the half-breed Atala, "daughter of Lopez," half-Indian and half-European, Christian in spirit and pagan in her passions, would appear to be a good candidate for the role of mediator.

A problem, however, arises—something Terry Eagleton might characterize as one of his "niggling details"—when we start looking closely at Atala's body as bridge.[11] Though supposedly dead, her body appears very pliable and certainly not stiffened by rigor mortis. Our eyes tell us she is very soft to the touch; her upper arm bulges over the priest's hand, his fingers push into her side, close to her left breast. Her head lolls to one side, revealing a soft white neck and rounded shoulder. The smooth whiteness of Atala's illuminated skin contrasts sharply with the hardened muscles and brown skin of Chactas. The position of Atala's body reflects the soft curvature of the Edenic landscape through the rock bridge; the horizontal folds in the green undulating valley behind echo the lines and angles of her midsection and thighs, connecting her womb visually with the fertility of the wilderness.

The transparent shroud wrapped around her body—a significant change from the text's opaque linen—further heightens the erotic appeal of Atala, as it contributes to the implied softness of her skin, especially over the breasts that are very clearly delineated, the right breast starkly outlined in white against the dark brown cross. Her breast, in fact, obstructs our view of the cross cradled in her arm; our gaze is required to pass first over this part of Atala's anatomy before arriving at the traditional Christian symbol. The average Christian viewer cannot fail to be troubled by the close proximity of these two icons (a reaction somewhat akin to that experienced upon seeing a popular rock artist displaying the crucifix between partially exposed breasts). It is not as if Girodet did not want our eyes to be drawn to the breasts; on the contrary, they constitute the most brightly lit area of the canvas.

Even more troubling, however, is the realization that we have been trapped into admiring the beautiful breast of a dead girl, a mode of necrophiliac behavior that should give most viewers pause. And, as a defense against this, I would argue that we cannot allow ourselves to think of Atala as anything *but* "asleep." In other words, we are psychologically forced into wishing Atala alive again because the only beauty acceptably admired in this painting is *living* beauty. As such, there is no harmony of death and life: death is rejected outright. Atala's body does not form a bridge between oppositions: it valorizes life, the flesh, and fertility, represented in the Indian on the left, while at the same time it rejects their opposites, namely, death, the spirit and celibacy, all of which are associated with the Christian monk on the right. Atala lives paradoxically in death, beautiful, radiant and highly eroticized, causing the viewer to concentrate more on the physical perfection of the dead martyr's body than on the spiritual victory won for virginity. The final sign of the painted half-breed, like that of her textual sister, is the white lily of a breast rising above all, triumphant, irreducible, and forcibly alive. Girodet's Atala thus perfectly embodies in visual terms Chateaubriand's novel brand of Romantic Christianity, a post-revolutionary religious hybrid that privileged life over death, flesh over spirit, and jouissance over abnegation.

Notes

1. All Chateaubriand citations come from François-Auguste-René de Chateaubriand, *Mémoires d'outre-tombe*, 3 vols. (Paris: Livre de Poche, 1973); *Oeuvres complètes de Chateaubriand*, 18 vols. (Paris: Garnier, 1929); and *Oeuvres romanesques et voyages*, 2 vols., ed. Maurice Regard (Paris: Gallimard, 1969). I shall refer to the first as *M*, the second as *OC*, and the third as *RV*. All translations are mine. See *RV*, I, 26.

2. For example, Doris Y. Kadish, *Politicizing Gender: Narrative Strategies in the Aftermath of the French Revolution* (New Brunswick: Rutgers UP, 1991), and André Maurois, *Chateaubriand: Poet, Statesman, Lover*, trans. Vera Fraser (New York: Greenwood Press, 1969).

3. Chateaubriand, *M*, I, 460.

4. Chateaubriand, *M*, I, 461.

5. Chateaubriand, *OC*, II, 9.

6. Chateaubriand, *OC*, II, 706.

7. Chateaubriand, *OC*, II, 703-4.

8. Chateaubriand, *OC*, II, 63.

9. Chateaubriand, *OC*, II, 71-73.

10. Chateaubriand, *OC*, II, 85.

11. Terry Eagleton, *Literary Theory: An Introduction* (Minneapolis: U of Minneapolis P, 1983).

The Postponed Narratives of Desire in Ludwig Tieck's Novel *Franz Sternbalds Wanderungen*

Heather I. Sullivan

Ludwig Tieck's novel *Franz Sternbalds Wanderungen* (1798) should perhaps be titled "The still-untold Tale of Sternbald." As an unfinished fragment, it is a pastiche of poems, discussions of art, lush descriptions of nature, and a plethora of tales connected to the life of young Franz who travels from Germany to Italy studying art. Franz's story is still untold, however, not only because Tieck never finished writing it, but also because the assorted personal narratives within the story that would probably explain the origins of its protagonist are repeatedly begun and then postponed. The novel is itself Franz's story, but without the introduction to his family and childhood typical of a Bildungsroman, and without the conclusion where he finds his place in or outside of society. Critical literature has already considered the implications of this novel as a fragment and as a paradigmatic example of the developmental novel about a young artist in German Romanticism.[1] This article explores instead the issue of desire in relation to the sharing or postponing of personal narratives. By focusing on both the individual narratives told by several minor characters to Franz, and the interruptions and postponements of the other narratives that would likely explain his heritage, we discover a pattern describing Tieck's sense of the self that comes into being only in the act of telling its story.

Franz Sternbalds Wanderungen follows a tradition of much popular fiction of its era: it presents a promising young man whose heritage is first unknown but is finally revealed to be aristocratic or at least well-connected. The postponed revelation of information is a common strategy in many forms of literature, and is similar to the mystery whose solution is given to the reader only at the end of the text after many harrowing escapades, and usually with everything resolved for the best under the circumstances. The postponements of the particular narratives in *Sternbald* that may contain vital information about the mysterious background of the protagonist are, however, more than a strategy for evoking the desire in the reader to keep reading. They are, instead, related to the formation of what I call the "narrative self," or the self that establishes itself in small outbursts of narration in a specific context. While the self already exists, its personal story line is often frustratingly open-ended and the hopeful narrator-to-be may spend more time listening than telling his or her own story. This unresolved narrative self may better describe the Romantic individuals portrayed in Tieck's work than the term "subject" as a creator-of-a-world so often associated with German idealism and Romanticism. Franz is not simply the stereotypical Romantic ego perceiving the world only as a reflection of himself; instead, he is the self who desires to tell or at least hear his own story and never completes this task. In the meanwhile, he hears the tales of several other characters, all of which help structure that part of his story that is told in the novel.

Setting the stage for the exploration of this self is Franz's discovery during a short visit home before continuing to Italy that the parents who raised him were actually only his adopted parents; hence his educational trip takes on the additional connotation of a search for his biological and cultural origins. Just as his father, that is, the man who is supposedly his father, lies on his deathbed and wishes to reveal to Franz his real story, he is interrupted and whispers "tomorrow," only to die that evening. This promised information is never provided, and the rest of the novel uneasily attempts to relate the untold story. The desire for it to be told reappears regularly. Roderigo, a wandering monk and temporary companion of Franz, for example, twice begins to speak of an unusual old Italian who reminds him somehow of Franz, but twice he is interrupted. Restless and uncertain of what path should be his chosen one in life,

Franz is driven frantically onwards by these postponements. The question arises as to whether each life story must be told by the person living it or whether it just needs to be told. In Franz's case, the act of hearing others' tales replaces his own narrative; they form his incomplete life story in the novel.

These personal narratives told by various characters whom Franz encounters thus establish a framework for the untold story of Franz and for the novel itself (which are, of course, the same thing), and interpenetrate in distinctive ways. Rudolf, a friend of Franz and a poet, first tells the story of Ferdinand to Franz and his friends. This story is unusual in being the only one of the four that is poetic rather than historical in nature. It is an exception in that it functions as an allegory and possible foreshadowing for Franz's life, rather than telling a past history of one of the figures. Its significance lies both in its position as the first of all of the tales, and in its clearly aesthetic origin that is emphasized by Rudolf throughout the act of narration. This emphasis appears, for example, when Rudolf mentions a war-devastated countryside as a setting and then refuses to pin down what war he means. He claims it makes no difference for the aesthetic function of the narration that should simply attract the interest of the listeners for its own sake. This disclaimer of intended fictionality is all the more pertinent when we realize that it doubles as an apparently "accurate" representation of Franz's own life as we read of it in the novel. The only possible version of Franz's story that we have is an openly fictional one, one told as entertainment by a poet. The implications for the narrative self are many; it is perhaps always a fiction of sorts, but not one characterized by absence but rather endlessly retold or postponed and often by multiple voices.

Rudolf begins with a description of Ferdinand, who finds a small portrait and falls in love with it. (Similarly, Franz briefly sees a beautiful young woman who immediately disappears but remains in his thoughts; not too much later he comes across a portrait of her.) Ferdinand, Rudolf explains, sets out on an adventure to find this beautiful girl portrayed in the picture, maddened by love and impervious to the sensible advice from his friend Leopold about the impossibility of success. Emerging out onto a field after long days of despair and a particularly exhausting night of marching through the forest, he spots a lovely pilgrim dressed in white and praying. He approaches her at the very moment as a knight swoops out of nowhere and attempts to drag her away; not to be outdone, the valiant young hero stabs her antagonist and saves her. It turns out, of course, that she is the woman he has been seeking. They end up spending the night in a hermit's hut somewhere in the woods, only to discover on the next day that the hermit is the father of both the rescued girl and the marauding knight who shows up ready to fight again and is instead reunited with his family ready to celebrate the young couple's engagement.

The importance of this story is its clear parallel to Franz's life; he, too, has fallen in love with a vision of a young woman whose picture he later obtains, and he also is searching for her as the object of his desire. It is this, along with his sought-after education in art, that drives him forward in his travels. Franz understands the entire tale as a soothing promise of hope for himself, and hearing the story clearly helps him in his own goal of establishing his narrative self.

The second story narrated is also one of an absent lover and a portrait. The countess, Adelheid, tells the sympathetic Franz about her painful emotional situation: on the morning of her wedding, her fiancé disappeared and never returned. Before and after Franz hears the countess's story, he is in the process of painting her portrait. He is to combine this picture with the painting she has of her missing fiancé. Later we discover that he is Roderigo, who, in turn, tells his own story in the fourth personal narration. Linking these three figures together is a mixture of chance occurrence and, more importantly, the painting of a portrait, an act closely associated with the telling of personal narratives in the novel. Franz reacts strongly to her story, an indication of the impact these other stories have on his own life. He listens sympathetically to the countess's tale and then, in turn, impresses his own character onto her life story in the act of painting the separated lovers together. Hence, he works to establish his own narrative self even while being overwhelmed by those of others, but his story is actually told only in the context of the personal narratives of these other people.

The third narrative occurs when Franz seeks out Anselm, an "inspired" hermit and painter, in his forest abode. Anselm shows the young artist his paintings and then proceeds to explain his situation. His sad loss of his wife, child, and entire fortune lead him to choose a life in the forest where he can at least maintain a basic level of sustenance. Warmed to the older man after his narration, Franz offers to buy one of the paintings in order to make a friendly donation. He suddenly notices a small portrait he had not seen before, one of a beautiful blond girl—who else but the mysterious Marie, the woman of his dreams—and presses a gold coin into the hermit's oblivious hand. Briefly elated by his discovery, despite the usual melancholy that plagues him after listening to someone else's sad story, Franz later sinks into a terrible gloom when Adelheid reports to him that the picture is of her deceased sister. This eccentric artist and hermit might just be the unusual Italian of whom Roderigo twice begins to speak before being interrupted. The answer is not given in the incomplete novel, but there is certainly a parallel to the hermit in the story that is told by Rudolf and that so closely reflects what we know of Franz's life. In any case, this little portrait of Maria, Franz's beloved whom he finally discovers in person in the last few pages of the unfinished novel, somehow links together the hermit, Marie, the countess, and Franz.

In the fourth narrative, we hear the story of an injured knight, Roderigo, who is the missing fiancé of the countess and the man depicted in her precious portrait to which Franz adds her picture. Roderigo explains his present condition to the sympathetic young listener: he is an Italian and has led a wild youth, traversing the world in search of adventures with his even wilder friend Ludoviko. After returning from a long journey, Roderigo met the countess and fell in love. They quickly set a marriage date, but the approaching celebration caused the knight to think only of his lost freedom and the embarrassment of having to report to Ludoviko that he is married. Distraught and wanting to see his friend once again, Roderigo left. He is now having second thoughts about his departure and longs to see his beloved once again. The narrator of this final tale is the same Roderigo who twice begins and is twice interrupted in telling the story of the Italian who so mysteriously resembles Franz.

The second attempt to tell this story follows immediately after he narrates his own story. The connections of these four tales and of the still untold tale of Franz's life are thus firmly established, both by some unknown historical relationships and in Franz's act of hearing them. They provide the frame for the untold story desired by Franz's narrative self.

The narratives told to Franz by various figures in the novel therefore supplement the thrice-untold tale of Franz's heritage. The most significant aspect about these personal tales related by minor figures in *Franz Sternbalds Wanderungen*, besides filling in historical information demonstrating the relationships among them, is that they allow the speakers to formulate their "selves," their origins, their desires, their goals, and, at the same time, to link this self to the listeners in the act of storytelling. As Wayne Booth describes it: "What is essential about that self is not found primarily in its differences from others but in its freedom to pursue a story line, a life plot, a drama carved out of all the possibilities every society provides: the amount of overlap with other story lines matters not a whit. The carving is done, both consciously and unconsciously, by a self that is social at birth and increasingly socialized, colonized in a response to penetrations by other selves."[2] Describing each individual self as a story line carved out in response to others fits most appropriately with Tieck's figures who (in most all of his texts, including *Franz Sternbalds Wanderungen*) establish and, I would assert, create, their identities while telling their life story to others. It is not so much a question of the realism of the narration or whether the narrator is reliable, unreliable, or even mad, but the act of narrating itself that matters. I would therefore add to Booth's statement the fact that the carving of a life plot is often done in precisely this form of relating personal narratives to other individuals.

Hence, the discussion of the narratives whether told or postponed in this novel of early German Romanticism has everything to do with an understanding of the self, particularly in terms of its composition as a story line told in the context of many other story lines. The act of narration both establishes the self, composes its line, and creates new ties and even debts to others. In the absence of a personal account, as in the case of Franz, the narratives of others influence and even write his life in the process of being told. It is perhaps the sense of being written that both fills so many of Tieck's characters like Franz with the hope of eventually telling their own personal story, and yet greatly disturbs them, for they are drawn into desires linking their narrative selves to others in unexpected and often uncontrollable ways.

Desire has another important role in the four personal narratives in *Franz Sternbalds Wanderungen*. Each of them is associated with a portrait of an unknown but desired person or a long-lost lover. Ferdinand, the figure in Rudolf's story possibly foreshadowing Franz's life, finds a portrait of a beautiful girl and travels the world until he finds her; Franz paints the countess's portrait, combining it with the already existing picture of her missing fiancé, Roderigo, who later tells his own story; and finally, Franz buys the portrait of his beloved Maria from the old hermit, Anselm. In the absence of the desired individual, the portraits painted by or handed over to the teller or listener draw him into a new sort of intimacy in the act of telling or hearing each tale. The desire felt for the lover is closely linked to the significance of the narrative and it creates an additional debt of emotional investment between speaker and listener. Both the narrative and the portrait are potential sites at which the narrative self can present its tale.

In addition to the desire resulting from viewing or hearing about the portraits in the four narratives, each of them is prefaced with a statement directly evoking desire from the listeners in the form of expected sympathy, offers of friendship, direct association with love or explanations of attachments. Peter Brooks has demonstrated the inevitable association of narrative and desire, suggesting that: "Narratives both tell of desire—typically present some story of desire—and arouse and make use of desire as dynamic of signification."[3] He explains this connection between narrative and desire as a basic human drive: "Narratives portray the motors of desire that drive and consume their plots, and they also lay bare the nature of narration as a form of human desire: the need to tell as a primary human drive that seeks to seduce and to subjugate the listener, to impli-cate him in the thrust of a desire that never can quite speak its name . . ."[4] While the need to narrate is most likely a basic human drive, I would argue, at least in the case of *Franz Sternbalds Wanderung-*

en, that the narrators are not acting primarily on the drive to seduce and subjugate the listener or unconscious infantile satisfactions as Brooks suggests, but rather out of a desire to create their own story in the context of others (or of themselves at a later time when rereading the written) who hear or read it.

The latter aspect of narration within such a context, the following of a contract of sorts based on speaking and hearing or writing and reading, is as significant as the very weaving of the personal tale. There are enormous social consequences at stake when telling one's life story, as Franz expresses after hearing each tale, and as anyone knows who has had to sit and listen to the painful details of an intimate story told by a stranger: the listener is left with a sense of debt or obligation or at least an inkling of connection, desired or not. It is not the seduction, subjugation or infantile satisfaction that causes this sensation but rather the fact that one's own story line, made up of many such stories linked together, has merged, however briefly, with the story line of the other. The portraits of the missing loved ones in *Franz Sternbalds Wanderungen* allow the basic desire for narration and self-representation an additional mode for setting up the emotional context binding presenter to presentee.

Another example of the relationship of the personal narratives or individual story lines to particular paintings in *Franz Sternbalds Wanderungen* is the first picture done by Franz whose content and process of creation is explained in detail. He paints it for the local church after learning from his dying father that he has another set of biological parents, about whom his adoptive mother can tell him nothing. It is a picture of the proclamation of the birth of Christ, a picture of promised origins at the site that was supposedly Franz's own origin, but turns out to be merely the site of his youth. He thus creates a scene of expected birth and connection to family, of the expectation of unification, after discovering his own uncertain heritage, his untold story. His response to this representation upon its completion is oddly mixed as he claims there is something intimately personal and yet foreign and strange in it, leaving him unsettled. His painting is a reaction to his life that is both intimately known to him in his memories and yet still unknown and untold—the beginning of every life story, after all, can only be told by others and his is painfully uncertain at this stage in the novel. Each of the paintings associated with the four narratives depicts that which the figures are missing, or more precisely, absent family members or loved ones. While Franz never has the chance to tell his story in a narration, he "tells" it, creates it, even if hardly to his satisfaction and only partially, with his paintings.

Tieck's depiction of the desire for sharing self-representation is a desire to be able to create part of the context of one's life. Our human consciousness enters into our lives only after the beginning of the story; that is, we become aware of ourselves only after two or three years of life, whereas our own context actually began, of course, before we even emerged into the world or recognized our existence. Even with the missing beginning, the overabundance of memories and their associations and the endless input of new environmental information still cannot be maintained in a solid and singular story line without some creative narration (exclusion), and this therefore requires that every living being, human or otherwise, create a context of relevance for itself. Perception of external events and the processing of sensory input is more a matter of exclusion of information, of selection of what is important for survival, than it is of being aware of all of the input. It is, then, always a creation of a narration based on this material (and most likely on the stories of others). The acts of narrating a story and forming a representation are processes similar to the general assimilation and recapitulation of our lives in a specific context. It is, however, less a matter of ordering chaos than of establishing the narrative self's place in the world in the face of so many other stories. An audience expands one individual's narration over a greater surface and finds a more complete (although such a thing always remains fragmented) context.

Understanding the creation of contexts in the formation of works of art also provides insight into the more general creation of the context for personal narration. The discussions of art in *Franz Sternbalds Wanderungen* appropriately concentrate on the what is necessary to create context, both as a reaction to external stimuli and as a task of a good painter. The great German painter, Albrecht Dürer, who makes several appearances as Franz's teacher at the beginning of the novel, claims that aesthetic contexts should reflect nature's abundance, but in such a manner as to draw the viewer into a world with a certain internal logic, whatever that may be. He explains that it is better to present a familiar context to viewers than to alienate them with overly unfamiliar details. He often presents the figures in his paintings, for example, with contemporary clothing so that the object loses its foreignness. This is, in fact, one of the central ideas in Tieck's theory of art, one that he develops at length in one of his rare theoretical essays. In that essay, Tieck discusses Shakespeare's expert creation of literary and stage contexts and hence worlds that unite multiple life stories while captivating the audience.[5] Essentially, Tieck asks how Shakespeare forms such inviting contexts in his plays that live on their own and are thus easily linked to the worlds of the viewers.

Similarly, we find Dürer's and Lucas von Leyden's discussion of paintings at the end of part one of *Franz Sternbalds Wanderungen* primarily addressing issues of context. These master artists tell Franz that no artwork is truly original. Instead, it is a conglomeration of experiences, memories, and ideas gathered and put down in a specific context. These painters agree that when imitating nature, one should not copy the objects, but rather the composition, the bringing together of many things in a particular pattern. And no art is too extreme in oddity or in utilizing the supernatural, because all representations are of things that have been seen, heard, or dreamt and are thus "natural." The only unacceptable art is that which has a false composition or *Zusammensetzung*. Art in this novel is first and foremost a matter of creating a sort of context capable of attracting the viewers and linking them to its unique qualities, just as the telling of narratives is the creation of a life story in relation to others.

While Franz's story is still untold, it consists of parts of many life stories somehow linked to his own. His narrative self remains in a fragmentary state, yet this perhaps exemplifies most every narrative self that is still living. The completion of a life story is always postponed by the continuation of life. Most importantly, no life story exists entirely on its own, for each beginning and ending must finally be told by others.

Notes

1. Richard Alewyn has published the fragment of Tieck's plan for continuing the novel, evaluating its implications for the open-endedness of *Franz Sternbalds Wanderungen*. Heinz Hillmann criticizes the novel for lacking not only a conclusion but also a general development, whereas such authors as Ernst Behler, Lothar Pikulik, and Ernst Ribbat consider it to be a prototype of the Romantic novel and the groundwork for German Romanticism. See Richard Alewyn, "Ein Fragment der Fortsetzung von Tiecks *Sternbald*," *Jahrbuch des freien deutschen Hochstifts* (1962): 58-68; Ernst Behler, *Frühromantik* (Berlin: de Gruyter, 1992); Lothar Pikulik, *Frühromantik: Epoche, Werke, Wirkung* (Munich: Beck, 1992); and Ernst Ribbat, "Ludwig Tieck: *Franz Sternbalds Wanderungen*," *Romane und Erzählungen der deutschen Romantik: Neue Interpretationen*, ed. Paul Michael Lützeler (Stuttgart: Reclam, 1981). The primary texts are Ludwig Tieck, "Der Sturm: Ein Schauspiel von Shakespear, für das Theater bearbeitet, nebst einer Abhandlung über Shakespears Behandlung des Wunderbaren," in *Tieck: Schriften*, ed. Achim Hölter (Frankfurt am Main: Klassiker, 1991), and *Franz Sternbalds Wanderungen*, ed. Alfred Anger (Stuttgart: Reclam, 1966).

2. Wayne C. Booth, "Individualism and the Mystery of the Social Self, or, Does Amnesty Have a Leg to Stand on?" in *Freedom and Interpretation: The Oxford Amnesty Lectures 1992*, ed. Barbara Johnson (New York: BasicBooks, 1993), 60-101.

3. Peter Brooks, *Reading for the Plot: Design and Intention in Narrative* (Cambridge: Harvard UP, 1984), 37.

4. Brooks, 61.

5. This essay, "Der Sturm: Ein Schauspiel von Shakespear, für das Theater bearbeitet, nebst einer Abhandlung über Shakespears Behandlung des Wunderbaren," from 1796, is an analysis of *The Tempest*. Tieck evaluates Shakespeare's use of the supernatural in a manner that draws in the viewers rather than alienating them (a most anti-Brechtian notion). He bases it on four criteria that he believes are essential for Shakespeare's success:

    1) the unity of the supernatural in a cohesive world;

    2) a presentation of manifold supernatural beings or objects so that no single one stands awkwardly alone in an otherwise "normal" world;

    3) the comical element that self-consciously distracts from any aspects that

may seem unbelievable; and
   4) the use of music to establish a mood that harmonizes the depicted actions.

Notes on Contributors

STEPHEN C. BEHRENDT is George Holmes Distinguished Professor of English at the University of Nebraska. Among his recent books are *Shelley and His Audiences* (1989), *Reading William Blake* (1992), and *Royal Mourning and Regency Culture: Elegies and Memorials of Princess Charlotte* (1997), as well as two collections of poetry. He has edited *History and Myths: Essays on English Romantic Literature* (1990) and *Romanticism, Radicalism, and the Press* (1997), as well as collections of essays on the teaching of key Romantic texts. Among his major research and teaching interests are women writers of the Romantic period, William Blake, the Shelleys, and the relations among the arts.

MICHAEL J. CALL is Associate Professor of Humanities at Brigham Young University. He is the author of *Back to the Garden: Chateaubriand, Senancour, and Constant* (1988), and has published essays in a number of journals including *Eighteenth Century French Studies*, *Romance Notes*, and *Woman's Art Journal*. His research specialties include eighteenth-century French women writers, the arts of the Romantic period, and the problem of female infertility in post-revolutionary France.

JULIE COSTELLO teaches in the Sophomore Core Course Department at Notre Dame University. She has been managing editor of *Nineteenth-Century Contexts* and serves currently as business manager for *Bullan: An Irish Studies Journal*. Her essay on Maria Edgeworth and the politics of wet nursing is forthcoming in 1998.

CLARK DAVIS is Associate Professor of English at Northeast Louisiana University and author of *After the Whale: Melville in the Wake of Moby-Dick*. His essays have appeared in *Studies in American Fiction*, *ESQ*, and *American Transcendental Quarterly*; he has contributed reference articles on Nathaniel Hawthorne, Zenas Leonard, and William Goyen.

DIANE LONG HOEVELER is Associate Professor of English and Coordinator of the Women's Studies Program at Marquette University. A member of the Advisory Board of the American Conference on Romanticism, she has authored and coauthored several recent books including *Romantic Androgyny: The Women Within* (1990), *Approaches to Teaching Jane Eyre* (1993), *The Historical Dictionary of Feminism* (1996), and *Charlotte Brontë* (1997). Her *Gothic Feminism: The Professionalization of Gender From Charlotte Smith to the Brontës* will appear in 1998.

RICHARD KAPLAN has taught at Whitman College and is now an editor and independent scholar. His book on Dostoevsky and Melville is forthcoming, and a co-written screenplay *Sentences* has been a finalist in competition at the Sundance festival.

KAREN KARBIENER is a graduate student in the Department of English at Columbia University.

DEBBIE LOPEZ is Assistant Professor of English at the University of Texas, San Antonio. Her dissertation *Adam's Nightmare: Keats's Legacy to Herman Melville and Nathaniel Hawthorne* won the Howard Mumford Jones Prize in 1994 at Harvard University.

LARRY H. PEER is Professor of Comparative Literature at Brigham Young University. The editor of *Prism(s): Essays in Romanticism*, he has published essays and reviews in *Colloquia Germanica*, *Italian Quarterly*, *Comparative Literature Studies*, *Essays in Literature*, *Comparative Literature*, and elsewhere. His poetry has appeared in several outlets. His books include *Beyond Haworth: Essays on the Brontës in European Literature* (1984), *The Reasonable Romantic: Essays on Alessandro Manzoni* (1986), and *The Romantic Manifesto* (1988).

FRED V. RANDEL is Associate Professor of Literature at the University of California, San Diego. He is the author of *The World of Elia: Charles Lamb's Essayistic Romanticism* and essays on various English Romantic poets and prose writers. He is completing a book on the intertextuality and meaning of English Romantic mountains and caves.

MARGARET REID is Assistant Professor of English at Marquette University and a recent Harper Postdoctoral Fellow at the University of Chicago. She has published in *The Journal of Narrative and Life History*.

DONELLE R. RUWE is Assistant Professor of English at Fitchburg State College. She serves on the governing board of the Eighteenth- and Nineteenth-Century British Women Writers Association and edits the association newsletter. Her recent publications have appeared in *Children's Literature*, *Religion and Literature*, and *Indiana Review*, and she has contributed to a volume on teaching Romantic women poets.

HEATHER I. SULLIVAN is Assistant Professor of German at Trinity University in San Antonio, Texas. She has just published her first book (*Intertextuality of Self and Nature in Ludwig Tieck's Early Works*), and is currently working on an interdisciplinary project examining eighteenth-century geology and German Romanticism.

INDEX

Allen, Paul 77n.
   A History of the American Revolution 77n.
American Revolution 59-62
Atwood, Margaret
   Lady Oracle 117
Austen, Jane 123
   Northanger Abbey 117
Baillie, Joanna 18, 23, 24, 155n.
Barbauld, Anna Laetitia 20
Bildungsroman 223, 233n.
Black, John 135
   Life of Torquato Tasso with an historical and critical account of his writings 135
Blackstone, William 108
   Commentaries on the Laws of England 108
Blackwood's Edinburgh Review 163
Brontë, Charlotte 123
   Jane Eyre 116, 117, 121, 122, 124
Brontë, Emily 123
   Wuthering Heights 117, 121
Burke, Edmund 17, 18, 20, 200, 201
   A Letter to a Noble Lord 207
Burns, Robert 90
Byron, George Gordon 6, 26, 52, 91, 135, 144, 153, 155n., 160, 191, 201
   Don Juan 26
   "The Lament of Tasso" 136, 137, 139, 141
Calderón de la Barca, Pedro 13, 196
Carlyle, Thomas 91
Carter, Angela 117
   Nights at the Circus 117

Chateaubriand, François-René de 7, 211, 212
   Atala 8, 211, 214-218
   Genie du Christianisme 211, 212, 214
   René 214
Chaucer, Geoffrey 13
Coleridge, Samuel Taylor 20, 31n., 144, 160, 161, 207
   "Frost at Midnight" 24-25
   "Kubla Khan" 24
Cooper, James Fenimore 76
   The Spy 77n.
Cruikshank, George 26
Dante Alighieri 144, 196, 216
Dickens, Charles
   David Copperfield 27
Donizetti, Gaetano
   Lucrezia Borgia 84
Dostoevsky, Fyodor 4, 47, 56
   Notes from the Underground 48
   Poor Folk 5, 47-49, 55-57
Drake, Nathan 135
   On the Government of the Imagination, or the frenzy of Tasso and Collins 135
DuBois, W. E. B. 107
Dunlap, William 77n.
   André: A Tragedy in Five Acts 77n.
Ellison, Ralph 107
Ferrier, Susan 23
French Revolution 12, 24
Freud, Sigmund 114-115
   "A Child is Being Beaten" 115
Fulton, Alice 13
Gibbon, Edward 204, 206

History of the Decline and Fall of the Roman Empire 204-205
Girodet-Trioson, Anne-Louis 7, 8, 211
   The Entombment of Atala 218-221
Goethe, Johann Wolfgang von 1, 45n., 92, 93, 99n., 135, 142-143, 144, 153, 155n., 191
   Torquato Tasso 6, 133, 136, 137, 139, 142-143, 144, 146-148
   relationship to Spinoza 2
Gogol, Nikolai 51
   "The Overcoat" 51
gothic novel 5, 103-109, 127-128, 130n.
Grant, Anne 24
   "Familiar Epistle" 24
Grosholz, Emily 13
Hawthorne, Nathaniel 45n., 160, 162
   "Endicott and Red Cross" 70, 80n.
   The Scarlet Letter 59-77
   theory of language 78n.
   "Wanton Gospeller" 70
Hazlitt, William 160, 163
Hegel, Georg Wilhelm Friedrich 7, 188n., 198
Hemans, Felicia 5, 6, 13, 23, 133, 136
   Records of Women 25
   "Scenes and Passages from the 'Tasso' of Goethe" 138-154
Hemingway, Ernest 53
   "Big Two-Hearted River" 53
Hicks, Elias 90
Homer 89
Hone, William 26
   The Political House That Jack Built 26
Hoole, John 136, 155n.
   "The Life of Tasso" 137, 148-149
Hume, David 18, 20, 28, 172-175, 180
Huneker, James Gibbons
   Overtones 87
Hunter, Anne 24
Hutcheson, Francis 173
Ingersoll, Robert 87
Irving, Washington 61
   The Life of George Washington 77n.
Ives, Charles 13
Kant, Immanuel 172, 175-177, 180
Karamzin, Nikolai Mikhailovich 192-193
   Letters of a Russian Traveler 192
Keats, John 5, 6, 52, 160, 170n.
   Endymion 160, 161-162, 165
   Lamia 6
Kenzuboro, Oe 47
Kozlov, Ivan Ivanovich 191
Landon, Letitia 13, 23, 24
   Improvisatrice 24, 25
Leibniz, Gottfried Wilhelm von 2-3
   relationship to Spinoza 2
   theory of knowledge 2-3
Locke, John 69
Manzoni, Alessandro 7, 198
Marsh, James 79n.
   Aids to Reflection 79n.
Marx, Karl 45n.
Maurier, Daphne du 117
   Rebecca 117
melopoetics 82, 92, 96n.

Melville, Herman 4, 6, 33-46, 47, 56
  "Bartleby, the Scrivener" 43
  "Cock-A-Doodle-Doo!" 33-34, 35, 38, 41
  The Confidence Man 34-40
  criticism of Romantic optimism 35-43
  "Jimmy Rose" 41, 46n.
  Mardi 162-163, 164-169
  Moby Dick 163, 167
  Pierre 5, 33, 47-48, 52-57, 162-163
  "Poor Man's Pudding" 40
  "Rich Man's Crumbs" 40
  The Scarlet Letter 5
  White Jacket 44n.
Montagu, Elizabeth
  "Essay on the praeternatural beings in Shakespeare" 106
Moody, Elizabeth 21
Murdock, Iris 117
  The Italian Girl 117
  The Time of Angels 117
  A Severed Head 117
Napoleon Bonaparte 21
Nietzsche, Friedrich 171
North American Review 87
Oates, Joyce Carol 117
  Bellefleur 117
  A Bloodsmoor Romance 117
  Mysteries of Winterthurn 117
Opie, Amelia 23
Patai, Raphael 160
Pix, Mary 23
Plato 200
"The Political Dessert" 26
Pratt, Samuel Jackson 18
  "Bread" 18-19
  Sympathy; or, a Sketch of the Social Passion 19
Prussian legal code 177-178
Pushkin, Alexander Sergeevich 7, 191-198
  Boris Godunov 191-193, 196
  draft paper on classicism and Romanticism 195
  Ruslan and Ludmila 193
The Quarterly Review (John Murray) 163
Radcliffe, Ann 103, 104, 116, 121, 129n., 130n.
  The Italian 103, 108
  The Mysteries of Udolpho 103, 108, 114-115, 122, 124
  La Vallée 117, 124
Rhys, Jean 117
  Wide Sargasso Sea 117
Robinson, Mary 18, 20, 23, 24
Roethke, Theodore 13
Romantic artist 160-165
Romanticism
  and American identity 66-77
  and canonicity 6
  and Christianity 8, 201, 215-218
  and contemporary criticism 14-15, 16
  definition 1, 4, 7, 11-13, 27-28, 192-198
  and Enlightenment aesthetics 173-177
  and Freudian psychology 6, 112-114
  and gender 5, 6, 22, 45, 124-126, 129n., 140-146, 150-151
  and history 5, 60-62
  and imagination 19
  and language 4, 41-43, 62-63, 64-72, 73-77, 109-110

and motherhood 171-185
and narratology 8, 25, 224-232
and realism/naturalism 54-57
and Regency culture 14-20, 25-26
and sensibility 17-19, 31n.
and sentimentalism 4-5, 15, 17-22, 23-24, 47-57
and solitude 7-8
and the Victorians 27
and women writers 4, 14-15, 104-128
Rossini, Gioacchino Antonio 89, 92
Ryleev, Kondraty Fyodorovich 191
Sacher-Masoch, Leopold von 114
Sade, Marquis de 114
Sand, George 48
Schelling, Friedrich von 197
Schlegel, August Wilhelm 5, 92, 179
Schlegel, Friedrich 5, 7, 172, 198
   Athenäum fragments 196
   and feminism 168n.
   Ideas 178-179, 180
   Lucinde 6, 172, 181-185
Schleiermacher, Friedrich 186n.
Scott, Sir Walter 91
Serassi, P. A. 135
   Vita di Torquato Tasso 135
Shakespeare, William 13, 89, 90, 153, 196, 232
Shalikov, Pyotr Ivanovich 193
Shelley, Mary 23, 123
   Frankenstein 26, 116, 117
   Mathilda 117
Shelley, Percy Bysshe 6, 20, 52, 135, 160, 161

   Adonais 163, 164
   The Cenci 23
   A Defence of Poetry 18
   Prometheus Unbound 21, 28
   Zastrozzi 23
Siddons, Henry 112
   "The Sicilian Romance, or The Apparition on the Cliff" 112
Smith, Adam 172, 174-175, 180
Smith, Charlotte 13, 18, 23, 24
   Elegiac Sonnets 24
Snyder, Gary 13
Southey, Robert 20
   Thalaba, the Destroyer 31n.
Spark, Muriel 119
   Driver's Seat 119
Spinoza, Benedict 1
   metaphysics 1-2
Staël, Germaine Necker (Madame de) 115n.
   Corinne 155n.
Sterne, Laurence 20, 27
   Sentimental Journey 17
Tasso, Torquato 6, 131-137, 144, 157n.
   Gerusalemme Liberata 139
Tennyson, Alfred (Lord) 91
Tieck, Ludwig 7, 223
   Franz Sternbalds Wanderungen 8, 223-232
Traubel, Horace 88, 90, 92
Tytler, Alexander Fraser 143
   Essay on the Principles of Translation 143
Virgil (Publius Vergilius Maro) 201
   Aeneid 202-204
Voltaire (pseud. of François-Marie Arouet) 191
Voss, Johann Heinrich 191

Vyazemsky, Prince Pyotr Andreevich 194
Wagner, Richard 4, 5, 81-95
  "The Artwork of the Future" 83
  Der Ring der Nibelungen 81, 88, 94
  Tannhäuser 86
  "The Work and Mission of My Life" 87
Weber, Carl Maria von 89
Wellek, René 4
Whitman, Walt(er) 4, 5, 81-95
  "A Backward Glance O'er Travel'd Roads" 84, 93, 94
  "A Boston Ballad" 83
  Grashalme 92
  Leaves of Grass 82, 83, 85, 87, 91, 93
  "Memoranda" 89, 90
  "The Nibelungen Lied" 86
  "November Boughs" 90
  "The Old Bowery" 90
  "Our Eminent Visitors, Past and Present" 90
  "Out of the Cradle Endlessly Rocking" 81
  "The Poetry of the Future" 87
  "Proud Music of the Storm" 83
  review of *Ernani* 84
  "Song of Myself" 83
  "Specimen Days" 89
  and music 84
Williams, Helen Maria 13, 20, 23
Wollstonecraft, Mary 17, 117, 118, 131n.
  Mary, A Fiction 17
  Vindication of the Rights of Woman 104
Woolf, Virginia 153
  A Room of One's Own 122
Wordsworth, Dorothy 53
Wordsworth, William 4, 6, 17, 18, 20, 25, 31n., 33-34, 35, 40, 41, 44n., 53, 141, 144, 156n., 199
  "Elegiac Stanzas" 200
  The Excursion 15, 206
  Lyrical Ballads 25
  "Ode on the Intimations of Immortality" 21
  "Peter Bell" 201, 203, 208
  The Prelude 201, 207
  "Tintern Abbey" 199, 201, 204, 205-208
  "The Tuft of Primroses" 206
  The White Doe of Rylstone 199, 203, 207